ARISTOCRACY IN
GREEK SOCIETY

ASPECTS OF GREEK AND
ROMAN LIFE

General Editor: Professor H. H. Scullard

ARISTOCRACY IN GREEK SOCIETY

M. T. W. Arnheim

THAMES AND HUDSON

TO MY

MOTHER AND FATHER

Any copy of this book issued by the publisher as a paperback is sold subject to the condition that it shall not by way of trade or otherwise, be lent, resold, hired out or otherwise circulated, without the publisher's prior consent, in any form of binding or cover other than that in which it is published, and without a similar condition including these words being imposed on a subject purchaser.

© 1977 THAMES AND HUDSON

All Rights Reserved. No part of this publication may be reproduced or transmitted in any form or by any means, electronic or mechanical, including photocopy, recording or any information storage and retrieval system, without permission in writing from the publisher.

PRINTED IN GREAT BRITAIN BY
LATIMER TREND & COMPANY LTD PLYMOUTH

CONTENTS

PREFACE 7

INTRODUCTION 9
Definitions – Aristocrats, Aristocracy and Oligarchy

I KINGS AND HEROES 13
Homeric Aristocracy; Homer and History

MAP OF THE GREEK WORLD 24-5

II HEYDAY OF ARISTOCRACY 39
Royal-Clan Aristocracies; Athens
Aristocracies of First Settlers; Military Aristocracies
Ruling Groups of Fixed Size; Aristocracy by Conquest

III THE REPUBLIC OF DEMIGODS 72
The Metamorphosis of a Social System
Aristocracy Old and New; Council and Assembly
The Ephors; Athens and Sparta Compared; Disaffection
The Breakdown of the Lycurgan System
A Second Lycurgan Revolution

IV ALTERNATIVE TO ARISTOCRACY 121

V ARISTOCRATS AGAINST ARISTOCRACY 130
Aristocrats in Athenian Democracy; Solon and the Aristocracy
Nobles and Tyrants; Aftermath of Tyranny
Cleisthenes' Reforms; Two Political Types
Aristocrats against Aristocracy

VI THE ARISTOCRATIC ETHOS 158
*Plato against Democracy; The Old Oligarch
Pericles' Funeral Oration; Justice and Equality; Euripides
Justice in Plato's Republic; Two Platonic Paradoxes
Aristotle on 'Good Birth'*

CONCLUSION 182

NOTES 189

BIBLIOGRAPHY 209

INDEX 217

PREFACE

This is in a sense a 'companion volume' to my book on *The Senatorial Aristocracy in the Later Roman Empire* (Oxford, 1972). Its purpose is roughly the same, namely to discover the role of the aristocracy in society, but it tackles the question from a somewhat different angle. In this book I shall be concerned not only with the aristocracy, in the sense of the nobility as a social group, but also with aristocracy as a form of government, with the role of individual aristocrats in non-aristocratic forms of government and also with aristocratic ways of thinking about politics. The period dealt with runs from Mycenaean times roughly to that of Alexander the Great, though an earlier or later terminal date has been adopted in the discussion of particular areas wherever that has seemed appropriate. All dates in the book are BC unless there is some indication to the contrary.

There has never before been a full-scale work devoted to a study of Greek aristocracy. The nearest one can get to it is the admirable book by that great Cambridge polymath, Leonard Whibley, entitled *Greek Oligarchies, their character and organization*, which was first published in 1896. Despite the apparent similarity of titles, however, the subject matter of the two books will be found to overlap hardly at all, for Whibley, writing as he did at a time when Progress was the presiding deity and Constitutionalism her ministering angel, devoted his book largely to the constitutional side of the question. This book, on the other hand, is more concerned to analyze the underlying nature of government and the way in which people thought about it. Did the Greeks have an aristocracy? How aristocratic was Mycenaean society? What bearing does the aristocratic society of the Homeric epics have upon history? How did monarchy turn into aristocracy in the Dark Age? Why did so many aristocratic governments succumb to revolution in the seventh and sixth centuries, and what was the nature of these revolutions? Was Sparta an aristocracy? What was the role of aristocrats and aristocracy in Athens? Was Greek political thought really egalitarian at any time? Those are some of the questions with which this book is concerned.

The book is aimed as much at the Greekless reader as at those who are familiar with that ancient tongue. All quotations from the sources have, therefore, been translated into English, the translations all being my own except in the case of one passage quoted on page 153.

Most of the ideas in this book have been tried out in some shape or form at one time or another upon my unsuspecting supervision pupils at St John's and other Cambridge colleges, and the value of such a sounding-board is inestimable. I must thank St John's College for giving me this opportunity and also the requisite facilities for research by electing me into a Fellowship in March 1971. The manuscript has been read at one or other stage of composition by Mr John Crook, Professor H. D. Westlake and Professor H. H. Scullard, the general editor of this series, all of whose comments, criticisms and suggestions have made the book freer of faults than it would otherwise have been. Not least, I owe a debt of gratitude to my parents, Dr and Mrs W. Arnheim, for their constant and unflagging encouragement, and it is, therefore, to them that I dedicate this book.

St John's College, Cambridge, 1975 M. T. W. A.

INTRODUCTION

DEFINITIONS – ARISTOCRATS, ARISTOCRACY AND OLIGARCHY

Was Bertrand Russell an aristocrat? In one sense, of course, he was, because he was the third Earl Russell and related to the Duke of Bedford. But in another sense he was equally obviously not an aristocrat, namely in regard to his political opinions. This case exemplifies the ambiguity of the words 'aristocrat' and 'aristocratic' in English. The terms can refer either to people of noble birth or else to a political outlook or governmental structure. It would be quite correct, therefore, to say that Bertrand Russell was an aristocrat but not an aristocratic politician. It would probably be clearer to say that he was a nobleman who did not have aristocratic political views, and the terms 'noble' or 'nobleman' are used in this book interchangeably with 'aristocrat' and 'aristocracy' when referring to people's descent and lineage. The adjective 'aristocratic', however, has generally been reserved to refer to a political outlook rather than to birth, on much the same lines as the word *aristo* was used in the French Revolution to refer to anyone, however humble, who supported the *ancien régime*. It may now be possible to understand how a Peisistratus or a Pericles can be described as an 'anti-aristocratic aristocrat'.

Nowadays the word 'democracy' is used only in reference to forms of government (though, since there is hardly a government in the world today which does not claim this appellation, it is hard to know exactly what it means or whether it has any meaning at all). As little as a century ago, however, 'democracy' had the same sort of ambiguity as 'aristocracy' still has. 'The democracy', or, in other words, the lower classes, was thought to be the dominant element in a democracy, in just the same way as aristocracy is thought of as rule by 'the aristocracy'. When seen in this light it is not difficult to understand how the same word could come to be used for the dominant element in a type of government as for that form of government itself. As 'aristocracy' has both these meanings in current English and as there is very little risk of ambiguity, since the context will generally make it quite plain in which of the two senses the word is being used, I have used 'aristocracy' to refer both to the nobility and to a form of government.

But when may a constitution be termed aristocratic? Was Sparta an aristocracy, for example? The image that 'aristocracy' conjures up in the modern mind is one of velvet, ermine and coronets, luxury and ease. The Spartans, on the other hand, or, to be more precise, the Spartiates (i.e. the dominant element in Sparta) are renowned for their hard and austere way of life. Even by normal Greek standards the Spartiates could not all be classified as nobles. All the same their form of government was undoubtedly aristocratic, in the sense that the state was dominated by a section of the population whose position was hereditary. In terms of numbers, it is true, the Spartiates formed a higher proportion of the total population than we normally expect an aristocracy to do, but more of that in Chapter III.

One of the favourite pastimes of Greek philosophers and political thinkers was the classification of constitutions, the normal pattern being a twofold division, one on the basis of the numerical size of the ruling element and the other on a moral basis. In other words, each category in the numerical classification is divided into a 'good' variety and a 'bad', Plato's criterion (in the *Statesman* and the *Laws*) of good and bad being respect for law and Aristotle's rule in the interests of the whole community as against rule in the interests only of the dominant element itself. The resulting classification is as follows:

	Good	Bad
Rule by one man:	Monarchy	Tyranny
Rule by a minority:	Aristocracy	Oligarchy
Rule by the many:	Democracy	Democracy

Plato uses 'democracy' for both varieties of rule by the many, but Aristotle sometimes uses *politeia*, probably best translated as 'constitutional government', for the 'good' variety. The term 'ochlocracy', or 'mob rule', was first applied to the 'bad' type of democracy by the second-century Hellenistic historian Polybius. It will be noticed from the table that the ancients used 'oligarchy' for the 'bad' type of rule by the few, and the word has retained a pejorative connotation to the present day. In this book, however, the word 'oligarchy' will be used as a generic term for all types of government by a minority class or group, whether the criterion of membership of this dominant element is wealth, race, ability, birth, religion or freckles on the nose. Aristocracy, or rule by a hereditary social group, is seen, therefore, as a sub-species of oligarchy. In fact, though, whatever the initial criterion of oligarchy, there is a tendency for oligarchy to turn into aristocracy. This tendency could be counteracted only by the abolition of the family. But as it is there seems to be a natural desire on the part of parents to hand on to their children the same benefits and advantages that they have themselves enjoyed and, if possible, to add to them. This does not necessarily entail a change of criteria, because the criteria of oligarchy tend themselves to be inherited. Wealth and religion are obvious examples of this. But even where membership of the oligarchy depends upon personal qualities of individual ability not only is there an element of genetic heredity involved but the environment tends to be inherited as well, including such features as educational opportunities and psychological incentives.

But how dominant is the dominant element in an oligarchy? How much power does a ruling group actually wield? And, for that matter, what constitutes a group or class? The word 'class' is much bandied about and is also a highly emotive word. Nowadays, under the impact of the writings of Karl Marx, classes are thought of as primarily economic divisions, and, in Marxist terminology, the 'ruling class' is essentially that class which owns the 'means of production'. Other schools of political thought employ different terminologies and different systems of classification. The concept of an 'élite' derives from two early twentieth-century Italian thinkers, Gaetano Mosca and Vilfredo Pareto, who were the first to use the word in this political sense. Mosca preferred to call his dominant element the 'political class' and his conception of it is somewhat narrower than Pareto's, because it includes only those who play an active part in government. All this also impinges on that favourite hobby-horse of political theorists, the question of 'sovereignty', which I have no intention of discussing here.

There are three basic heads, it may be suggested, under which any dominant group must be considered: recruitment, cohesiveness and power. By 'recruitment' is meant the degree of ease or difficulty with which outsiders can become members of the dominant element in society. 'Cohesiveness' refers to the degree of 'solidarity' which exists within the dominant element, and by 'power' is meant the degree of control which the dominant element can exercise over government and society as a whole.

From our earliest records of Greek history, as we shall see presently, until the upheavals of the seventh and sixth centuries aristocracies were the order of the day in most parts of the Greek world. Membership of the dominant element in society was closed to all except those actually born into it and there was a strong *esprit de corps* that knit all members of the aristocracy together and that even seems to have produced a fellow-feeling among aristocracies in different states, which was cemented by marriage. The fact that one was an aristocrat was evidently of much greater importance than the fact that one was an Aeginetan, a Megarian or an Athenian. But this cohesiveness or 'solidarity', which we may regard as a centripetal force within the aristocracy, was balanced by a centrifugal force, rivalry between noble families and individuals within the same state. As was recognized by Aristotle, a spirit of equality within the aristocracy itself was a binding factor. It is no accident, for example, that the English word 'peer' should mean both 'equal' and 'nobleman'. Even though there have long been different degrees of nobility, and a baron or a viscount is a very low form of life by comparison with a marquess or a duke, the ancient aristocratic egalitarianism – which was limited to the aristocracy itself – has survived in the word 'peer'. The same concept is found in the aristocratic fear and hatred of any form of monarchy or dictatorship, the best known example of this being the Roman senatorial anathematization of the word *rex*, or 'king', and of the reality underlying that word. Hence the collegiate magistracies, short terms of office and rotation that are the hallmarks of the Roman Republican constitution, as of so many Greek aristocracies and oligarchies.

Greek aristocracies of the archaic period, therefore, were closed hereditary groups with a high degree of cohesiveness. Their power was economic and social as well as political, since they combined their control of government with wealth and dignity. The widespread wave of revolutions of the seventh and sixth centuries which toppled these aristocracies replaced them, as is argued in Chapter IV, with popular dictatorships, but within a generation or two there was usually a counter-revolution which established a wealth-based oligarchy. But birth had never been superseded as a basic criterion of worth in Greek political thinking, so the passage of time saw the emergence of new aristocracies out of the oligarchies of wealth, aristocracies which in some cases survived right into Roman times.

CHAPTER I

KINGS AND HEROES

HOMERIC ARISTOCRACY

When Menelaus, king of Sparta, first sees Odysseus' son Telemachus and Nestor's son Peisistratus he knows at once that they are of noble birth though he has not set eyes upon either of them before:

> Help yourselves to food, and welcome. Then after you have dined we shall enquire who you are. Your ancestry is not hidden, but you are clearly of the stock of sceptred kings cherished by Zeus, for no base-born [*kakoi*] parents could produce sons like you.[1]

This is no isolated text. The same concept of nobility runs right through both Homeric epics. To give another instance from Telemachus' visit to Sparta, when Telemachus is about to leave Menelaus he is offered gifts, as was traditional, but he has to refuse the offer of horses, to which his own country, the rugged island of Ithaca, was not well suited. His little speech on the subject impresses Menelaus, who then comments: 'The way you speak, dear child, shows that you are of noble [*agathon*] blood. I shall therefore change my gifts, which I am certainly able to do.'[2]

A man's worth in the eyes of Homer is determined both by his lineage and by his actions. But these are not two independent criteria; they are closely bound up together. It is possible for a non-noble to act nobly (in both senses of the word), and he is then suitably commended by the formula: 'You do not look like a man who is either base [*kakos*] or foolish.'[3] This formula occurs only twice, each time in the *Odyssey*, and it is important to note that on both occasions it is addressed to a person who is either known or assumed to be a commoner: in the one case Odysseus addresses it to the herdsman Philoetius and in the other it is used by Nausicaa to Odysseus himself when they first meet.⁴ It is similarly possible for a noble to act basely, the prime example here being the behaviour of Penelope's suitors, who, Penelope believed, were killed by a god 'angered by their galling arrogance and evil [*kaka*] deeds. For they esteemed no one on earth that they encountered, neither the base [*kakos*] nor the noble [*esthlos*].'⁵ This lack of respect for all and sundry, including their rudeness to strangers (who were regarded as being under the special protection of Zeus), as when one of the suitors hurls a footstool at Odysseus and another an ox's hoof, is a serious breach of the noble code of correct behaviour. Yet the suitors are themselves of noble birth, indeed the noblest (*meg'aristoi*) young men in Ithaca, as Odysseus himself tells us.⁶ But these cases, of non-nobles acting nobly or of nobles acting dishonourably, are exceptions. In general in the two epics men's actions reflect their social rank and lineage. That is why the words denoting nobility of birth are the same as the words describing commendable personal qualities, and the words denoting lowly birth are the same as those referring to bad personal qualities. The Greek words concerned are on the one hand *agathos, aristos, aristeus* and *esthlos*, and on the other *kakos* and the plural comparative *cherées*. The ambiguous usages of these words are not unparalleled in modern English, in which we use the word 'noble' to refer both to a person's birth and to the quality of his deeds – or even of his wine. But to Homer there probably was no ambiguity, because his characters generally act out the parts allotted them by birth. Not only that, but they looked the part naturally as well. When covered in seaweed, as Odysseus is when he is washed on to the shore of Scheria, or when dressed in rags, as he is when he first returns to Ithaca, it may be a little more difficult to discern the nobility of the aristocrat, but it is not normally at all problematical, and the same applies to the qualities that distinguish the lowly.

In the touching scene in the last book of the *Odyssey* in which Odysseus is reunited with his father, Laertes, after twenty years, he finds the old man working in his vineyard dressed in a tattered tunic. Odysseus at first acts as a stranger and pretends to take Laertes for a slave, but then remarks: 'It is clearly not on account of idleness on your part that your master fails to care for you, nor is there any indication from your appearance and build that you are a slave, for you look like a nobleman [*basileus*] who, when he has bathed and eaten, should sleep on a soft bed.'⁷ Odysseus is cheating here, since he knows full well that Laertes is not a slave, but it is a good reflection of the way in which the Homeric mind operates. Thersites, the insolent commoner who dares to insult Agamemnon, the king of Mycenae and commander-in-chief of the expedition against Troy, is described in great physical detail:

> He was the ugliest man who came to Ilios; he was bandy-legged and lame in one foot; his rounded shoulders converged upon his chest. Above was a twisted head, from which sprouted sparse stubble.[8]

There can be no doubt from this as to what Thersites' origin and character are. Is it coincidence that of all the Greek gods it is the smith-god Hephaestus alone who is portrayed as a cripple? Generally speaking, gods can be distinguished from mere mortals as easily as nobles from commoners. It is extremely flattering for a Homeric hero to be mistaken for a god. But Hephaestus' portfolio is a menial one: hence no doubt his misshapen appearance.

Homeric studies have never been the most fertile ground for the cultivation of scholarly unanimity, and today less than ever. Some scholars even deny that Homeric society is aristocratic. Their main argument rests precisely upon Homer's ambiguous usage of words of moral approbation and condemnation. They point to cases where *agathos*, *esthlos* or *kakos* refer to purely personal, as against social or 'class', attributes, as if that proves that those words never refer to birth or social rank. There is no denying that such words often do refer to personal qualities such as courage or prowess in war, and when a man of humble origins displays qualities properly befitting his betters, or vice versa, these words are applied across the barriers of rank and birth. It is worth noticing, though, that Eumaeus the swineherd, the only slave, and indeed the only commoner, to have more than a walk-on part in either of the epics, is duly invested with a suitably noble – in fact a royal – pedigree, together with a tale of woe to reconcile it with his present lowly status. His father, he tells Odysseus, was ruler of the island of 'Syria', on which there were two cities.[9]

There can be no doubt that there are class barriers in Homeric society. The episode sparked off when Agamemnon's attempt to embolden his army back-fired is perhaps the best known example. Odysseus goes round persuading the men not to clamber aboard the ships. But the way in which he addresses them differs according to their social (which is no doubt also reflected in their military) rank. To anyone who is a nobleman (*basileus*) or a man of distinction (*exochos anēr*) he would speak in terms of sweet reasonableness, but the lower orders he handles rather more roughly:

Any man of the people [*dēmos*] that he saw or found calling out he would strike with his staff and upbraid in the following words: 'Hey you, sit still and pay attention to the words of those who are better men [*pherteroi*] than you – you, who are cowardly and weak, and of no account either in war or debate.'[10]

Here again, it is worth noting, the lack of manly qualities is taken for granted as a concomitant of low social rank.

Another telling example occurs in the *Odyssey* when Odysseus in the guise of a beggar asks to be allowed to try to string the bow, which none of the suitors has been able to do. The suitors are against allowing him to try, but Penelope then intervenes, saying that he should be permitted. The prize in the bow-stringing contest was to be Penelope's hand in marriage, but, in extending to Odysseus the privilege of testing his skill as an archer against that of the suitors, Penelope (who is still unaware that the beggar is actually Odysseus) by no means intends to allow him to compete for her hand, as she makes very clear: 'Do you expect that, if the stranger bends Odysseus' great bow with main strength, he will take me home with him and make me his wife? I am sure such a thought has not even crossed his own mind.'[11] Why not? She gives the answer herself, 'it is not fitting' (*oude eoiken*), which is echoed in the reply of Eurymachus, one of the suitors:

> Daughter of Icarius, wise Penelope, it is not that we think this man will take you home with him. That would not be fitting. But what we do fear is the gossip of men and women, in case one of the common people should say one day: 'Greatly inferior men are courting the wife of a man of excellent worth; they cannot even bend his polished bow. But some wandering beggar man who came there easily strung the bow and set it through the iron.' So people will speak and it would become a reproach to us.[12]

Eurymachus makes two points here. First, that it is inconceivable that a beggar should marry a queen. Secondly, there is the fear that a non-noble may act more nobly than the noble suitors and thus put the suitors to shame. In Homeric society such behaviour is obviously regarded as being sufficiently rare as to cause comment – and in this case, ridicule.

Not even wealth can bridge the gap between noble and commoner. The worst insult to fling at a nobleman is to call him a merchant. When

Euryalus, one of the Phaeacian merchants, taunts Odysseus with being a merchant, it is because Odysseus has refused the invitation to join in the athletic contests. This is another example of the Homeric idea that a man's behaviour reflects his lineage. Lack of skill in games is a clear sign of lack of nobility. On this occasion, of course, Euryalus is wrong; Odysseus' excuse for not wishing to participate is genuine. But the taunt spurs Odysseus into activity and his adept handling of the discus is sufficient to convince the Phaeacians – who do not yet know who Odysseus is – that Euryalus has made a serious mistake. So grave an insult requires a profuse apology and a handsome gift to make amends.[13]

The big divide in Homeric society is this one between nobles and commoners, rather than between kings and nobles. In fact it is very difficult to discern any social gap between kings and nobles, and the word *basileus*, the ordinary classical Greek word for king, is often used by Homer in the sense of 'nobleman', though he also uses it to mean 'king'. We have a good example of this confusing ambiguity in the first book of the *Odyssey*, in which Antinous, one of the suitors, reacts to Telemachus' new-found boldness by saying: 'May Zeus never make you king in sea-girt Ithaca, though this is your heritage by birth.' Telemachus returns a soothing answer: 'It is no bad thing to be a king [*basileuemen*]. One's house is at once enriched and one's honour enhanced. But there are many other nobles [*basilēes*] in sea-girt Ithaca, both young and old, one of whom may have that position, since glorious Odysseus is dead. But I shall be master [*anax*] of our house and of the slaves whom Odysseus captured.'[14] This discussion is then rounded off by Eurymachus, who says that the question of who was to be king rested in the lap of the gods, but that, whatever happened, Telemachus would be guaranteed the retention of his house and possessions. This discussion makes it quite plain that Ithaca was a monarchy, though we are left in some doubt as to how the kingship was transmitted, since it was clearly not by automatic hereditary succession. We cannot even be sure that the kingship was held for life, since Odysseus' father Laertes, though still alive, is certainly no longer king – if he ever was.

It is also worth noticing that the Ithacan who had the earliest ties with King Agamemnon was not Odysseus or any member of his family, but one of the suitors, a man otherwise unknown called Amphimedon, who was a guest-friend (*xeinos*) of Agamemnon's and who had put him up when he came to persuade Odysseus to join him in the Trojan expedition.[15]

From all this we must conclude that kings and nobles belonged to the same social grade. Modern parallels are not hard to find. Until the sixteenth century English kings, for example, were generally addressed as 'Your Grace', a title which they shared with dukes and archbishops. It is no accident that the styles 'Your Highness' and 'Your Majesty' appear at a time of monarchical self-assertion.

It is very difficult to estimate the proportion of the population of Homeric society made up by the aristocracy. The nobles seem quite numerous if judged in terms of the number of suitors – and, as we have seen, the suitors were 'by far the noblest' (*meg' aristoi*) of Ithacan youth. All in all, according to Telemachus, there were a hundred and eight suitors, representing only Ithaca and its three neighbouring islands, none of them particularly big.[16] Furthermore, the suitors cannot be regarded as the whole aristocracy of those islands, since they are all young and unmarried. In absolute historical terms the number is probably meaningless. Homer did not venerate statistical accuracy quite so much as it is now fashionable to do. We are told by the archaeologists, for example, that not even the great halls of the palaces of Mycenae and Tiryns – and Odysseus' palace was undoubtedly a punier affair than these – could have held anything like that number. Even taken in relation to other Homeric figures it makes little sense. We are told that Odysseus had fifty female slaves in the palace, but that figure does duty for Alcinous' female household establishment as well.[17] In Alcinous' mythical land of Scheria, which, like Ithaca, is a monarchy, the body of nobles, here also called *basilēes*, is smaller, numbering only a dozen – exactly the same number as the suitors who came from the island of Ithaca itself. Whatever the proportion of the population that the nobility comprised in Homeric society, we cannot but see it as a time of weak monarchies. Indeed, Alcinous seems hardly more than the chairman of a board. In his description of the constitution of Scheria he says that the twelve *basilēes* rule (*krainousi*) over the Phaeacians together with himself, and he urges the others to contribute a share equal to his own towards Odysseus' parting gift.[18] But there is nevertheless no doubt about his superiority to the others, and his palace, as described by his daughter Nausicaa, clearly stands out as the main building of the city.[19]

The political picture in the *Iliad* is complicated by the fact that we do not see the Greek leaders in their natural habitat but as an invading army on foreign soil. As for Trojan political institutions, all we can say is that, like the Homeric Greek state, Troy is a monarchy. It would appear to be a hereditary monarchy, since Priam is portrayed as an old man and since it is assumed that one of his sons will succeed him.[20] In the military setting of the Trojan War Agamemnon is clearly the most important of the Greeks. But is that only because he is commander-in-chief or does it reflect a more permanent political hegemony of Mycenae over the rest of Greece? If the latter, the political structure of Greece as a whole must have been essentially that of the individual states writ large, with the relation between the king of Mycenae and the lesser kings being similar to that between each local king and his own aristocracy. This would give us a three-tier aristocratic hierarchy of great king, lesser kings and nobles. But is that the picture presented to our gaze in the Homeric epics?

The state of Mycenae – quite apart from Agamemnon himself – certainly holds a special position in the *Iliad*. It is, for example, the only state to be described by the epithet 'rich in gold' (*poluchrusos*). Now it is still maintained by some scholars that Homeric epithets are meaningless formulae, the choice of which is determined by exigencies of metre rather than by sense. But as time goes by more and more of Homer's epithets are seen to make some sense as identification tags. Troy is the only city called by Homer *eupōlas* ('abounding in horses'), and his stock epithet for the Trojans – and for no other people – is *hippodamoi* ('tamers of horses'). And the Trojans were just that: the archaeological site of Homeric Troy is strewn with horse bones.[21]

When Achilles objects to Agamemnon's recouping himself for the loss of his own slave-girl by taking Achilles', he explains why it was that he came to Troy in the first place. He had no quarrel, he says, with the Trojans; they had never ravaged his land or stolen his cattle. 'But we followed you, you shameless creature,' he says to Agamemnon, 'so as to give you joy and in an attempt to secure satisfaction for Menelaus and for you, you cur, from the Trojans.'[22] It is difficult to know how to interpret these lines. Was Achilles in some way obliged to join Agamemnon? Odysseus certainly was not, and he took some persuading, so much so that he delayed the expedition.[23] But, if Achilles was not subject in any way to Agamemnon, it seems strange that he should always have had to hand over to him the greater part of the loot from the sacking of a city for which he alone had been responsible. That is one of the things about which Achilles complains in the initial quarrel with which the *Iliad* opens. The best arguments in favour of Agamemnon's exercising an overlordship in Greece are probably to be found in the second book of the *Iliad*. When Agamemnon assembles the troops we are given the full pedigree of his sceptre, which, we are told, signifies that he rules (*anassein*) over 'many islands and the whole of Argos'.[24] Now Greece as a whole has islands aplenty, but if you cast your eye along the coastline assigned to Agamemnon in the Catalogue of Ships in the second book of the *Iliad* you will have the greatest difficulty in picking out any at all. In fact there is not a single island there, the coastline in question lying on the north of the Peloponnese and stretching from Aegium to Corinth.[25] As for Argos, it is assigned by the catalogue not to Agamemnon but to Diomedes. But clearly, whatever the extent of Agamemnon's own kingdom, the phrase 'many islands and the whole of Argos' is intended as a general description of the whole of Greece, as is the expression met with several times in the *Odyssey* to describe the fame of Odysseus, which was renowned 'throughout Hellas and mid-Argos'.[26] The word 'Argives' is similarly used, synonymously with 'Achaeans' and 'Danaans', to represent the Greeks in general, and 'Argos' itself also turns up occasionally in Homer in the loose sense of 'Greece'.[27] Agamemnon's sceptre would, therefore, appear to signify his supremacy over the whole of Greece. The seven cities, moreover, which he offers Achilles as part of his conciliatory gift are none of them anywhere near his own kingdom, but in Messenia in the southwest of the Peloponnese, an area which belongs according to the catalogue to the kingdom of Nestor of Pylos. Indeed, in offering them Agamemnon specifically calls them 'the last cities of sandy Pylos', using the same phrase as that used in the singular by Nestor himself when referring to the town of Thryoessa, a town which it is obvious from the context was within his kingdom.[28] How then could Agamemnon promise them so airily to Achilles? – for there can be no mistake about it; Achilles was to become their sovereign ruler: 'In them live men rich in sheep and cattle, men who will honour him with gifts like a god and who, acknowledging his sceptre, will pay him rich tributes.'[29] Agamemnon could not have been thinking of capturing the seven towns, since they were not in enemy territory. Not only Nestor of Pylos and his sons Antilochus and Thrasymedes, but also Crethon and Orsilochus, the twin sons of King Diocles of Pherae, one of the seven cities, fought in the Greek army at Troy.[30] The only explanation of Agamemnon's offer is that he had some overlordship over the cities, and presumably over Nestor as well as over the kings of the individual cities like Diocles. This explanation ties in with the description of Agamemnon as master of 'many islands and all Argos', or, in other words, of the whole of Greece.

This interpretation is corroborated by other evidence which on its own would not be conclusive. Agamemnon's sceptre is clearly a very special sceptre. As we have seen, Homer carefully traces its pedigree, not failing to mention that it was originally made by Hephaestus for Zeus.[31] When Odysseus tries to restore order among the troops he first goes to Agamemnon to get this sceptre, and with it he strikes the noisy soldiers and Thersites.[32] It is during that same episode that Odysseus addresses his little homily on obedience to the rank and file, the concluding words of which are: 'A multiplicity of rulers [*polukoiraniē*] is not a good thing. Let there be one ruler, one king [*heis koiranos estō, heis basileus*], to whom the son of crafty Cronus [i.e. Zeus] has given sceptre and jurisdiction in order to make decisions for his subjects.'[33] The ruler of whom he is speaking is, of course, Agamemnon, and the language does not seem to indicate only a military sense. Another indication that Agamemnon's rank is superior to that of other kings is Achilles' ironical remark when turning down the proffered hand of any one of the daughters of Agamemnon: 'Let him choose another of the Achaeans who suits him and is more kingly [*basileuteros*] than I.'[34]

Just as the kings of single areas, like Alcinous or Odysseus, were far from being autocrats but shared their power to some degree with the aristocracy, so Agamemnon is obliged to take into account what the other kings – or some of them – recommend, as Nestor reminds him in his usual tactful manner when proposing the sending of a deputation to Achilles.[35] There are references to a 'council of great-souled elders', but it is hard to tell whether that includes all kings properly so called or only some of them. It certainly does not include all *basilēes*, as we can see from the very explicit statement in Book Ten of the *Iliad* that Nestor's son Antilochus and Meriones, nephew and squire of the Cretan king Idomeneus, are invited to attend a particular council meeting.[36] A passage in the second book of the *Iliad* when Agamemnon summons the 'senior leaders of the Panachaeans' is revealing.[37] Only seven names follow, after which the proceedings begin, leading one to believe that these seven are the sum total of the council. If so, this is probably to be regarded as a war council and need not necessarily represent all the normal councillors of the great king when at home. The seven, predictably enough, are Nestor, Idomeneus, the two Aiantes, Diomedes, Odysseus and Menelaus, all of whom are kings, of Pylos, Crete, Salamis, Locris, Argos-Tiryns, Ithaca and Sparta respectively. Since they are also the only real Greek kings (as against *basilēes* in the sense of 'nobles') to play a significant role in the *Iliad*, this could mean that all Greek kings were *ex officio* members of the council of the great king of Mycenae. If so, it might seem strange that Homer should have no word for king in this sense. But is it the case that Homer has no such word? The answer, I believe, is 'No'.

There is a word which sometimes seems to be used as a synonym for *basileus* and whose range of meaning undoubtedly does overlap with that of *basileus* but which a detailed examination of instances will reveal to be essentially different, namely the word *anax*. The first difference that must be noted is that *anax* but not *basileus* can be used of gods as well as of men. Secondly, as a political title, *anax* (or its verb *anassein*) is used only of real kings and their sons, but not of mere nobles. It is thus used to describe such men as Nestor, Idomeneus, Diomedes, Achilles, Menelaus, Alcinous, Priam, his son Helenus, Anchises and his son Aeneas, but *not* any of Penelope's suitors or Alcinous' twelve *basilēes* in the *Odyssey* or any of the large number of noble warriors who appear in the *Iliad*. The man of whom it is used more often than of anyone else is, not surprisingly, Agamemnon himself. The reason why the meaning of *anax* has not generally been seen as clearly as this is that, when used in regard to slaves, the word naturally refers to the master of the household. But there is no ambiguity: the context always makes it quite plain which of the two meanings *anax* will have in any given passage.

What emerges from all this is a political hierarchy embracing the whole Greek world and culminating in the great king of Mycenae. Next in rank are the other *anaktes*, the kings of the several regions (e.g. Nestor, Diomedes or Menelaus), who act as the great king's counsellors. Beneath them are the kings of smaller areas and of individual cities, and then come the ordinary nobles. Some kingdoms, like Odysseus' Ithaca, were probably too small to have sub-kingdoms within them, but we know of at least two which did have them, namely Nestor's Pylos, and Phthia, the kingdom ruled over by Achilles' father Peleus. Pylos seems to have had three tiers of kings – or at least the possibility of having three tiers, because it is hardly likely that Agamemnon contemplated deposing the kings of the seven cities that he offered to Achilles. We do not know for certain that all seven had their own kings, but, as we have seen, Pherae certainly did, and its king, Diocles, was a loyal ally whose father had ruled the city before him. Achilles' position would probably, therefore, have been as a sort of super-king over the rulers of the individual cities but no doubt subordinate to Nestor. In Phthia we know that Phoenix, who had fled there to escape a family feud, was given the Dolopians, a people living in the furthermost part of the kingdom, to rule over (*anassein*), but clearly as subordinate to Peleus, as we can see from the fact that he was engaged as Achilles' tutor and went to Troy together with him.[38]

Achilles is told by Agamemnon that the seven cities are inhabited by rich farmers who would 'honour him with gifts like a god' and 'pay him rich tributes [*themistas*]', but it is difficult to know how he would share the revenue with Nestor and the city kings. In Mycenae itself, in which there is no evidence of sub-kings, we know at least of the military obligations that the aristocracy had to Agamemnon, presumably in his capacity as king of Mycenae rather than as great king of Greece. His mare, Aethe, we are told, had been given him by Echepolus (i.e. 'horse-owner') of Sicyon in lieu of military service. A scholiast remarks on this passage that Agamemnon probably 'thought it more useful to take a warlike horse than a man with no experience of war', but the choice clearly lay with Echepolus rather than with Agamemnon, as is well demonstrated by the other case we have of the same obligation. This is the case of Euchenor of Corinth, who preferred to serve in the army rather than pay 'a heavy fine' (*argaleēn thoen*).[39] Both Sicyon and Corinth are listed as part of Agamemnon's kingdom in the Catalogue of Ships, and there can be no doubt that Echepolus and Euchenor, both of whom are described as coming from rich families, are nobles and that what we have here in these two passages is evidence for some form of military obligation on the part of the aristocracy to the king.

HOMER AND HISTORY

Homeric society has been discussed as a self-contained world without relation to its historical bearings. It is now necessary, however, to turn to the vexed question of which period, if any, it essentially reflects. This question has taken the place of the discussion on whether Homer was one man or many, which was so fashionable in the last century, as *the* Homeric question. It must be clearly understood, though, that, even if Homeric society is thought – as it is by some scholars – to be so hopeless a jumble as to yield nothing of value in the understanding of any particular historical period, it nevertheless reflects an aristocratic view of society which, as we shall see, is never entirely absent from any period of Greek history.

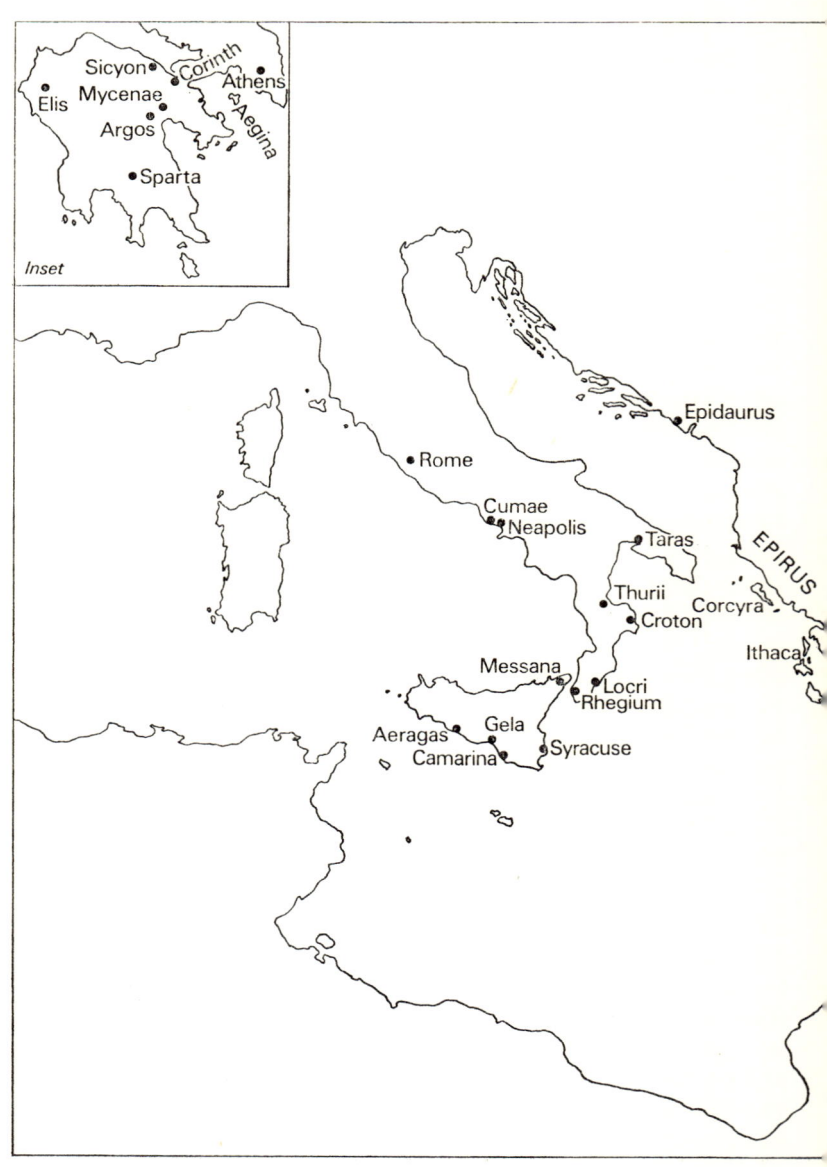

Map of the Greek World in ancient times

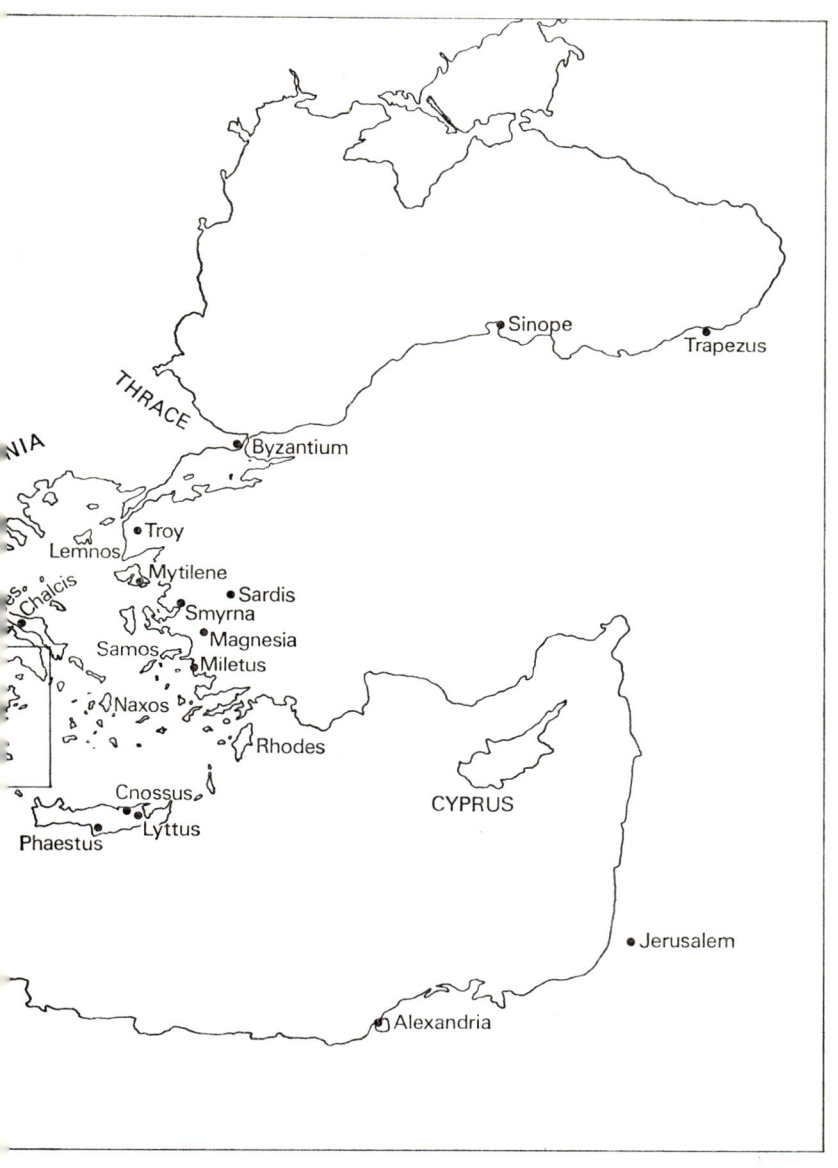

So completely negative an attitude to Homer's historical value is rare, confined to those who believe that the epics are not each a single work of literature but rather a composite heap of fragments of widely differing authorship and date, 'ein übles Flickwerk' (a sorry patchwork), as von Wilamowitz-Möllendorff called it. Studies of modern 'bards', however, especially of the illiterate 'guslari' of Yugoslavia, who compose epics of great length relying entirely upon oral tradition, together with studies of the formulaic nature of Homeric language, has convinced most scholars that the epics were each composed as a single work by a single poet. Whether the poet of the *Odyssey* was the same as that of the *Iliad* or not is a different, and much less important, question. Now that this unitarian view has become the scholarly consensus only two historical periods are generally thought to be reflected in the poems: the Mycenaean period, which the epics claim to be describing, and the period when the poems were written.[40] The traditional date for the Trojan War, as calculated by the third-century Alexandrian scholar Eratosthenes, is 1184, though some modern scholars would place it as early as 1260; and the end of the Mycenaean period as a whole is generally dated between 1200 and 1100. The composition of the epics themselves is placed by different scholars at various points between the ninth and the seventh centuries, so there is a gap of at least three hundred years between the period with which the poems purport to deal and the time when they were composed. It might seem strange, therefore, that scholars should find any difficulty in distinguishing the two strata and deciding how much belongs to the one and how much to the other. Yet that difficulty certainly does exist.

The range of opinion extends from those who believe that the epics contain a fair amount of reliable information about the Mycenaean period to those whose charity will credit Homer with virtually no knowledge of Mycenaean times. More important, perhaps, than the arguments marshalled by the various protagonists is the very fact that such an argument can take place at all. Elements from two periods so widely separated as the Mycenaean age and the late 'Dark Age', it might be thought, should be easily distinguishable. One reason why they are not is undoubtedly the fact that our knowledge of both periods is, to say the least, very defective. But could not another reason be that the two periods were not so different from each other – especially in regard to social and political affairs – as is usually thought? That possibility remains to be explored.

It should be remembered that, if one ignores the epics for the time being, the evidence for these two periods is confined to archaeological remains and, for the Mycenaean period, to the Linear B tablets, the interpretation of both of which is fraught with problems. This needs stressing, especially since modern scholars sometimes write about Mycenaean society as if our knowledge of it were far more firmly based and interpretations more clear-cut than is actually the case. Thus one modern writer, whose scepticism will not allow Homer to get away with anything, has no hesitation in speaking of the 'centralized bureaucratic social organization of Pylos and Mycenae'. This author expresses the view elsewhere that 'there were no feudal, or comparably conditional, tenures in the Homeric world ... The Mycenaean tablets, on the contrary, suggest that in their world conditional tenures were the rule.'[41] Are we to understand from these statements that Mycenaean society was at the same time both a centralized bureaucracy and 'feudal' in structure? If so, we should be more than a little intrigued, for these two types of organization, far from co-existing in the same society, are generally mutually exclusive. Centralized bureaucracy has tended to be associated with strong monarchy, as in Pharaonic Egypt, the heyday of the Byzantine and Ottoman Empires, and France under Louis XIV, in none of which did the aristocracy play an important part in government. In feudalism, on the other hand, the prime examples of which are medieval Europe and medieval Japan, the landed aristocracy tends to be predominant and the central government and monarchy tend to be weak. Can Mycenaean society really be said to partake of both these very different patterns?

Let us assemble what social and political evidence of the Mycenaean age there is of which we can be certain. First, there can be no doubt that it was a period in which states existed which were far larger than the city-states of classical Greece. The Linear B tablets found in Cnossos mention cities scattered over the whole of Crete, but (except for a reference possibly to Cyprus in connection with spices) no place outside the island. The kingdom of which Cnossos was the capital probably embraced the whole of Crete. The Pylos tablets reflect a kingdom made up of two provinces, and the names of sixteen towns occur, nine in the one province and seven in the other. In Mycenae unfortunately no palace records have been found, but the archaeological remains of a palace building have certainly been turned up by the excavator's spade. The palace at Mycenae is only one of several Greek palaces that have been discovered dating from the same period, and it is far from being the best preserved. Built on top of the acropolis it has been exposed to the worst ravages of the weather and part of it has actually fallen over the hill. The palaces of Tiryns and Pylos are in the best state of preservation on the mainland, and palaces have also been unearthed at Athens and Thebes. A glance at the map will show that Mycenae and Tiryns are extremely close together, with less than twenty miles separating them. This puzzling fact is easily understood if we return our gaze to Homer. For, from the Catalogue of Ships included in the second book of the *Iliad*, we learn that Tiryns is in the kingdom of Diomedes whereas Mycenae is in Agamemnon's realm.[43] It is important to emphasize that the Mycenaean age is the only period in Greek history in which there were regional kingdoms of this kind. Homer could certainly not have sucked this idea out of his thumb, however succulent it may have been. We must conclude that the Homeric state is a reflection of Mycenaean actuality in this regard, a view which is not invalidated by certain discrepancies between Homer and the tablets in points of detail.[44]

Let us turn now to what the tablets tell us of the government of Mycenaean states. The word *wanaka*, which has been read in several tablets, both in Pylos and in Cnossos, has been identified with the Greek word *anax* and is thought to refer to the king. It is significant that the word occurs only in the singular, presumably because it refers to the head of state, of whom there was only one. In this regard *wanaka* corresponds exactly to the human application of *anax* in Homer which we have already established as being confined to real kings. Besides the fact that the states, whose capitals were Pylos and Cnossos, were monarchies headed by a *wanaka* the tablets yield very little unambiguous constitutional information, despite the elaborate hypotheses which have sometimes been elicited from them. One of the most vexed problems is the nature of the tenure of land, the main evidence for it being a Pylos tablet interpreted by Ventris and Chadwick, the decipherers of Linear B, as listing the landholding of the king and his 'fief-holders'.[46] The word taken to represent the king's 'preserve' is *temeno*, identified as the Greek word *temenos* which again occurs in Homer in a very similar sense. In the epics it is used only of land held by a king or a god, the use of the latter alone surviving into classical Greek.

A modern writer, intent on demonstrating that Homer cannot be considered a source for the Mycenaean period, has tried to show that his use of the word *temenos* is inconsistent by pointing to the passage in the *Odyssey* where Odysseus, in his visit to Hades, is reassured by his mother that his *temenea* are being held intact by his son Telemachus.[47] Telemachus is not himself a king, but it is clear that what he is doing here is just looking after the land until such time as Odysseus returned – or, presumably, until a new king was installed. This passage can certainly not be used as evidence that the *temenos* was not automatically attached to the kingship, as some would argue.[48] There are also two other passages that refer to a non-king in the same connection. In the one Achilles mockingly imputes to Aeneas as the motive for his courage in facing him in single combat the ambition of gaining the kingship of Troy or the award of a *temenos*.[49] The other passage similarly tells the story of Meleager, son of King Oeneus of the Aetolians, who, when sulking in his bedroom and taking no action against the invading force of Curetes, is offered a *temenos* in return for his renewed co-operation.[50] It should not be forgotten that both Aeneas and Meleager were members of royal families. In the Aeneas passage the grant of the kingship and the award of a *temenos* may be taken as a hendiadys, a common device in Homer.[51] Aeneas certainly pays no separate attention to the taunt about the *temenos* but answers Achilles as if all he had mentioned was the kingship. Similarly, in the case of Meleager there is no specific offer of the kingship or a share of the kingship, but it is emphasized that the offer of a *temenos* is *mega dōron*, 'a great gift', and we are, therefore, a little puzzled when we go on to read that this 'great gift' amounted to only fifty acres of land, though admittedly of the best land. But it is perhaps more important to notice who offered Meleager the *temenos*. It was, we are told, 'the most distinguished priests of the gods', sent by the elders (*gerontes*) of the people. Why priests? This perhaps shows us that we cannot ignore the fact that Homer uses *temenos* to refer to divine precincts as well as royal demesnes. Further evidence of the connection between divine and royal *temenē* is to be found in the *Odyssey*, where we are specifically informed that the *temenos* of King Alcinous abuts upon the grove of Athena.[52] That divine and royal domains should share the same word is perhaps not entirely coincidental. The king was, after all, the head of the state religion as well as of the state, and, indeed, long after monarchy had utterly disappeared from the political constitution a religious official called 'king' survived in some states, among them Athens with its *archon basileus* and Rome with its *rex sacrorum*. Could not the *temenos* therefore, have been attached to the king *ex officio* in his religious capacity?

But the king is not the only person in the tablets to be listed with a *temenos*. Someone called the *lawagetas* also had one, according to our Pylos tablet, though his is only a third of the size of the king's. Here too, it should be noted, as in Homer, *temenē* seem to have been rather small, though it is difficult to know how to interpret the measurements, which are given in terms of yield rather than of area.[53] But who or what was the *lawagetas*? It is identified with the classical Greek word *lagetas* used by Pindar in the rather general sense of 'leader of men', and Ventris and Chadwick translate it as 'the military leader', though the word does not occur in any military context. But, whatever his functions, the *lawagetas* clearly was second only to the king in importance. But do we not find a Homeric parallel here again? Of the twenty-nine contingents listed in the Greek Catalogue of Ships eight are described as being under the main command of two men rather than of one.[54] In some cases the two men, especially when they are brothers, are regarded as equal leaders, but in others it is clear that they are not on a par. The best known example of this latter joint leadership is that of Idomeneus and Meriones of Crete, in addition to which there is the case of Sarpedon and Glaucus on the Trojan side. In both of these cases one member of the pair is king and commander-in-chief of his men, and the other is second-in-command. Meriones is also Idomeneus' nephew and Sarpedon and Glaucus are cousins. Could such cases not offer us a parallel to the connection between the king of Pylos and his *lawagetas* in the tablets? If they too were related to each other we could also the more easily understand the *lawagetas*' holding of a *temenos*.

The next entry on the same tablet, which follows after a blank space, presumably so as to distinguish *temenē* from other land, is interpreted as representing the landholding of three *telestai*, each of whom had the same amount of land as the *lawagetas*. The word *telestas* (if indeed that is the correct reading of what the tablet actually says, namely *tereta*) has been interpreted variously. Some scholars prefer to equate it in sense with the classical Greek word *telestēs* which usually refers to a priest or to the initiate of a mystery cult, but others have translated it rather as 'fief-holder' or 'baron', seeing it as meaning essentially 'man of the service-burden [*telos*]' and, therefore, as a semantic (though not an etymological) equivalent of the word 'baron' itself. This ingenious explanation gains no support, however, from the evidence. The town (or district) of Pakija, we learn from another Pylos tablet, contained no less than fourteen *telestai*, and a Cnossos tablet lists forty-five *telestai* in the town of Aptara.[56] These forty-five *telestai* also appear in rather unsuitable company for 'barons', namely together with five carpenters. From this it would seem unlikely that this interpretation is right. The fact that *telestai* appear on our *temenos*-tablet may perhaps favour a religious interpretation of their position, but we cannot be sure. It would certainly be very strange to have the land held by 'fief-holders' on the same tablet as the royal demesnes, because a list of royal tenants would surely not include the king himself. Quite what the purpose of our *temenos*-tablet could have been is impossible to say.

It is generally accepted amongst scholars that the Linear B tablets portray a 'feudal' type of society, but as we can already see, this view rests largely upon the interpretation of technical terms which are at best ambiguous. In addition to the official titles that we have examined there are the terms *kotona kitimena* and *kotona kekemena*, which have been interpreted to mean 'cultivated land' and 'fallow' or 'private' and 'communal' land respectively.[57] But even if the latter is the right interpretation, it is difficult to know what to make of the large number of tablets describing the size (or yield, or portion of yield?) of private plots, together with the names of the tenants (if that is what they are) on them.[58] The owners of such private plots are not said to be holding them from anyone or in return for anything, so why are there records of their land at Pylos at all? The answer must surely be that what we have here is a tax register. Nor are the 'communal plots' very much more promising for a picture of a 'feudal' society. There are several tablets describing land as held *paro damo*, which is taken to mean 'from the village', but there is no indication that the arrangement here is anything other than a commercial lease.[59] There is one long tablet, as well as several short ones, which is thought by Ventris and Chadwick to record the obligation to render services in return for the tenure of communal land, but the meaning of the key words is once again in doubt, notably that of the word *woze*, which, transcribed as *worzei*, is translated 'he performs [an obligation]', a possible meaning of the classical *rhezo/erdō*, with which it is identified.[60] It has also been suggested that the word be translated 'he cultivates, ploughs', but that is a meaning which is more remote from the classical sense. There is a meaning, however, which both forms of the classical verb often have and which in addition fits the tablet in question very well, and that is, 'he offers a sacrifice'. No less than four of the ten sentences in the tablet contain some religious reference, one of them in fact to a *ijerowoko* or *hieroworgos* (*hieroergos*), translated as 'sacrificing priest', the verbal part of which is precisely the verb *rhezō*.[61] This religious association is no isolated phenomenon in the tablets. Indeed, the overwhelming majority of tablets dealing with land contain some mention of a priest, priestess or slave of a god as a tenant. It would seem from this either that the tablets give only a very partial picture of Mycenaean landholding or else that the central government did not keep a complete land-register but interested itself only in particular categories of land.

When we turn our attention from land tenure to administration our understanding is no less baffled by terminological ambiguities in the tablets. A good number of titles occur which have been taken to represent official designations. The only one which is undeniably connected with the military is the title *eqeta* (*heq^{u}etas*), which is equated with the rather rare classical *hepetēs*, 'follower' or 'attendant'. It appears both in tablets listing the names of officers and the number of men under their command, and in some land-tenure tablets. In the former it occurs in a formula of the type 'and with them the *heq^{u}etas* Alektruon son of Etewoklewes' tacked on to the end of each 'platoon' list.[62] Palmer, followed by Ventris and Chadwick themselves, sees the word as equivalent in sense to the Homeric *hetairos* and interprets it as 'companion of the king' on the analogy of *comes* ('count') in later Latin.[63] Ventris and Chadwick suggest that the *heq^{u}etai* may have been 'liaison officers representing the central authority, the command being in the hands of the local lords'.[64] They also believe that the addition of a patronymic in several cases where a *heq^{u}etas* is named corroborates their importance. There is also a tablet which seems to indicate that the *heq^{u}etai* wore a uniform, mentioning as it does 'twenty-five cloaks with white *onuke* [edges?] suitable for *heq^{u}etai*'.[65] The reason for the record is presumably that the uniforms were supplied by the central government, which really gives us no clue as to their rank. One fact that might make us doubt the illustrious rank assigned to the *heq^{u}etai* by Ventris, Chadwick and Palmer is that in the military tablets they are attached to quite small contingents of men, often no more than twenty or fifty, and in one case ten.[66]

This should warn us not to try to work out the rank and meaning of a title from purely etymological and semantic considerations. Such studies are of the greatest value in the study of the history of an office or position but cannot stand alone. If we were to use the same method to work out the meaning of modern titles such as 'knight', 'peer', 'marshal' or 'chancellor' we would be very misinformed indeed, for

KINGS AND HEROES

all those titles have very different functions today from those which they had originally. A field marshal, for example, might be excused for feeling slightly piqued at being taken for a groom or farrier, which is his title's original sense.

Several other titles have turned up in the tablets which are thought to represent regional officials. But here again the evidence is unclear, and, even if we accept such words as *moropa, korete, porokorete* and *damokoro* as indicating the titles of local officials, we can still infer very little from either the titles themselves or from their contexts as to the work they did or their relation to the king and his government.[67] The title which has probably attracted the greatest interest, however, is *pasireu*, which has been identified with the Greek word *basileus*.[68] Ventris and Chadwick suggest that the *pasireu* has a similar position in the outlying towns to that occupied in the capital by the *lawagetas*, because a Cnossos tablet that seems to be a list of administrative officials has the title *lawagetas* associated with Cnossos, but the two other towns listed have a *pasireu* instead.[69] To add to this impression we have the word *kerosija*, which occurs in connection with a man who is probably described in another tablet as *pasireu* and which is identified with *gerousia* (council).[70] If this is right, we are pretty close here to the Homeric conception of the *basileus*. Unfortunately, however, all is not plain sailing. In a Cnossos tablet that is thought to be a tribute-list of gold from the leading men the contribution from the *pasireu* is at a rather low level, the same in value as that from the *porokorete*, Palmer's 'assistant district officer'.[71] If we could be sure that what we have here is a tribute-list (rather than, say, a salaries register), we might see it as a parallel to the *themistes* in Homer.

After reading this very sceptical and negative account of the picture of Mycenaean society emanating from the Linear B tablets the reader may find it difficult to understand how scholars could ever have been so certain that it was a 'feudal' or a bureaucratic society. The fact that scholars often speak as if Mycenaean society was both of these at the same time should in itself, as we have already pointed out, have given the game away. It is a fault into which even Ventris and Chadwick slip, as, for example, when they speak of the *pasireu, moropa* and *korete* as 'officials' in one place and as 'chieftains' in another.[72] All we can really say about Mycenaean society from the tablets is that it appears to have been highly organized, but we have no idea at all about its power-structure. Was the *wanax* the autocratic head of a tightly controlled bureaucratic machine with tiers of officials reaching down into the localities? Or was he merely the highest of the nobles in the land, a head of state sharing his rule with the aristocracy? The fact that there were scribes keeping elaborate records at the centre does not necessarily indicate a powerful and centralized bureaucracy because we really do not know what the purpose of all this record-keeping was, or, in many cases, even the meaning of the records themselves. On their own the tablets give us very little insight into the nature of Mycenaean government and society. With the aid of extraneous evidence, however, we could perhaps begin to understand the tablets better and be able to select with some discretion from the welter of ambiguous alternative interpretations which confronts us in the tablets. But what other evidence is there? Only Homer, who, after all, claims to be dealing with the Mycenaean world of a date not very remote at least from the Pylos tablets. There is, moreover, a fair degree of agreement between the Homeric picture and that which is discernible in the tablets.

First, the states in both Homer and the tablets are regional monarchies of a kind never again to be found in the annals of Greek history. In both sources these states are headed by a king styled *wanax* or *anax* who possesses a demesne known in both cases – and in no other period of Greek history – as a *temenos*, a name which in both cases is also used to denote the sacred precincts of a god. The fact that the tablets found in Cnossos are not only stylistically indistinguishable from those found in Pylos but also use the same titles and deal with the same subjects indicates that Crete and Pylos were states of the same type and make it more than feasible to see them as parts of a larger state system. This is corroborated by archaeological evidence, which shows more uniformity in the pottery of the various parts of the Mycenaean world than at any other period of Greek history. Precisely such a state system does indeed appear in Homer, as we have seen, with the king of Mycenae at the head not only of an allied army but evidently also of the whole Greek world. Once again, nothing resembling this pattern was ever to recur in Greek history. Within each state, according to Homer, there was a hierarchy of aristocrats, with power shared by the various aristocratic tiers. Here the tablets are rather ambiguous, but there certainly is a hierarchy, one of whose members shares his title with Homeric nobles, namely, *basileus* – a usage confined to the tablets and to Homer: in classical Greek the word always means 'king'. In both Homer and the tablets, furthermore, there is some mention of the paying of tribute to the king – another feature which marks off Homer and the tablets from the records of all later periods. These parallels, it should be noted, are not in incidentals but concern the basic structure of society. Most important of all, they are common only to Homer and the tablets. The conclusion that Homeric society is essentially Mycenaean society is inescapable.

The identification is not without its difficulties and there obviously are features in the Homeric picture, usually points of detail, which do not belong to the Mycenaean age. Homer knew, for example, that in the Mycenaean period swords were made of bronze, but on five occasions in the *Iliad* he seems to forget this and allows them to be made of the more modern metal, iron. But in several things that Homer was thought to have got 'wrong' he has been vindicated as archaeology has turned up more and more evidence. Bronze greaves and armour, which Homer often mentions, have now been shown not only to have existed in the Mycenaean age, but also not to have existed at any other time.[73] Similarly, Homer was regularly accused of anachronism for putting temples and lifesize cult images into his epics, but two temples have come to light on Delos and a further one on the island of Ceos off the coast of Attica, in which, moreover, lifesize cult statues have been found.[74] One of the most serious differences between Homer and the Mycenaean archaeological remains is that Homer cremates his dead while the Mycenaeans generally buried theirs. But, here again, further evidence has come to Homer's rescue in showing the growing incidence of cremation towards the end of the Mycenaean period, precisely, that is, the period with which Homer claims to be dealing. Examples have turned up from places as far apart as Prosymna in the Argolid, Pylos, Attic Perati, Rhodes, Cos, Naxos and Crete.[75] It should also be remembered that Homer's cremations take place in Troy, which certainly practised cremation throughout the Mycenaean period.[76] But probably Homer's most vexed 'anachronisms' are his treatment of spears and chariots. Homeric heroes are usually thought of as armed with two throwing-spears, while Mycenaean warriors are thought of as having a single thrusting-spear, but here again a close examination will show a much less clear-cut picture. Homeric heroes carry two spears in surprisingly few cases in the epics and evidence of Mycenaean throwing-spears has now come to light.[77] As for chariots, Homer is usually accused of misunderstanding the correct use of a chariot in battle and mocked for using his chariots merely to taxi his warriors to and from the battlefield instead of massing them in charges as he should have done.[78] In fact we really know nothing about the Mycenaean use of chariots in war. Arguments from analogy prove nothing, and there are parallels for both uses.[79] Moreover, Greek terrain is hardly suitable for massed chariot charges, and, if horses could be used in later times, as they were, merely to transport the warrior to the battlefield, where he would dismount and fight on foot, it is no more unreasonable for chariots to have been used for the same purpose in the Mycenaean period.

The remaining arguments against accepting Homer as a source for the Mycenaean period are mostly negative. If Homer had really known anything about Mycenaean society, runs the argument, then we should surely find references in the epics to the elaborate bureaucracy with its tiers of officials with their various titles, to conditional tenures of land and to the written word, all of which the proponents of such arguments accept axiomatically as important features of Mycenaean society.[80] But the picture of Mycenaean society that emerges from the tablets is not nearly so well defined as such critics seem to think. If there is a lack of evidence of 'centralized bureaucratic social organization' in Homer, it is no more in evidence in the tablets. Likewise, if the epics show no sign of conditional tenures of land (though there is good Homeric evidence for other sorts of 'feudal' obligation, e.g. military obligation and tribute), the tablets are equally unhelpful here. If the epics fail to use all the varied titles that appear in the tablets, we should hardly be surprised to find that the language of the bard differs from that of the scribe. It should also be noted, for example, that in classical times poets do not always use technical terms and titles very accurately, even contemporary ones. Thus, the head of state might have the title *archagetas* (as in Sparta) or *prutanis* (as in several oligarchies) and nevertheless be described in literature as *basileus*. As for the art of writing, its importance is exaggerated out of all proportion. With the exception of some fifty inscriptions on jars and one solitary graffito on a wall in Cnossos, Linear B is confined to clay tablets evidently written by professional scribes numbering about thirty in Pylos and approximately the same number in Cnossos.[81] That is hardly what one would call a 'literate society', and it also enables us to understand how the art of writing could disappear in the 'Dark Age'. Much is made by some modern writers of the contrast between the elaborate scribal records of property embodied in the tablets and the fact that Odysseus' swineherd Eumaeus can recite the whole of his master's property by heart.[82] But, despite Eumaeus' very proper pride in the extent of his master's fortune, Odysseus' wealth must have been small beer by comparison with that of a Menelaus or a Nestor, as we can tell from the way in which Odysseus' son Telemachus gapes at the sight of Menelaus' palace.⁸³

Those features of Homeric society which it shares with the tablets but which never recur again in Greek history must be Mycenaean, as we have seen. But there are other features of Homeric society, notably cremation, which are to be found in the 'Dark Age' as well as in the Mycenaean period. In these cases we cannot know whether Homer's account is based on Mycenaean traditions or on the practice of his own day. But much more important than that, some of these features which survived the Mycenaean age evidently continued right through the 'Dark Age' as well and reappear when the curtain goes up on Greek history once more in the seventh century. In the light of this we should perhaps reconsider the generally accepted view that, just as 'the archaeological record in Greece is marked by a very sharp downward break after the destruction of Mycenae . . .', so 'the very structure of society (not merely the scale) had changed'.⁸⁴

Once again the archaeological evidence is much less clear-cut than some would like to think. So much so that it has even been quite seriously suggested and plausibly argued that the Mycenaean period did not come to an end as a result of an invasion,⁸⁵ as most scholars still believe, though the Dorians, who were once generally regarded as the culprits, are no longer held responsible but are thought to have arrived on the scene after the Mycenaean civilization had already come to an end. But even those who believe that that civilization owed its demise to an invasion have to admit that 'there is no single object or custom which can be associated with the invaders in any region passed through by them . . . Not only have we no evidence of any alien objects, we have no evidence of any settlement at all.'⁸⁶ From this the conclusion is drawn that 'the invaders did not settle in any of the areas which they overran, but departed.'⁸⁷ Can we really believe that invaders overran Mycenaean Greece in sufficient numbers to disrupt the whole society without leaving any traces whatsoever? There can be no doubt that there was a fair amount of disruption, the chief feature of which being the abandonment of some of the main centres of Mycenaean life, notably Laconia and Messenia, the areas covered by the kingdoms of Sparta and Pylos. This was associated with a general and severe reduction in the population of Greece as a whole, though outlying parts of the Mycenaean civilization such as Achaea, East Attica, the Cyclades and Ionian islands, Rhodes, Cyprus and the coast of Asia Minor gained an influx of settlers. What was the cause of this depopulation and shift in population is unknown, but continuity with the Mycenaean past was certainly not entirely broken. Close connections persisted between East Attica, the Dodecanese and Miletus, as can be seen from pottery. Tombs excavated in Rhodes, Cos, Naxos and Perati, moreover, 'include a fair amount of gold, and semi-precious stones are commonly used for beads, and it is possible to conclude that the standard of living was fairly high'.[88] Outside this limited area the unity of the Mycenaean age was indeed fragmented, but the overall picture that now emerges from the archaeological remains is of a much more gradual decline, stretching over a period of more than two centuries, from the thirteenth to the eleventh centuries. The striking feature is the lack of any intrusive element in the archaeological remains to explain this decline. Whether it is explained in terms of internal conflict, which seems unlikely in view of the destruction and wholesale desertion of certain sites, or in terms of the advent of other Greek-speaking peoples whose culture was indistinguishable from that of the Mycenaeans, which might gain some measure of support from the diversification of Greek dialects, the fact remains that the cultural break was not nearly so clean as is often thought. In this regard, it is perhaps worth noting, the picture of early Greek history as presented by archaeology is not so remote as it might previously have seemed from that presented by Thucydides.[89]

CHAPTER II

HEYDAY OF ARISTOCRACY

The curtain goes up on Greek history again in the seventh century and we notice at once that the backdrop has changed. There is no sign now of the palace that adorned the stage in the Mycenaean scene. What we see instead are temples, smaller buildings and a stoa surrounding a central *agora*. The *polis*, the city-state, has made its début. Some critics would have us believe it is not only the stage-set that has changed, but that we are now watching a different play altogether. 'In all Greek history this is one of the most mystifying vanishing acts,' writes one such scholar in referring to the disappearance of monarchy and its replacement by aristocracy.[1] If it is a vanishing act it is a singularly clumsy one, and as for mystification the reader will have to judge for himself. But, considering that the monarchies that we found in Homeric society, which is to say in the late Mycenaean period, were decidedly weak, and that power seems already to have resided largely in the hands of the aristocracy, we should hardly be very surprised to discover that monarchy has now altogether disappeared in the majority of Greek states. Whether the Mycenaean kings had ever been autocrats lording it over all they surveyed is impossible to say and the tablets give us no idea of the power relations in Mycenaean society. But in the society which Homer portrays, which we have identified essentially with the late Mycenaean world, there can be no doubt that monarchy is weak. The time of troubles that then supervened cannot but have had an adverse effect upon the power of the kings. As the disorder swept the central royal governments away, so it must have enhanced the power of the landed aristocracies. We do not have any details of this process, but, seeing the situation both before and after the period of disorder, we may be excused for believing that the sum of two and two is four. It is also worth noting that similar results have occurred in similar circumstances at other times and in other societies, the obvious example being the case of the 'decline and fall' of the Roman Empire.[2]

The novelty of the city-state has also undoubtedly been exaggerated. It was not unknown even in the Mycenaean period, though within the framework of larger regional monarchies and the over-all supremacy of the king of Mycenae. We have already had occasion to mention Pherae as a city-state of this kind with its own king, but even some of the regional kingdoms in the Mycenaean period were no bigger than the city-states of the classical age. Odysseus' Ithaca and Ajax' Salamis are the first examples that spring to mind, but the kingdoms of Diomedes and Agamemnon as defined in the Homeric Catalogue of Ships were not themselves appreciably bigger than their classical successor-states of Argos and Corinth respectively, though their borders were very different, and Menelaus' Sparta as defined in the same source formed only a small part of the area of the classical state of the same name.[3]

ROYAL-CLAN ARISTOCRACIES

It is significant that the commonest of the early forms of aristocracy was one which limited power to the descendants (and possibly collaterals) of the last king, which would seem the natural sequel to weak monarchy in a time of disruption. A good many states are known to have had this form of government, including Corinth, Mytilene, and probably also Thessaly, Epirus, Chios, Scepsis and the majority of Ionian towns on the coast of Asia Minor, notably Erythrae, Clazomenae, Ephesus and Miletus.

On most of these we have very little information. In the case of Mytilene all we know is that the ruling group claimed descent from King Penthilus, who is made the son of Orestes in mythology.[4] We cannot be certain that this claim of royal descent on the part of the Penthilids was genuine, but it is nevertheless significant that it should have been made; and we also know that the Penthilids did not include the whole aristocracy of Mytilene, since two other noble houses are named by the lyric poet Alcaeus, the Cleanactidae and the Archeanactidae.[5] That these two families were noble is clear from Alcaeus.[6]

Miletus was similarly under the Neleidae, descendants of Neleus, Nestor's father according to Homer, who was traditionally thought to have founded the city.[7] The government seems to have retained the outward appearance of monarchy, as power (*archē*) is described by Aristotle as being transferred from one man to another and we also know from Nicholas of Damascus of a certain Laodamas, who 'ruled the Milesians as king' (*ebasileuse*).[8]

Several other Ionian cities on the coast of Asia Minor seem to have had a similar form of government. Herodotus tells us that some of them chose as their 'kings' (*basileus*) the descendants of the Lycian king Glaucus, who appears in Homer on the Trojan side and who rather stupidly swops his gold armour for the bronze armour of Diomedes; that others chose the Caucones of Pylos, descendants of Codrus, son of Melanthus; and that yet others chose both.[9] The house of Glaucus, it should be noted, was of native Lycian blood, whereas the descendants of Codrus were the Neleidae, who probably ruled other Ionian cities in addition to Miletus and who are here interestingly identified as Caucones, a pre-Greek people originally inhabiting Triphylia in the western Peloponnese and near neighbours, therefore, of the Pylians.[10] This identification ties in with the persistent tradition that, when expelled from the Peloponnese by the Heraclidae, Nestor's family (i.e. the Neleids) made for Asia via Athens.[11] The form of government seems to have started off as monarchy, and, in those states in which power was entrusted to both a native Lycian dynasty and a Greek one, possibly a dual monarchy. But it turned eventually into rule by the royal clan or clans. Strabo tells us that the descendants of Androclus, one of the sons of King Codrus of Athens and traditional founder of Ephesus, were still in his own day (the Augustan age) called kings and were accorded certain honours, such as the right to sit in the front row at the games, and the privilege of wearing purple and carrying a staff as a sign of their royal descent.[12] At Erythrae, similarly, we learn from Aristotle that there was an 'oligarchy of the Basilidae', which means literally the 'sons of a king' and at Chios the same name recurs in Herodotus as the patronymic of an oligarchical opponent of the tyrant Strattis, who had presumably overthrown the aristocratic government of the royal house.[13] In the more remote parts of Greece this form of government evidently persisted for a long time, for when Thucydides introduces us to the Chaonians of Epirus during the Peloponnesian War he tells us that they had no king but were led by Photius and Nicanor, members of the 'ruling clan' (*ek tou archikou genous*) who held the annual presidency (*prostateia*) at the time.[14] The same seems to have applied to the Thesprotians, also from Epirus.[15]

The best known case of a royal clan monopolizing power in an aristocratic constitutional framework is that of Bacchiad Corinth. The Bacchiads were a family tracing their origin back to the first Dorian king of Corinth, Aletes. Bacchis, who gave the family its name, was, according to tradition, the fifth of the Dorian kings and a direct descendant of Aletes himself, who was sometimes regarded as the original Dorian conqueror of Corinth and sometimes as arriving on the scene about a generation later.[16] There were thought to be either ten or twelve Dorian kings of Corinth, all of the same line, after which the headship of state was vested in an annually elected *prutanis*, still drawn from the Bacchiad family until the tyranny of Cypselus about a century later. There are slight divergences in the various accounts – all of them very brief – which have come down to us, especially in regard to the end of the monarchy. Pausanias has the last Bacchiad (or Bacchid, as he prefers to call it) king as Telestes, who, he tells us, was murdered by two men whose names he gives as Arieus and Perantas, after which there were no more kings.[17] Telestes, according to Diodorus Siculus, was killed by relatives and was succeeded by Automenes, who reigned for one year, after which the Bacchiads, who totalled two hundred in all, monopolized power as a body, electing an annual *prutanis* from among their own number to be head of state.[18] Herodotus adds the significant piece of information that the Bacchiads married exclusively within their own clan.[19] The only fixed date in all this is that of Cypselus' accession to power in 657, estimates of the duration of the Bacchiad aristocratic republic varying between ninety and 119 years.[20] Pausanias' statement that after the introduction of the *prutanis* there was no longer a king has been challenged on the ground that Cypselus bore the title 'king', but we shall have to return to this question when we discuss him.[21] The over-all picture in Corinth is very similar to that in the other cities which we have already examined, though Corinth was a Dorian state, but the change from monarchy to aristocracy took place ten generations after the Dorian conquest – ample time for the Dorian monarchy to suffer the same stresses and strains as its Ionian and Aeolian counterparts.[22]

ATHENS

In Athens there was also a royal house that retained prominence after ceasing to hold the kingship, but it is probably not quite a parallel case to the ones already mentioned, because only one member of the royal family, rather than the whole clan, appears to have held office at any one time. This family was the Neleids once again, who were traditionally thought to have taken refuge in Athens when expelled from Messenia – which is not so implausible as used to be thought, especially in view of the depopulation of Messenia and the influx of people into Attica at the end of the Mycenaean period, as we have already seen.[23] One branch of the Neleid clan was believed to have remained in Athens and the rest to have sailed across to the coast of Asia Minor. The first Neleid kings of Athens, according to tradition, were Melanthus and his son Codrus, whose son Medon was regarded as the first life-archon.[24]

In the second book of Thucydides we find an interesting description of the early constitution of Athens. Attica, we learn, had originally been divided into autonomous towns, which, though nominally under the suzerainty of the king of Athens, had sometimes even made war on him.[25] This picture corresponds remarkably well with the general picture of Mycenaean government that we analyzed in the last chapter and also with what little Homer has to say about Athens: in the Catalogue of Ships the king of Athens seems to be the ruler of the whole of Attica, and in the *Odyssey* Cape Sunium, the southernmost tip of Attica, is described as the 'headland of Athens'.[26] Thucydides goes on to explain how Theseus, ninth on the traditional list of kings, reorganized the state and made it more centralized. In classical times not only did the king survive as one of the nine archons (though he is always called just *basileus* not *archon basileus*), but there were four *phylobasileis* (literally, 'tribal kings') as well. In classical times their functions were very vestigial, since all we know about them is that they sat together with the *basileus* himself in the rather futile murder trials where there was no accused or in cases of homicide where the 'guilty' party was an animal or an inanimate object.[27] But could not this committee of the five kings have been the original council of the realm? – again something with which we are familiar from the Mycenaean period. And could not the four *phylobasileis* have been the sub-kings of the regions of Attica as well as the heads of the four original tribes? According to Aristotle's *Athenian Constitution* the decline of the monarchy occurred in three stages. The life-kingship was first replaced by a ten-year term and then later by an annual one.[28] This brief analysis is usually rejected by modern scholars as too schematic or 'improbable in itself', though the explanations offered in its place are often no more plausible.[29] In any case, we do know of cases in other periods where the tenure of an office was gradually extended with a view to increasing the power of its holder – the best known example of this being Julius Caesar's dictatorship – so why can we not believe it possible for the same process to happen in reverse?

The decline of the monarchy is related to the question of the creation of the new posts of archon and polemarch, and there were two schools of thought on the subject among the ancients: those, like Aristotle in his *Athenian Constitution*, who believed that the monarchy continued indefinitely, albeit greatly weakened politically; and those, notably Pausanias, who regarded the accession of the Medontidae as marking the end of monarchy and the replacement of the king at the head of the state by the archon:

> At that time [743 BC] there were not yet in Athens annually elected archons. For the people at first stripped the descendants of Melanthus, known as the Medontidae, of most of their power, and converted their office into a responsible magistracy instead of monarchy, but they later set a ten-year limit on their tenure of office.[30]

Pausanias seems here to mean that the Medontidae lost the title of king as well as the power that had gone with it. Yet he was certainly well aware of the fact that there was still a *basileus* in Athens in his own day.[31] More puzzling than that, he is at pains in another passage to insist that the monarchy continued until the reign of Clidicus, the last king but one on the traditional list.[32] The easy explanation of this inconsistency – and it did not take nineteenth-century scholars long to think of it – is that it reflects Pausanias' use of two different sources.

In view of the recurrence in Roman sources of the idea that the Athenian monarchy came to an end on the death of King Codrus, Medon's father, this *Quellenforschung* explanation may possibly be right.[33] We know that the monarchy, or at any rate the existence of someone called a *basileus*, did not come to an end then – nor at any subsequent classical time, as is vouched for by Plato.[34] The double tradition could have arisen from a confusion. There can be no doubt that the period of Athenian history dominated by the Medontidae marks a political watershed of one kind or another, and our best guide in this matter is probably Aristotle's *Athenian Constitution*, which tells us that the archonship first came into existence in the reign of Medon or of his son Acastus (traditionally dated to about a century after the Trojan War).[35] Athenian archons, we are told in addition, took an oath 'as in the days of Acastus'.[36] Most authorities, according to Aristotle, date the institution of the archonship to the time of Medon, but some prefer to date it to Acastus on the basis of the oath 'on the ground that it was in his time that the Codridae [i.e. the Medontidae] retired from the kingship in return for the privileges granted to the archon.'[37] Several other sources make the death of Codrus and the accession of his son Medon the turning-point, including the Eusebius-Jerome chronology, the epitomator Justin and Velleius Paterculus, the last two connecting the constitutional change with the heroic self-sacrifice of Codrus.[38] An oracle had pronounced that the invading Peloponnesians would capture Athens – unless they killed the king. Codrus duly disguised himself as a shepherd, made his way to the enemy camp, where he provoked a scuffle and so managed to get himself killed without being recognized.[39] Considering that this heroic deed was in the interests of Athens we might think depriving his family of the kingship immediately afterwards a strange form of gratitude. The tradition that no one was now thought worthy to succeed Codrus in view of his heroism and that this was the reason for the end of the monarchy derives only from late sources, notably Justin's brief history written in the fourth century of the current era. It also rings extremely hollow and is probably to be regarded as an attempt on the part of a historian to reconcile what would otherwise appear to be two incompatible facts: Codrus' heroism and the end of the monarchy. A different and much more ordinary explanation of the end of the monarchy offered in Aristotle's *Athenian Constitution* is that 'kings were no longer chosen from the family of Codrus because they appeared extravagant and had become soft.'[40] But this by no means solves our problem. It must be remembered that the kingship was not abolished but only ceased to be held by the Medontids, who, however, to complicate matters still further, were not deprived of all political power, because they now monopolized the archonship, which was long to remain the most important political office in Athens. The Medontids had presumably gone down rather than up in the world but they clearly were not entirely eclipsed, the period of their predominance ending, according to the traditional chronology, only three and a half centuries after the death of Codrus. Though at first held for life the archonship was evidently elective rather than hereditary, and the position of *basileus* presumably became so as well, as must the post of polemarch (the military commander-in-chief) whenever it came into existence.[41] These three offices were traditionally thought to have been held for life until 752, then for ten-year terms until 683, which date, a generation after the end of Medontid supremacy, was supposed to mark the transition to the familiar classical system of nine archons (including the *basileus*) elected annually.[42]

How much importance the Medontid clan had as a whole is impossible to say.[43] It is likely that only the archon himself had any power, the rest of the family being roughly on a par with the electors.[44] By contrast with the states already discussed the picture here seems to be one of aristocratic rule rather than rule by a royal house, and the Medontids do not appear to have been an exclusive caste, as, for example, were the Bacchiads of Corinth, since several names belonging to other noble Athenian families appear in the archon-list during the period of Medontid supremacy, which continued, according to the traditional dating, to 712.[45] Such names are Megacles and Alcmaeon, which are associated with the famous Alcmaeonid family, Ariphron and Agamestor, which are connected with the Buzygae and Philaidae respectively. The obvious explanation for the appearance of these names on the list is intermarriage between the families which they represent and the Medontid house.[46]

It should be noticed that the Medontids were not in the strict sense Eupatrids, since they were, as we have seen, traditionally regarded as Pylian immigrants who arrived in Athens a century after the time of Theseus.[47] The Eupatridae, on the other hand, by which term is meant the old hereditary aristocracy of Athens, are said by Plutarch (possibly on the authority of Aristotle) to have been separated out from the rest of the population by Theseus.[48] The attribution of the division of society into classes to the work of a single individual at a particular point in time is nonsensical, but Plutarch's statement is by no means incompatible with the account of Theseus' constitutional reform as given by Thucydides, who says that in reorganizing the government Theseus dissolved all the local councils and magistracies and established a single central council and administration for the whole state.[49] Thucydides does not actually describe the composition of Theseus' centralized council, but it is a safe bet that it was made up entirely of Eupatrids.[50] What evidence we have of the nature and functions of the Eupatrids points strongly in this direction. 'Those who are called Eupatrids', reads an anonymous anecdote, 'live in the city itself, share royal descent and are in charge of religious affairs.'[51] The royal descent referred to here must mean descent from the original local rulers of Attica. Plutarch similarly tells us that Theseus 'assigned to the Eupatrids the duty of religious knowledge, of filling the magistracies and of being teachers of the law and interpreters of religious and sacred matters.'[52] With the end of monarchy and the institution of an elective headship of state in the archonship the power of the Eupatrids was probably enhanced, and as their power grew, so they shortened the tenure of the archonship.

We know nothing about the method of election to the archonship except the tantalizingly vague statement in Aristotle's *Athenian Constitution*, purportedly embracing all three major offices (i.e. the positions of archon, polemarch and *basileus*) through the periods of life-tenure, ten-year terms and annual election down to the reforms of Draco (traditionally dated to 621): 'They appointed [*kathistasan*] the holders of the chief offices by birth [*aristindēn*] and wealth.'[53] But to whom does the 'they' refer, and to whom the phrase 'by birth and wealth'? In a later chapter of the *Athenian Constitution* we read that 'in ancient times' the Areopagus Council had the independent right of selecting the magistrates.[54] This statement, corresponding as it does with the view airily expressed in a passage of Isocrates' *Areopagiticus*, is not generally accepted, but, according to Hignett, 'may safely be dismissed as one of Isocrates' inventions to glorify the Areopagus.'[55] Despite this, there is, however, no reason to believe that Aristotle got the idea from Isocrates in the first place. If, moreover, the description of Draco's reforms is accepted, then the two passages fit neatly together. According to this, Draco gave the electoral power to those who provided themselves with arms, or in other words, to the hoplites.[56] Modern scholars do not generally, however, accept the Draconian constitutional reform as historical, partly because Draco is nowhere else mentioned as a constitutional (as against a judicial) reformer, partly because the property qualification for the nine archons and the Treasurers of Athena which Aristotle here also associates with Draco's reforms is thought to be anachronistic, and partly because the whole idea is regarded as reeking 'of the doctrinaire oligarchism of the late fifth and early fourth centuries'.[57] But, if we accept the Draconian constitutional reform, we can believe both the statement that 'in ancient times' the magistrates were elected by the Areopagus Council and also the statement in Aristotle's *Politics* that Solon made no change in regard to the Council or the election of magistrates.[58] If we put these three passages together the following chronology emerges: Stage I (before Draco): the magistrates are elected by the Areopagus Council. Stage II (probably 624/1): Draco transfers the elections to the hoplites and eligibility for office is decided by a property qualification. Stage III (c. 580): Solon extends the franchise to all citizens.

This sequence is far from implausible, the only snag being that Aristotle speaks of Stage I as if it belonged to the immediate pre-Solonian constitution, though he uses a vague phrase 'in ancient times'.[59] Most modern scholars refuse to believe that there ever were any Draconian laws other than a law of homicide, which Aristotle's *Athenian Constitution* tells us was the only piece of Draco's legislation that was not repealed by Solon.[60] The very existence of Draco has been called into question, and, since his name means 'snake' in Greek, it has been suggested that he is just a personification of the snake which lived on top of the Acropolis and acted as the watchdog of Athens, signalling the approach of an enemy by refusing to eat its monthly honey-cake.[61] A more serious objection to the historicity of Draco's constitution is, as mentioned above, that it bears an uncomfortably close resemblance to the doctrines of the late fifth-century oligarchs, who were always anxious to claim that their blueprint had the imprimatur of antiquity and was none other than the 'ancestral constitution' (*patrios politeia*).[62] But perhaps the question of the historicity of Draco or of his constitution is less important than has sometimes been thought. According to the above sequence, Draco and Solon represent two phases in the transition from a system of government based upon birth to one based on wealth. The two men were, moreover, separated in time by only one generation – or at most by two.[63] But whether we regard Solon's reforms as being anticipated to some degree by those of Draco or whether we reject the historicity of Draco's constitutional reforms, there can be no doubt that the transition from birth to wealth as the criterion of eligibility for political office dates from the period 650–570 or, to limit it further, probably 624–570 – a period of turbulence and change in Greece, as we shall see in the next chapter.

But that by no means disposes of the question of classes in pre-Solonian Athens. Aristotle tells us in his *Athenian Constitution* that, in his organization of the constitution, Solon 'divided the population into four classes according to wealth, as it had been divided previously as well'.[64] This seemingly straightforward statement has occasioned much scholarly controversy.[65] The tendency is to accept either the first half of Aristotle's statement or the second, but not both. Rejection of the first half is the product of the belief that Solon was not a reformer but merely a recorder of what the law already was[66] – a view so totally at variance with the evidence that it is difficult to believe that it could be seriously held. But more of that presently. Rejection of the second half of Aristotle's statement, which would probably be able to claim a large body of scholarly support, is the natural corollary to the dismissal of Draco's constitutional reforms as bogus.[67] But, if looked at from a different angle, Aristotle's statement as a whole could be regarded as yet further evidence, in addition to what has already been cited above, of the genuineness of Draco's reforms. Stage II of the three-stage scheme outlined above would then include a division of the population into wealth-based categories, upon which eligibility for office was based. Aristotle's belief that the population of Athens had already been divided into wealth-based classes before Solon's reforms can indeed refer only to Draco's supposed constitutional reforms. Aristotle clearly saw Draco as the originator of a wealth-based rather than a birth-based political system, as we can see from the reforms which he attributed to that legendary figure. He may have been trying to square that belief with the view that regarded Solon as responsible for the timocratic class divisions, but no one in antiquity ever thought of attributing this reform to anyone other than one of these two men. The earliest possible date for the change was, therefore, in about 680 and the latest 570 – despite the attempts of some modern scholars to push it back to the remote past.[68]

This discussion also raises another question, one which exercised the ancients as well as modern scholars: was there an Areopagus Council before Solon? Plutarch inclined towards the view that there was, though he was evidently in the minority in his own day, when the establishment of the Areopagus was generally attributed to Solon.[69] Plutarch reached his conclusion by logical deduction, but there was also a tradition, reflected in Aeschylus' *Eumenides*, that the Areopagus Council traced its origin – at least as a law court – to the earliest days of Athenian history. Plutarch's reason for believing in the pre-Solonian existence of the Council was that Solon himself mentioned it in one of his laws as already in operation.[70] Here again we hear of the Council only in its judicial capacity as a murder and homicide court, but we are not entitled to brush this evidence aside, as Hignett does, as being irrelevant to the question of whether it also acted as a council.[71] Of all its functions that of being a murder court was one of the few of which the Areopagus was not deprived by Ephialtes' reform of 462. There is no reason to doubt that the Areopagus Council that acted as a murder court in the fourth century was the same body as the Areopagus Council that acted as a murder court in the days before Solon. But we also know that, until 462, the post-Solonian Areopagus had very general supervisory powers over government and administration. We know, furthermore, that that council comprised all ex-archons and was in practice an aristocratic body. It would be quite out of keeping with Solon's reforms for him to invent such a council, but, on the other hand, we would expect to find some general council in pre-Solonian Athens. It seems almost certain, therefore, that the Areopagus court was that council, and it is probably to be regarded as the descendant of the king's council of early Athens. Considering that according to Aristotle's *Politics* Solon is said not to have altered the Areopagus Council, we ought not to be surprised (as Hignett is) that the composition and powers of the council listed in the *Athenian Constitution* as applying to the pre-Solonian period are the same as those listed for the post-Solonian period.[72]

Whether membership of the Council was already automatically vested in all ex-archons or not, there can be no doubt that the Council was recruited entirely from the ranks of the Eupatrids, who, as we have already seen from Plutarch, were regarded as monopolizing the magistracies as well as the control of religion and law from the time of 'Theseus'.[73] But who were the Eupatrids? That they were a hereditary aristocracy is recognized by all, but were they the whole of the Athenian aristocracy or only a part? Scholarly opinion on the subject ranges between equating the Eupatrids with all those who belonged to *genē* ('clans') on the one extreme and, on the other, regarding the Eupatrids themselves as only a single *genos*.[74]

Until the reforms of Cleisthenes in 507 the people of Athens were divided into four tribes (*phylai*), which were made up of several phratries (*phratriai*) (literally, 'brotherhoods'), each of which in turn comprised several *genē*, membership of each of these groupings being hereditary. Members of a *genos* traced their descent from a common ancestor and, though this ancestor was always mythical, that is no reason for dismissing the alleged blood-tie as fictional.[75] According to Aristotle's *Athenian Constitution* these divisions were instituted by 'Ion', the mythical ancestor of all Ionian Greeks, and were numerically fixed: thus, according to this, not only were there four tribes but also twelve phratries, each consisting of thirty *genē* comprising thirty men apiece, yielding a total of 10,800, which is clearly meant to be the total number of male citizens.[76] The division of the population into tribes, phratries and *genē* is as unlikely to have been the work of 'Ion' as their division into classes is to have been that of 'Theseus', and the fixed numerical totals are clearly an anachronistic reflection of the Cleisthenic reformed tribal structure, which is also indicated in the equation of the phratries with *trittues* ('thirds'), another Cleisthenic innovation. It is clear, though, that the tribal structure of Athenian society was not the arbitrary creation of a law-giver but a natural growth of great antiquity, as can be seen from parallels in other Greek states. Miletus, Cyzicus, Perinthus and Tomi all had tribes which to some extent shared the names of the Athenian tribes, Cyzicus having all four of the Athenian names plus a further two – thus perhaps further corroborating the tradition of the Athenian colonization of Ionia.[77] In Dorian states such as Sparta, Sicyon and Argos, similarly, the population was divided into the three traditional 'Dorian' tribes, Sicyon and Argos having an additional tribe, which, like the two additional tribes in Cyzicus, were presumably for the non-Dorians.[78] But, despite its anachronism on this score, the explanation of the Athenian divisions offered by the *Athenian Constitution* is not entirely without value. Ion was regarded as living long before Theseus, so the *genē* were clearly considered to embrace the whole of the original population, nobles and commoners alike. There is no basis here for believing that the members of the *genē* were all Eupatrids, nor that the Eupatrids were merely one *genos*. This is further corroborated by Diodorus' equation of the Eupatrids in Athens with the priestly caste in Egypt.[79] There are those, like Hignett, who believe that the term 'Eupatrid' was the name of a single *genos* as well as serving to describe the aristocracy as a whole, but the evidence for this belief is dubious, to say the least.[80] By contrast with modern scholars the ancient sources show unanimity on the definition of the Eupatrids that cannot but reflect the true situation. This brings us back to the description of Eupatrid functions that Plutarch gives in his *Life of Theseus*, which agrees with what is said by the definition given in the *Anecdota* quoted above, with Diodorus Siculus and also with Aristotle's *Athenian Constitution*, which sees Athenian society as made up of three social elements: Eupatrids, farmers and artisans.[81] In view of this impressive array of authorities there seems no reason why we should not regard the Eupatrids as essentially the whole of the Athenian aristocracy, in whose hands political power was vested until the reforms of Solon in 594.[82]

ARISTOCRACIES OF FIRST SETTLERS

Athens was not by any means the only Greek state to have an aristocratic government of this kind, broader, that is, than the royal-clan aristocracies of places such as Mytilene, Miletus and Corinth. It is sometimes known how the aristocracy in question came into existence, but by no means always. In Syracuse, Samos, Miletus, Thera and the

Apollonia on the Ionian Gulf and, probably, Byzantium, Cyrene and the Apollonia on the Black Sea, the original settlers and their descendants formed a closed group which monopolized power.[83]

In Samos and Syracuse the ruling aristocracy was known as the *geomoroi* or, in Doric, *gamoroi*, meaning 'those with a share of the land', which presumably refers to the original settlers. In Samos the *geomoroi* seem to have been in power by 620 or 600 and, after a three-generation interlude of tyranny lasting from about 572 to 522, they evidently returned to power, though not necessarily straightaway.[84] The details of Samian history that have come down to us are tantalizingly scanty. From Plutarch we are given the impression that the *geomoroi* came to power initially by the violent overthrow of the 'monarchy' of one Demoteles, about whom nothing further is known.[85]

They were certainly back in power before 440, when a sudden shaft of light illuminates Samian history. In that year, we learn from Thucydides, Samos and Miletus, both members of the Delian League headed by Athens, quarrelled over the possession of the mainland town of Priene. The Milesians got the worst of the ensuing war and appealed to Athens for help, an appeal which was seconded by some private citizens from Samos itself who wished to overthrow the Samian government. Being generally hostile to aristocratic or oligarchical regimes, Athens obliged, sending forty ships to Samos, where a 'democracy' was set up. But, although the Athenians took the precaution of demanding a hundred hostages, fifty men and fifty boys, from the aristocrats, and also of leaving a garrison on the island, their new government did not last long. With the help of seven hundred mercenaries the aristocrats regained power, which naturally resulted in an even stronger Athenian counter-attack than before. After a nine-month siege the Samians capitulated and the 'democracy' was presumably restored, as may be gathered from the anti-Athenian activities of exiled Samians, undoubtedly members of the defeated aristocracy, during the Peloponnesian War.[86] But the aristocracy was back in power by 412, when it was overthrown by a rising of 'the common people [*dēmos*] together with some Athenians who happened to be present on board three ships', as Thucydides puts it.[87] This seems not to have been a genuinely popular revolution, as may be gathered from another, and somewhat puzzling, passage in Thucydides, set in 411:

> Those who had previously risen up against the powerful men [*tois dunatois*] and were the popular party [*ontes dēmos*] changed sides

again, being persuaded by Peisander when he arrived and by his Athenian supporters in Samos. Numbering three hundred they became conspirators intent on attacking the others as being the democratic party [*hōs dēmō onti*].[88]

From this it would appear that the 'common people' of the anti-aristocratic revolution of 412 amounted to no more than three hundred men – less than half the number of the aristocrats themselves, since we know that two hundred of them were killed and a further four hundred exiled in 412, and there is no indication that this accounted for all of them. On the contrary, there clearly were some left, as we can see from the interesting decree of the revolutionaries that the common people were not to intermarry with any of the aristocracy.[89] What we have here seems to be a picture of oligarchical faction-fighting rather than of a genuine mass movement. In any event, the attempt of the three hundred to gain control of the government of Samos was thwarted by the presence of the crews of several Athenian vessels based on the island, the result being the victory, as Thucydides puts it, of 'the many' (*hoi pleiones*).[90]

In the case of Syracuse, which was a Corinthian colony, we know that in about 490 the *gamoroi* were overthrown and expelled by their Cyllyrian 'slaves' together with the *demos*.[91] That is what Herodotus tells us. Dionysius of Halicarnassus uses the word *pelatai*, the normal Greek equivalent of the Latin *clientes*, instead of 'slaves'.[92] The position is further clarified by fragments from Aristotle's lost treatise on the Syracusan constitution, and from Timaeus' *Histories*, who call the slaves in question Callicyrians rather than Cyllyrians and regard them as similar to the Spartan helots, the *penestai* of Thessaly and the *Clarotai* of Crete.[93] We are also told that they were very numerous.[94] What evidently happened in Syracuse, then, was the overthrow of the landed aristocracy by a combination of the indigenous serfs with the Greek townsmen who were not members of the ruling group. But the revolutionaries did not long remain in control. Within a few years, in 485, the *gamoroi*, now based in the inland town of Casmenae, appealed to Gelo, the tyrant of Gela, who duly took over Syracuse and made it his capital.[95]

In the collection of puzzle-problems which is generally known as Plutarch's *Greek Questions* is a discussion of the Milesian party called the *aeinautai*. Plutarch divides the term into two, producing the Greek words meaning 'perpetual sailors', on the basis of which he then proceeds to explain the origin of the party label.⁹⁶ This is probably a case of a popular and false etymology supplying a plausible, but fictitious, historical narrative. It has been more convincingly suggested that the party name derives not from the word *nautēs* ('sailor') but rather from the word *naiō* ('dwell, inhabit, settle'), and that what we have here is once again an aristocracy of the original settlers of the town, Miletus, like Samos and Syracuse, being a colony settled from the mainland of Greece.

The cases of Thera and the Apollonia on the Ionian Gulf are specifically mentioned by Aristotle as examples of the rule of an aristocracy of the first settlers, who accounted for a small minority of the total population but who evidently were the only free inhabitants in those states.⁹⁷

MILITARY ARISTOCRACIES

In some Greek states aristocracy had a military origin, with power in the hands of the cavalry. This form of government is linked by Aristotle with wealth, for, as he points out, horse-rearing is not easy for anyone who is not rich, and states whose strength depended upon their cavalry were, therefore, ruled by what Aristotle here calls oligarchies but which were undoubtedly hereditary aristocracies.⁹⁸ Elsewhere he maintains that this was the earliest form of government after monarchy, cavalry being more important than infantry in early warfare.⁹⁹ This plausible argument further corroborates the view that what we have here is aristocracy rather than oligarchy. The states mentioned by Aristotle as having this type of government are Eretria, Chalcis, Magnesia and 'many of the others throughout Asia'.¹⁰⁰ The rulers of Chalcis were actually called *Hippobotai* ('horse-breeders') and a fragment of Heraclides Ponticus tells us that each member of the ruling class in Cyme, which is said to have numbered a thousand, was obliged to keep a horse.¹⁰¹ Colophon, like Magnesia, was situated in a plain and the people of both (though not this time specifically their ruling classes) are called *Hippotrophoi* ('horse-rearers').¹⁰² It may be fairly certainly accepted that Colophon was one of the 'many other' Asian states ruled by a cavalry-aristocracy to which Aristotle was referring. As in Cyme, the ruling group in Colophon is said to have numbered a thousand.¹⁰³ If we are right in believing that the population of Colophon was about thirty thousand (or 7,500 households), then the ruling aristocracy formed a high proportion of the total population.¹⁰⁴

RULING GROUPS OF FIXED SIZE

Ruling groups of fixed size were not uncommon in Greece. Where we hear in the sources of ruling élites of this kind, there is no need to assume that the round number in question is merely intended to give a rough impression of the size of the ruling group.[105] There is good reason to believe, on the contrary, that such a number may well represent a numerically fixed and determined ruling group, or, in cases where the number is only an approximation – and not necessarily a particularly close one – a ruling group recruited on the basis of some specific criteria.[106] The number one thousand is found as the size of the ruling group in several states besides Cyme and Colophon. In Opuntian Locris the assembly was officially styled 'The Thousand' and the influence of this constitution is found in several Greek colonies in the West. In Locri Epizephyrii in the toe of Italy, a colony of Opuntian Locris, we find an assembly of the same size, as also in Croton, Rhegium and Acragas (or Agrigentum, as the Romans called it), though in the last case this form of constitution is known only after the end of the tyranny of Phalaris in the sixth century.[107] In the case of Rhegium we know that The Thousand were chosen in accordance with a property qualification and 'administered everything'. In Locri anyone proposing an amendment to the laws had to appear before The Thousand with a noose round his neck. If the amendment was defeated, then the unfortunate proposer was hanged straight away in full view of the assembly.[108] This placed an effective damper on constitutional innovation, and Locri seems to have retained the same constitution throughout antiquity. Though the only datable reference to this constitution in the mother-state of Opuntian Locris is in an inscription from the early fifth century, there can be little doubt that it had already had a long history by that time.[109] The assembly of The Thousand at old Locris seems to have been connected with the matrilineal aristocracy there called 'the hundred houses' and, if so, clearly had an early origin.[110]

The aristocracy of the Italian Locri similarly traced its descent from these noble houses in the mother-city, so that, if we accept the connection between the hundred houses and the assembly of The Thousand, the constitution must go back at least to the very beginnings of the foundation of the Italian Locri, which is thought to date from about 673.[111] The same form of government still seems to have been functioning in Polybius' day, five hundred years later.

Though a thousand was a favourite number amongst the Greeks it was not the only one to be found in constitutional arrangements. Hippodamus of Miletus, who was, according to Aristotle, the first non-politician to turn his mind to the question of the ideal constitution, thought that ten thousand was the best size for the citizen body of a state.[112] Plato himself showed considerable interest in such speculations and suggested in his *Laws* that the optimum number of citizens was 5,040, since, for a figure which was not too big, it had the largest number of possible divisors, fifty-nine in all, including all the numbers from one to ten.[113] The best known fixed-number constitution is probably that of the Five Thousand in Athens after the Peloponnesian War, but we also hear of assemblies of fixed size in Heraclea (probably the Pontic city of that name rather than the Trachinian one), Syracuse and Massilia, in all of which the number was six hundred. The smallest such assembly of which we know was the body of 180 men in Epidaurus who alone had the rights of citizenship, probably in the period before the tyranny of Procles, father-in-law of Periander of Corinth, which is to be dated to about 600.[114] It must be stressed that in all these fixed-number aristocracies, the élite group, however small, was the only part of the population to have any share whatsoever in politics, as is indicated by the terms which are used to describe it.

Thus The Thousand in Opuntian Locris are called *plētha* (i.e. the assembly); at Rhegium and Cyme they are said to have controlled the whole state (*politeia*); and at Pontic Heraclea the six hundred are identified with 'the oligarchy' by Aristotle. The term *synhedrion*, moreover, which is often used for these limited citizen-bodies, is otherwise applied to assemblies rather than councils.[115]

How was the ruling body selected under such a constitution? In some such states, according to Aristotle, a son could not belong to the ruling group at the same time as his father and in others only the eldest brother could participate – a system very similar to that still operative in the British House of Lords. It is in this connection that Aristotle mentions Heraclea, Massalia and also Istrus and Cnidus – and it is perhaps interesting to note that Heraclea's assembly only reached the six hundred mark as a result of the inclusion of some of the affronted relatives of the original, and much smaller, ruling group. This form of government may therefore best be regarded as rule by the heads of the noble families, which brings us back to the case of Opuntian Locris with its 'hundred houses' and its assembly of a thousand, presumably made up of the heads of sub-divisions of the noble houses.[116]

ARISTOCRACY BY CONQUEST

Probably the most significant and ascertainable origin of an aristocratic form of government is conquest. The best known example of this sort of aristocracy is Sparta, but it is not the only one. Several other states of the Peloponnese had similar constitutions, namely Argos, Sicyon and Epidaurus, as well as Thessaly, Thera and Crete. The ruling classes of Elis and Boeotia in addition owed their position essentially to conquest. With the exception of Elis, Thessaly and Boeotia all these states had been conquered by the Dorians, the latest wave of Greeks to descend from the North.

In Thebes, the main Boeotian city, membership of the ruling group depended upon possession of a *klēros*, or land-allotment, which was evidently supposed to be inalienable, as we know from the story told about the legislator Philolaus, who included in his enactments a special measure designed to preserve the number of these allotments.[117] If we accept the romantic connection between Philolaus and Diocles of which Aristotle tells us, then we have a firm date, since Diocles was an Olympic victor in 728, less than half a century after the first Olympic games. Philolaus himself, we are told, was a member of the Bacchiad aristocracy of Corinth and his presence in Thebes is explained by the fact that he had accompanied Diocles, who left Corinth to escape the passion he felt for his mother.[118] The two friends were buried in their adoptive home, with their graves so placed that Philolaus' afforded a view of Corinth while Diocles' did not – one of the rare intrusions of anecdote that Aristotle's aseptic scientific mind permitted him. We are not told for what section of the population these allotments were reserved, but it clearly was not for all the inhabitants of the state. Trade, for one thing, disqualified its practitioners for political office, and one had to have been clear of all commercial taint for ten years before regaining eligibility.[119] Though not Dorian, Thebes here displays similar criteria for political participation to those of Sparta, and it is not particularly daring to infer that here too the ruling group was racially distinct from the subject population, and especially from the peasantry, or 'clod-hoppers' (*krupezophoroi*, literally 'clog-wearers'), as they were called. The Boeotians themselves were comparative newcomers to the area which is named after them, their arrival being dated by Thucydides to the period immediately before and after the Trojan War, the earliest Boeotians coming before the war and the main bulk about sixty years after the war.[120] This does not altogether square with the Catalogue of Ships included in the second book of the *Iliad*, which devotes more space to the Boeotian contingent than to any other, attributing to it fifty ships and enumerating twenty-seven cities under five leaders.[121] The Catalogue is usually considered earlier than the rest of the poem in which it is embedded and, if so, the Boeotians had settled in Boeotia at an earlier date than Thucydides imagined, unless the Boeotian contingent in the Catalogue was made up of pre-invasion 'Cadmean' Greeks, which is denied both by Thucydides' account, by the fact that the Boeotians in the Homeric Catalogue are so called, and also by the fact that the Mycenaean palace in Thebes seems to have been destroyed before the time of the Trojan War.[122] Whatever the origins and racial composition of the 'Cadmeans' – and there is some evidence of Middle Eastern connections, both in legend and now in the shape of archaeological remains as well[123] – the Boeotian newcomers are said by Thucydides originally to have inhabited the region of Arne in Thessaliotis, and to have been driven south by the migrating Thessalians in their descent from Thesprotia in Epirus, from which the Boeotians may have come initially, if their dialect is anything to go on.[124]

The system of government in Thessaly bore an even closer resemblance to the classical Spartan type than did the Boeotian one. In classical times the whole of Thessaly formed a single state, a loose federation of four regions each under a tetrarch, though it is difficult to say when this arrangement was instituted. Whether the legendary Aleuas the Red, who, if he ever existed, is probably to be placed in the late seventh century, divided a united Thessaly into four or, as seems more likely, united four independent states into one, is not clear from the evidence, two fragments of Aristotle's lost *Thessalian Constitution*.[125] So loose was the structure of the state that it had no permanent head but only a military leader, the *tagos*, who was theoretically appointed only for the duration of the current war but who usually continued in office for longer periods, sometimes for life. Nothing is known of the constitutional position of the *tagos*, which is hardly surprising considering that, even in classical times, Thessaly was a byword for lawlessness and disorder.[126] The position of *tagos* was never held by anyone outside the three leading aristocratic houses of Thessaly, the Aleuadae of Larissa (descended according to tradition from Aleuas the Red), the Scopadae of Crannon and the Echecratidae of Pharsalus, who are called by Herodotus *basilees* and who dominated the regions surrounding each of those towns respectively. The Scopadae disappear from the scene towards the end of the sixth century but the other two houses continued to co-exist in bitter rivalry, as reflected in their diametrically opposed foreign policies at the time of the Persian Wars.[127] The normal form of government in Thessaly, according to Thucydides, was a 'dynasty' (*dunasteia*), a term of opprobrium which he also uses of the government of Thebes at the time of the Persian Wars.[128] This latter is a very interesting passage, because Thucydides here explicitly contrasts 'dynasty' not only with democracy but also with 'constitutional oligarchy' (*oligarchia isonomos*). 'Dynasty' is defined as a situation in which power is held by a few men in such a way as to be the form of rule 'most opposed to law and to the most moderate type of government, and closest to tyranny'. This way of classifying governments was systematized by Aristotle, and the same constitutional attitude still persists in modern times enshrined in such catch-phrases as 'a government not of men but of laws'.[129] Certainly, no one in ancient Greece would ever claim that his own state was a 'dynasty'.[130]

It is almost as if in reply to Thucydides' slight that Daochus of Pharsalus makes a point of insisting, in an inscription recording the twenty-seven *tageia* of his grandfather, also called Daochus, at the time of the Peloponnesian War, that the elder Daochus had ruled Thessaly 'not by force but by law'.[131] So far there has been little resemblance to Sparta, but in one important respect there was a close parallel, namely the subjection of the conquered inhabitants of the area by the conquerors, the Thessalians or, as they called themselves, Petthaloi. When they first arrived is difficult to say, but their eponym, King Thessalos, described as a son of Heracles, occurs in the Homeric Catalogue as ruler of Cos and several neighbouring islands.[132] As in Laconia, the conquered populations were not kept all on a par, but in both cases there were two tiers of the conquered, *perioikoi* and serfs. Six peoples fringing Thessaly proper all about were subject 'allies' who were obliged to pay tribute and give military aid when called upon.[133] These were the Perrhaebi in the north-east, and then, going round the map clockwise, the Magnetes, the Achaei, the Malians, the Aenianes and the Dolopes, all of whom, with the single exception of the Malians, are mentioned among the Greek allies in the Homeric Catalogue, though their location had changed somewhat in several cases.[134] The absence of the Malians is explained by Herodotus' remark that the Dryopes, the original inhabitants of the area called Doris, had been driven from there 'by Heracles and the Malians', the cult of Heracles being predominant among the Malians, whose dialect as well as this predilection for Heracles points to their affinity with the Heraclidae or 'sons of Heracles', namely the Dorians. The Phthiotic Achaeans also spoke a similar dialect, but the Magnetes spoke a type of Greek classified as Aeolic and generally recognized as a surviving descendant of the language of the Mycenaeans. Xenophon actually refers to all these subject allies by the same term used for their counterparts in Laconia, namely *perioikoi*, which means simply 'those living round about', and the eastern parts inhabited by the Perrhaebians, Magnetes and Achaeans were known collectively as the Perioecis.[136]

The serfs, the Thessalian counterparts to the Messenian helots, were called *penestai*, which literally means 'the poor', but, despite this purely economic description, there is little doubt that though undoubtedly of Greek stock they were of a different racial strain from their conquerors and probably also from the *perioikoi*, and they themselves emphasized their racial difference by claiming descent from an obviously mythical ancestor called Penestes.[137] Nothing is known about them in detail, but their position was probably similar to that of the helots, which is the way in which they and other parallel classes elsewhere were treated by the writers of classical antiquity as well.[138] Such were the picturesquely named 'dusty feet' (*konipodes*) of Epidaurus, the *gumnētes* – i.e. light-armed non-hoplites of Argos, the *katōnacophoroi* ('wearers of the peasant smock') or *korunēphoroi* ('clubbearers') of Sicyon, and possibly also the *kunophaloi* of Corinth, all of whom were probably Greeks of one sort or another. Outside Greece proper the serf class probably came from a pre-Greek conquered population, examples being the *kulikranes* (possibly 'with cup-shaped helmets') of Heraclea in Trachis, the Mariandyni (a tribal name) of Heraclea in Pontus, the *prouneikoi* ('burden-carriers') of Byzantium and the rather strangely named *kallikurioi* ('beautiful lords') of Syracuse, all these cities being Dorian colonies. In Crete, another Dorian area, the serfs, again belonging to the native pre-Dorian population, were called by various names, *mnoetae*, etymologically cognate with *dmōs*, a slave captured in war; *aphamiotai*; *klarōtai* (from *klaros*, an allotment of land), or even, rather confusingly, *perioikoi*. At Gortyn, the peasants were called *oikees*, which really only means 'those dwelling in houses', perhaps a sign that the peasants cultivated the soil for the absentee landlords.[139]

Sybaris, an Achaean colony on the instep of southern Italy, whose name is still a byword for luxury and voluptuous living, had a lifestyle which probably differed from that of its neighbours only in degree. Among the many stories told of this prosperous city is one about the two Sybarites watching some peasants hoeing a field. When the one complains that the very sight of their exertions has brought on a rupture, the other replies: 'As for me, just hearing you mention it tortures my side.'[140] In at least two states farming was considered no less disgraceful a pursuit than commerce, namely Thessaly and the Boeotian city of Thespiae. Of the latter we are specifically told that agriculture was held to be a shameful occupation, and in the Thessalian cities the so-called 'free' *agora* was out of bounds not only to all artisans but also to all farmers, which presumably means that these classes were excluded from citizenship.[141] That this situation was not peculiar to Thessaly is clear from Aristotle's general explanation:

> Since there are several types of constitution, it is inevitable that there should be several types of citizen, and especially of the citizen subjected to the rule of others, so that, whereas in one type of constitution the artisan and the labourer necessarily have citizenship, in other types it is impossible, as, for example, in any so-called aristocratic constitution, in which the honours are awarded in accordance with virtue [*aretē*] and merit [*axia*]. For it is impossible for anyone living the life of an artisan or labourer to practise deeds of virtue.[142]

Where these lower classes, and especially the peasants, were at the same time of a different genetic strain from the ruling element, it was all the easier to perpetuate the exclusiveness. In the Western colonies this is borne out by the fact that very little social and cultural influence seems to have been exerted by the native inhabitants upon the Greek settlers. The only piece of evidence, Polybius' discussion of Locri, is contradicted by other evidence mentioned by the same author as well as by archaeological remains.[143] The attitude of the Greeks to the indigenous populations, and particularly to the Sicels, the native inhabitants of Sicily, was not free from scorn, as is demonstrated by the popular Greek proverb, 'the Sicel and the sea', i.e. 'the islander does not know the sea', which is meant ironically, to signify those who know but pretend they are ignorant, in other words, the stock type of peasant cunning.[144] It is worth noting that this coincidence between social and racial divisions is particularly characteristic of Dorian states, though in some Dorian states the rights of citizenship were eventually extended to non-Dorians, for whom an extra fourth tribe was created, such as the so-called Aegialeis or 'men of the shore' at Sicyon, the Hyrnathii at

Argos and probably also at Epidaurus, though when these fourth tribes were introduced is a matter of speculation.[145]

Aristocracies of conquest, it is worth noticing, generally show more gradations of status than do other types of aristocracies, because an already stratified society is imposed upon a pre-existing population, which in itself is very likely to be made up of several different elements. It is such initial differences which probably best explain the distinction between serfs and *perioikoi*. In a state in which the energies of the conquerors are largely absorbed in holding down the conquered population, a growth of equality in their ranks may develop so as to eliminate internal friction and foster solidarity. The prime example of this development is to be found in Sparta, where, as we shall see in the next chapter, the consolidation of the ruling population was achieved by deliberate government policy. 'Harmonious oligarchy is not prone to self-destruction', as Aristotle puts it, giving the example of Pharsalus, the semi-autonomous segment of Thessaly under the Echecratidae, 'for', he explains, 'though they are few they are the masters of many, on account of their good relations amongst themselves.' But not all aristocracies or oligarchies followed this path:

> When the ruling elements form another oligarchy within the oligarchy, they are destroyed. This is when, though the body of citizens as a whole is small, not all of these few have a share of the highest offices.[146]

The example Aristotle gives of this is Elis, in which power was in the hands of a senate of ninety *gerontes*, or elders, who held office for life and whose election was 'dynastic', 'similar to that of the gerousia at Sparta' – in other words, where only the members of certain families were eligible. Whether these 'elders' are to be identified with the *dēmiourgoi* mentioned in Thucydides' transcript of the 'Hundred Years' Alliance' between Athens, Argos, Mantinea and Elis in 420, during the Peloponnesian War, is not clear.[147] The oath to abide by the treaty is to be sworn on the Elean side by the *dēmiourgoi* and the 'Six Hundred' and was to be administered by the *dēmiourgoi* and officials called the *thesmophulakes* (i.e. 'guardians of the law'). A variant of the title *dēmiourgos* also appears in the Elean (i.e. North-western) dialectal form *zamiorgia* in an inscription probably dating from before 580.[148]

The same title recurs a century later in another inscription, in which certain penalties are to be exacted by the *damiorgia* (as it is here called) and others by *basilaes* (presumably 'nobles') and by someone with the very general sounding title of 'the man in the highest position' (*or megiston telos echoi*), the latter probably being the head of state.[149] It is not by any means certain, however, what sort of state Elis was at the time.

According to Diodorus Siculus it was only in 471/70 that the numerous small communities, or *damoi*, of Eleia were united in a synoecism, and on the basis of letter-forms the date of the inscription is somewhere between 475 and 450.[150] It is not clear, therefore, whether the inscription gives us a picture of pre- or post-synoecism Elean government. There are also further difficulties, such as, can the *damiorgia* (or *zamiorgia*) of the inscriptions be regarded as the committee of *dēmiourgoi*, or was it a separate body altogether? Some scholars have claimed that there were two sets of *dēmiourgoi*, one at a local level, being the heads of the several *damoi*, and the other at the centre of the Elean state, forming a *Regierungskollegium* similar to that of the Athenian archons.[151] There is no way of resolving this doubt, and we are still left with our original question, namely, can *dēmiourgoi* or a *damiorgia* of any kind be identified with Aristotle's ninety elders? The main difficulty here is that Aristotle's oligarchy-within-the-oligarchy did not last. That, after all, is the reason he mentions it in the first place, as we have seen. The chances are, therefore, that our inscriptions refer to a different form of government. But when did the change take place, and what did it entail? There may be a reference to the downfall of the oligarchy of the ninety in a passage in Plutarch in which a certain Phormio is regarded as achieving in Elis what Ephialtes did in Athens, namely 'curbing an oppressive and oligarchic council'.[152] If this Phormio is to be identified with Plato's pupil of that name who is said to have been sent to reform the constitution of Elis, and if the 'curbing [of] an oppressive and oligarchic council' does refer to the ninety, then the change in government presumably took place within Aristotle's own memory.[153] If so, it is likely that the whole episode of the ninety was a short-lived fourth-century affair. This is contrary to the general scholarly view, which takes it for granted that the oligarchy of the ninety was earlier than the constitution reflected in the inscriptions.[154] But what sort of constitution is it to which we have these sparse epigraphical clues? The mention of a council of five hundred in inscriptions dated tentatively to between 500 and 475 has been taken as a sign of a democratic constitution, perhaps on the model of the Cleisthenic reforms in Athens.[155] This must remain conjectural, but, even if it is right, there is no reason to believe that all the features of government found in fifth-century inscriptions were new. As in Athens, a council of five hundred (which in Elis, for whatever reason, had become six hundred by 420) could have been superimposed upon the institutions of an aristocratic type of government. The most likely hypothesis, based on parallel cases, is that the *zamiorgia* was an aristocratic council, though what its relation was to the *basilaes* is difficult to say. The *dēmiourgoi* (whatever their relationship may have been to the *zamiorgia*) were certainly a privileged group, as we know from an inscription which confers status equal to that of a *dēmiourgos* and to a *proxenos* (i.e. the representative of a foreign state) upon a named individual.[156]

In Argos, another conquest-aristocracy, but this time a Dorian one, we meet *dēmiourgoi* (or, in Doric, *damiorgoi*) once again. In fact, the very earliest inscription that we have from Argos, dating probably from the seventh century, applies the title to nine men, who, if the restoration of the text is correct, 'ruled' (*e[an]assanto*) Argos. The similarity of some of the names to mythical heroes led Vollgraff, the discoverer of the inscription, to interpret it in a somewhat fanciful way, but a much more convincing, if also more prosaic, interpretation, has been put forward by N. G. L. Hammond.[157] The nine *damiorgoi*, Hammond argues, are a college of eponymous magistrates at the head of state at one particular time, three from each of the traditional Dorian tribes, and the inscription itself is simply the list of leading magistrates in office which was normally appended to Greek legislative decrees. A later inscription, dated to the sixth century, similarly lists six *damiorgoi*, but in a fifth-century inscription we find the eponymous magistrate in the shape of a *basileus* called Melantas.[158] Despite an attempt to identify this Melantas with Meltas, the last real king of Argos according to Pausanias, Melantas was undoubtedly nothing more than an elective annual magistrate, since the Argive monarchy had come to an end well over a century before his time and the Teminids, the most illustrious of all the royal houses of the Peloponnese, were in semi-exile in the nearby town of Cleonae.[160] But, as in Athens, so in Argos the title *basileus* did not die out, as we can see from the rather specious argument used by the Spartans to claim supreme command over the proposed alliance with Argos in 481, namely that, as they had two kings and the Argives only one, it would be invidious to deprive one of their own kings of his command.[161]

All this leaves us with a serious puzzle: why is there no mention of a king in the sixth- and seventh-century inscriptions? The solution may lie in the conflict between king and aristocracy of which we catch some glimpses in our sources. In Pausanias, for example, we read:

> Cherishing equality and independence as they had from time immemorial, the Argives reduced the power of their kings to the barest minimum, so that nothing but the royal title was left to Medon son of Ceisus and his descendants.[162]

(Ceisus, according to this account, was the son of the founder of the Dorian line, Temenus himself.) The Temenids nevertheless continued as kings of Argos for a further nine generations after Medon, but then 'the people condemned Meltas son of Lacedas, the tenth descendant of Medon, and deposed him from power altogether.' According to Diodorus the Argive 'kingship' (*basileia*) lasted 549 years, which is too short a time if the merely titular elected 'kings' are included but seems rather too long for the twelve generations of Temenids mentioned by Pausanias.[163] It is difficult to know which of the two figures, the 549 years or the twelve generations, is likely to be nearer the truth, but there is a story related by Plutarch which could serve to reconcile them. Plutarch's story is that, upon the extinction of the Temenid house, the Argives sought the guidance of the Delphic oracle as to who their next king should be. The oracle proffered one of its more straightforward replies, telling them that an eagle would point out their king to them, which, needless to say, it did.[164] There is nothing here, it is true, about the Temenids being deposed or exiled, but, on the other hand, the Argives seem intent on continuing a hereditary life-monarchy rather than on turning it into an elective annual magistracy. We are not in any case told, either by Pausanias or by anyone else, that Meltas was the last real king of Argos, only that he was the last Temenid king, which is rather a different matter.

The foundation of Dorian Argos probably dates from the eleventh century, so, on Diodorus' computation, the monarchy must have come to an end at some time between roughly the mid-sixth and the mid-fifth centuries.[165] The absence of the king's name from the seventh- and sixth-century inscriptions mentioned above may be accounted for by his supreme unimportance. Even in Sparta, it is worth noting in this connection, though the kings there retained a certain amount of authority, documents were dated, not by regnal years, as is customary in monarchies – British statutes are so dated to this day – but by means of an eponymous ephor.

But who were the opponents of royal power? In Pausanias' explanation of Meltas' exile it is the *dēmos* who condemned him, and the same word appears in Diodorus' somewhat fuller narrative of what is presumably the same event, though the king is not actually named:

> Getting the worst of it in the war which they had fought together with their king against the Spartans, and having restored to the Arcadians their native towns, the Argives reproached the king for returning their land to the exiles and for not portioning it out amongst themselves. The people [*dēmos*] united against him and desperately laid violent hands upon him, whereupon he fled to Tegea, where he lived honoured by those whom he had favoured.[166]

It is difficult to know quite what the meaning of this is, but it seems that Argos had lost some Arcadian territory which it had previously possessed and had restored it to its original Arcadian owners, with whom the king was evidently on good terms. These Arcadians may fall into the category of *perioikoi*, and we certainly know that Argos had such semi-autonomous subjects. The *dēmos* which, both in Pausanias and Diodorus, shows such antipathy towards the king, must clearly be the Dorian population of Argos, that is, the stock of the conquerors, as against the conquered, among whom the pre-Doric Arcadians are to be counted, speaking as they did a dialect showing marked affinities with Mycenaean Greek.

But Meltas is not the only Argive king known to have been involved in internal strife. His grandfather, Pheidon, undoubtedly the best known of the kings of Argos, is termed a tyrant by Aristotle, is regarded by Herodotus as having introduced several innovations, and met his death in a faction fight in Corinth.[167] Whatever Pheidon's date – and he has been placed at points as widely separated as 900 and 600 – his career clearly reflects the age-old conflict between the Argives and their kings, or, perhaps more precisely, between the Argive aristocracy and the kings, for our board of six or nine *damiorgoi* is more likely to represent an aristocratic than a democratic constitution. Both numbers, it is significant, are divisible by three but not by four, showing that eligibility was confined to members of the three Dorian tribes, but whether it was further limited, as elsewhere, to certain families only, we cannot say. If those kings who wished to stage a royal comeback in terms of power were forced to ally with the *perioikoi* – as seems to have been the case with Meltas and also possibly with Pheidon[168] – it is likely that the bulk of the Dorian population was aligned with the aristocracy.

By 420, when the 'Hundred Years' Alliance' between Athens, Argos, Mantinea and Elis was signed, a fourth, non-Dorian, tribe had evidently been added and was clearly active in politics as well, since one of the three Argive bodies which were to swear to uphold the treaty was called 'The Eighty', a number this time divisible by four but not by three.[169] The members of the new tribe were known as Hyrnathii, named after the legendary daughter of King Temenus, Hyrnetho.[170] It might seem surprising that a tribe of non-Dorians should be given so Doric a name, but there may be a reason for that, as we shall see below. The admission of the Hyrnathii to political life probably occurred in the confused period after the defeat of Argos by Sparta at Sepeia in about 494.[171] The ancient sources are agreed that the battle ushered in political change, but they all describe it differently. Herodotus' is the most puzzling account:

> Argos was so bereft of its men that their slaves [*douloi*] ruled and governed and retained possession of everything until the sons of those who had been killed grew up. These then regained control of Argos and threw out the slaves, who, on being expelled, took Tiryns by force. For a time there was concord between them, but then an Arcadian soothsayer from Phigalea, a certain Cleander, came to the slaves and persuaded them to attack their masters. From this time forth and for a long time there was war, until with great effort the Argives won the day.[172]

Who were these 'slaves'? The word used by Herodotus is the ordinary Greek word for a chattel-slave, *doulos*, but, as we have already seen, there was in Argos a class of men called *gumnētes* whose status, according to Pollux, was similar to that of the Spartan helots.[173] They were presumably therefore state serfs and, as their name indicates, they served as light-armed troops. It is surely not stretching Herodotus' text too far to explain the 'slaves' as being these *gumnētes*. The casualties in the battle of Sepeia were variously estimated at five thousand, six thousand and 7,777, but even the lowest of these figures must have represented a high percentage of the adult male population of fifth-century Argos.[174] In deriding the possibility that the battle accounted for as many as 7,777 lives Plutarch put forward his own version of what had happened:

> In making up for the shortage of men they did not wed the women to slaves, as Herodotus relates, but to the best of the *perioikoi*, whom they made citizens. The women seemed, however, to show contempt for their husbands as inferiors and to shun them in their marital relations, which was why the Argives passed the law ordering those women who had a beard to sleep together with their wedded husbands.[175]

This account corresponds with that found in Aristotle, who says simply that, because of the casualties, the Argives 'were forced to admit some of the *perioikoi*' (to citizenship).[176]

The statements of Aristotle and Plutarch are not necessarily in conflict with that of Herodotus. It is clear that Herodotus is not talking about exactly the same events as those to which Aristotle and Plutarch are referring. It is quite conceivable that, in the aftermath of the defeat, the *gumnētes* rose up and took over the government for a time, and that, in order to oppose them, the Argives allied themselves with some of the *perioikoi* and eventually prevailed. In this way the two narratives are combined without straining either. It is certainly not necessary to resort to the desperate expedient of identifying Aristotle's *perioikoi* with the *gumnētes*, as some scholars feel impelled to do,[177] nor, with others, so that the word to promote Herodotus' 'slaves' embraces any dissident elements one fancies. One such scholar defines the term as follows:

> The name might be applied to anyone outside the traditional ruling class, to new democratic leaders who were not aristocrats of the highest class, or even to aristocrats who were prepared to court the *dēmos*; or to Aristotle's *perioikoi*; or it could mean that the democratic leaders were criticised for their submission to some external power, to Kleomenes or even to Xerxes.[178]

There is nothing to prevent our accepting the most obvious and sensible solution: Herodotus' 'slaves' were serfs and Aristotle's (and Plutarch's) *perioikoi* were *perioikoi*.[179] It is not as if we lack evidence that Argos had semi-autonomous *perioikoi* under her control. On the contrary, we have a whole list of perioecic cities in Pausanias: Tiryns, Hysiae, Orneae, Mycenae and Mideia.[180] The only difficulty here is that Argive possessions were in a constant state of flux, and it is not certain when all these cities would have been simultaneously within the Argive orbit.[181] It was probably the selected *perioikoi* rather than *gumnētes* who were enrolled in the tribe of the Hyrnathii, and this may account for the very Doric name, since, unlike the *gumnētes*, who were the descendants of the pre-Dorian population, the *perioikoi* were probably at least partly Doric.[182]

Quite when the Argives regained power from the *gumnētes* is difficult to say, but is not particularly relevant to our present purpose. The question has been much discussed and the terminal dates at either end are 490 and 467.[183] The fact that a council (*boulē*) seems to have been all-powerful, or at least independent of any assembly, in the negotiations with Sparta over a thirty-year alliance in 481 has sometimes been taken as a sign of aristocratic government, but it is hardly conclusive evidence,[184] and an inscription dated to about 475 certainly mentions an assembly, the *aliaia*.[185] In the arrangements for the administering of the oath for the 'Hundred Years' Peace' in 420 three Argive bodies are involved: the council (*boulē*), The Eighty and the *artunai* but neither the functions nor the composition or method of appointment of any of these is known.[186] Not even the size of the council is known, unless one assumes that the 500 people trapped while holding a meeting in the *prutaneion* and burnt to death in 315 were the council and that its size had not changed for more than a century.[187] The Eighty were probably an entirely separate body and, as we have already suggested, their number undoubtedly reflects participation by members of four tribes, which is the only clue to the fact, mentioned by Thucydides, that the constitution of Argos was at this time 'democratic'.[188] How democratic it was we have no way of knowing, but a body as small as The Eighty is generally a sign of aristocratic or oligarchical government, and the *artunai* do not have a particularly democratic look about them either. What little information we can glean about them from inscriptions suggests that they had financial duties, as did the similarly named *artutēr* at Thera, who was in charge of the financial administration of the religious association there.[189] The *artunoi* of Epidaurus, a state which had had close political ties with Argos in the early days after the Dorian migration, were anything but the magistrates of a democracy, being elected by and from the only 180 men in Epidaurus who had any political rights at all.[190] Their functions in Epidaurus were probably the same as those of the *amnēmones* in the similarly constituted state of Cnidus, where the *amnēmones* (under the presidency of the *aphestēr*), sixty men chosen from the aristocracy holding office for life and not accountable to anyone, acted as both an executive and probouleutic council.[191] There have been some attempts to identify the Argive *artunai* with the *damiorgoi*, whose absence is conspicuous amid the political bodies mentioned by Thucydides, but this seems unlikely, since both are old titles and, if the *artunai* numbered anything near sixty, that would seem too large a body for *damiorgoi*.[192]

Without the explicit, though bald, assertion on the part of Thucydides that the constitution of Argos at the time of the Peloponnesian War was democratic we should have had difficulty guessing it. The only two specific pointers in that direction are the creation of a fourth tribe, probably soon after the battle of Sepeia in 494, and then, evidently around 450, the move away from tribal divisions and towards classification by phratry instead, as indicated, for example, in the division of the infantry into five sections, *lochoi*, each under its own *strategos*, and also the use of the phratry rather than the tribe as an adjunct to a man's name.[193] This may indicate a shift to a regional type of classification rather than one based on descent, as had happened in Athens under Cleisthenes in the late sixth century. But it never altogether replaced the old tribal divisions in Argos, since they are still in evidence in the organization of the cavalry at the turn of the third and fourth centuries, and even under the Roman Empire they were still passing honorific decrees.[194]

Whatever the constitutional theory of democratic Argos, on those very few occasions when we see government at work (which is, admittedly, mostly during wartime) power seems to reside in the hands of a general.[195] But, however that may be, the tone of government was clearly anti-aristocratic, as was very clearly demonstrated by the so-called *skutalismos* or 'clubbing' episode in 370, which, according to Diodorus Siculus, accounted for more deaths than were ever recorded to have occurred in civil strife anywhere else in Greece.[196] What happened was that 'certain demagogues spurred the masses on against the men of outstanding wealth and reputation. Those who had been so calumniated united in the resolve to overthrow the *dēmos*.' This unleashed even more hostility against the aristocracy and thirty of the 'most illustrious' citizens were arrested, put to death and their property confiscated, followed by more and more, until over 1,200 'influential men' (*dunatoi*) had met their deaths.[197] Isocrates, some twenty-four years after the event, said that the men killed were 'the most distinguished and richest of the citizens' and that the people had set about 'doing these things with such joy as no one else would feel even when killing their enemies.'[198] The descriptions of the victims makes it quite plain that they were not only rich but also noble. As for the rampaging *dēmos*, it is impossible to know its composition, but it is highly unlikely to have been confined to Dorian Argives.

*   *   *

Before making any attempt to draw together the factors characterizing aristocratic government it will be necessary to discuss the best known aristocracies of all, Sparta and Crete. But it might be salutary first to reflect that, despite the cursory treatment it is normally accorded in general works, the 'heyday of aristocracy' was for the most part no brief flash in the pan. In a good many states aristocratic rule was the normal form of government throughout classical antiquity and no Greek state escaped it entirely.[199]

CHAPTER III

THE REPUBLIC OF DEMIGODS

Sparta was a legend even in its own day and there has scarcely been an age in which it has failed to arouse strong passions, whether of adulation or disparagement, amongst political thinkers. Such judgments generally reveal more of the preoccupations of the societies from which they emanate than of the society which they purport to analyze. It is no accident that among the idolizers of Sparta are to be numbered such diverse spirits as, for example, Machiavelli, Thomas More, Montesquieu and Rousseau, each selecting a different facet of Spartan life for commendation.[1] It is from Rousseau's *Discourse on the Arts and Sciences* that the title of this chapter has been taken:

> Could I forget that it was in the very heart of Greece that this city was seen to arise, as famous for its blissful ignorance as for the wisdom of its laws, this republic of demigods rather than of men? – so greatly superior did their virtues seem to mere humanity.[2]

It is Sparta as the cradle of virtue which attracted Rousseau, and her state-controlled practical education to this end is contrasted with what he regarded as the effete over-intellectualized lucubrations of the Athenians. For Rousseau virtue is an end in itself, and he closes his *Discourse on the Arts and Sciences* with a paean of praise to 'Virtue, sublime science of simple minds . . . and true philosophy.'[3] This attitude would no doubt have puzzled the Spartans themselves and would probably have seemed to them no less academic and remote from reality than the Athenian outlook which Rousseau so scorned. Whenever they themselves spoke of virtue it was no abstract concept they had in mind. Thus, when Agesilaus, the early fourth-century king, was asked why Sparta was an unwalled city, his reply was that 'cities should not be fortified with stone and wood, but with the virtues [*aretai*] of their inhabitants.'[4] 'Virtue' was a practical need, not a remote ideal.

THE METAMORPHOSIS OF A SOCIAL SYSTEM

But Rousseau's 'austerité républicaine' had not always been the hallmark of Spartan social life. We know very little of early Dorian Sparta, but what little we do know would not lead us to believe that it was significantly different from any other Dorian state. The foundation of Dorian Sparta is probably to be dated to about 1000, but the earliest evidence of political life comes from the pens of the seventh-century poets Tyrtaeus and Alcman. Alcman's compositions seem mostly to have been hymns addressed to various gods and goddesses and sung by a choir of young girls. Whether he was a native Spartan or whether he had come originally from Sardis in Lydia – and a fierce controversy raged on this question in classical times – he was a Spartan poet writing for Spartan choirs and in the Dorian dialect. The significance of this early Spartan poetry, fragmentary though it is, is the fact that Tyrtaeus and Alcman were not only Sparta's first poets but also, together with the seventh-century poet Terpander, her only ones. Poets had no more place in classical Sparta than artists, craftsmen or tradesmen of any description. Among the many anecdotes revealing Spartan scorn for anything but military prowess is one from Plutarch's collection of sayings and stories connected with King Agesilaus:

> On one occasion he heard that the allies were restive on account of the ceaseless campaigning, for there were many of them accompanying the Spartans, who were few in number. Wishing to test their numbers he ordered all the allies to sit mixed up together and the Spartans separately by themselves. Then he announced, first, that the potters should stand up, and, when they had done so, the herald next summoned the smiths, then the carpenters, the builders and each of the other trades in turn. Consequently, all but a few of the allies stood up, but not one of the Spartans. For it was forbidden to them to practise or learn a handicraft. So, 'You see, men,' said Agesilaus with a laugh, 'how many more soldiers we send out than you.'[5]

The profession of arms was the only one befitting a Spartan citizen and Sparta was the only Greek state to have that attitude. This concern to instil the military virtues is already present in the poetry of Tyrtaeus, who wrote in the mid-seventh century, a generation before Alcman:

> It is beautiful for a good man to die fighting for his country in the front line, but to leave his city and his rich fields as a beggar is of all

things most tormenting, wandering with his dear mother and aged father, with little children and wedded wife. Such a man, a victim of want and dire penury, will be loathsome to those he meets, those whose help he implores. He is a disgrace to his lineage, a reproach to his handsome form, pursued by every kind of disgrace and misfortune. If then there is so complete a disregard for a wanderer and neither shame nor respect nor pity, let us put up a spirited fight for this land and, without thought for our own lives, let us die for our children.[6]

These poignant and pathetic lines encapsulate the explanation as to why the perfectly normal Sparta of the early days turned into the legendary regimented military machine of classical times. In Tyrtaeus' mind there is no middle ground between glorious victory over the foe and utterly hopeless despair. At first sight this may seem particularly strange in view of the fact that he was writing not about a war of defence against an invading force but about a war of conquest, the Second Messenian War, in which he himself evidently fought as a Spartan general.[7]

The battle for an unnamed town, which, according to Tyrtaeus, was fought by 'our fathers' fathers' and lasted nineteen years, is generally regarded as the First Messenian War and seems to have ended at some time between 720 and 710.[8] 'Our fathers' fathers' may be taken literally or may have the more general meaning of 'ancestors', but the date of the Second Messenian War, depending as it does upon the date for Tyrtaeus himself, can hardly be later than 650.[9] Sparta, situated in the Laconian plain, spent, therefore, over half a century in conquering the neighbouring but by no means easily accessible plain of Messenia. Why? We do not know, but it is clear that it was not unconnected with the causes that led to the founding of Taras, better known by its Latin name, Tarentum, Sparta's first and probably her only overseas colony. The story has come down in several versions, in all of which the foundation of the colony is linked with the revolution or attempted revolution of the so-called Partheniae, the offspring of Spartan virgins (hence their name) by young men sent back from the front in rotation after the first ten years of the First Messenian War. Being illegitimate these Partheniae were denied citizenship and they, therefore, allied themselves with the helots and planned revolution. The signal of revolt was to be when Phalanthus, their leader, pulled his helmet over his forehead, but the plot leaked out and, at the last minute, the herald simply proclaimed aloud that Phalanthus should leave his helmet alone. The thwarted revolutionaries were then persuaded, needless to say by an oracle, to found a colony at Tarentum.[10] The story may have been slightly embroidered, but there is no reason to disbelieve it in its essentials, which are that Sparta was threatened with a helot revolt in the aftermath of the First Messenian War. We are not told whether the helots concerned were from Laconia or Messenia or both, since there were helots in both areas. But since the Laconian helots are never known to have rebelled in later times it would seem unlikely that they were involved now either. If the threat came from the recently defeated Messenians, as it undoubtedly did, that in itself would explain the need to subjugate them completely, and the fact that this external threat had combined with an internal revolutionary movement enables us to understand why for Tyrtaeus there are only two prospects, victory or utter destitution and exile.

The helot threat is the *leit-motif* of Spartan history and it is only in terms of this challenge that Spartan social and political institutions can be understood. But perhaps before discussing these it will be best to know exactly what we mean in referring to helots and *perioikoi*.

As has already been mentioned, the helots were of two kinds, Laconian and Messenian, who were sharply distinguished by the Spartans themselves, the former being generally referred to as the 'old helots' and the latter simply as Messenians (*Messēnioi* or *to Messēniakon*).[11] The reason for that is not difficult to fathom, since the Laconian helots were the original inhabitants of Laconia at the time of the Dorian conquest in the tenth and eleventh centuries, whereas the Messenian helots were simply the Messenians who, as we have seen, were subdued only in the seventh and eighth centuries. There seems little doubt, therefore, though the question has often been debated by scholars, that the Laconian helots were essentially of 'Achaean' stock, or, in other words, Mycenaean Greeks, whereas the Messenians, conquered so long after the Dorian immigrations, cannot but have had at least some measure of Dorian blood mixed in with their Achaean corpuscles. There is no reason to believe, as some scholars have sometimes argued, that the 'old helots' were a pre-Greek population – except in so far as such stock had already fused with the 'Achaean' element.[12] There is no support for the fanciful pseudo-etymological explanations so popular with the writers of antiquity, who derived 'helot' (*heilōs*, *heilōtēs*, or *heilōtis*) from the town of Helos in Laconia.[13] The term is rather to be traced to the root ἑλ- meaning to take or capture in war.[14] Least of all is there any justification for the view put forward by some modern scholars that there was no ethnic distinction between the helots and their masters but that they had become subjugated as a result of purely internal political conflicts.[15]

The ethnic origin of the *perioikoi* is less easily ascertainable, largely no doubt because they were far from being a homogeneous body, though their diversity has not always been recognized. There are those who regard the *perioikoi* either as wholly Dorian or as wholly Achaean, but it is more probable that they contained elements of both, as is indicated by the linguistic evidence, since the Laconian Doric dialect shows an Achaean admixture.[16] It was in Laconia that the great majority of perioecic towns were situated, and their inhabitants shared the appellation Lacedaemonians with the Doric Spartans, or Spartiates, as they are more accurately termed.[17] As their name indicates, the *perioikoi* lived around the main nucleus of Spartiate settlement, and the names of eighty perioecic towns are known.[18] These towns were each autonomous but nevertheless under the general suzerainty of Sparta, which controlled their foreign policy. Though, as has been mentioned, the *perioikoi*, unlike the helots, were officially termed Lacedaemonians, they seem often to have been regarded as citizens of their individual towns. The perioecic towns seem, for example, to have entered the Olympic Games independently, as is indicated by the memorial set up in Acriae, a perioecic town a little further along the coast from Helos, to the victor of five foot-races, a man called Nicocles.[19] Nothing is known for certain about the internal government of these towns, but we read in Xenophon of aristocrats (*kaloi k'agathoi*) among the *perioikoi* being sent out on campaign with King Agesipolis in 381.[20] If this is the correct interpretation of this phrase – found nowhere else in reference to the *perioikoi* – then the perioecic towns are likely to have been aristocratically governed. There is no evidence of helots in the perioecic regions, though some scholars have assumed that there were.[21] Isocrates' belief, accepted by many modern writers, that the ephors had the right to execute *perioikoi* without trial is probably wrong.[22] Isocrates is probably confusing *perioikoi* here with helots, though we know that Sparta exercised a certain amount of control over the strategically important island of Cythera by sending a specially appointed magistrate, the so-called Cytherodices, there once a year, and also by keeping a garrison there.[23] But Cythera was a special case, and in general the *perioikoi* seem to have been left pretty much to themselves so far as internal affairs were concerned. Their main obligation to Sparta was to supply troops, but, though they had no say whatsoever as regards foreign policy, they seem to have been loyal to Sparta throughout her history – and they are recorded as fighting in the Spartan army down to the third century.[24] The location of the perioecic towns is largely to be explained in terms of Spartan defence needs. They acted as a buffer between Spartan territory proper and outside foreign states. The Sciritis and Aegytis areas in the north, for example, insulated Sparta itself from the Arcadians. Another major perioecic area, the eastern seaboard of the Peloponnese from the Thyreatis in the north to Cape Malea in the south, together with Cythera and several other neighbouring islands, had originally been Argive territory and was the theatre of war between Sparta and her inveterate foe, and the Spartan conquest of the greater part of it seems to have been finalized by the mid-sixth century, though the Thyreatis itself remained a bone of contention in the fifth century.[25]

It is important to stress that of all the subject peoples it was only the Messenian helots who were restive, because they never reconciled themselves to their lowly status. They thought of themselves, and were thought of by others, as Messenians, and retained this feeling of national consciousness until they were released from the Spartan yoke by Sparta's disastrous defeat at the hands of Thebes in 371. Before the Spartan conquest Messenia had been a single state with its own king and an assembly made up from all its cities. The names of three kings are known, Euphaes, Aristodemus and Aristomenes, all of whom were involved in the struggle against Sparta.[26] It is not certain how many Messenian revolts there were, but there can be no doubt that the Spartiates felt threatened by the Messenians throughout. In 369 the Theban general Epaminondas claimed to have refounded Messenia after an interval of 230 years, which seems rather too short a period on the usual calculations of the date of the Second Messenian War, so it has been suggested that the Messenian state did not actually cease to exist until a third war or revolt in about 600.[27] Another rising is mentioned by Plato as occurring in 490 and then comes the well-known revolt of 464 – the so-called Third Messenian War.[28]

There can be no doubt that it is to this constant Messenian threat that we must attribute Sparta's social and political metamorphosis. For the purposes of our present discussion the main element of this transformation seems to have been a change in the composition of the aristocracy.

In view of the great volume of writings on Sparta in recent years it is surprising to see how little attention this question has attracted. Some scholars have embraced the view that Sparta had no hereditary nobility, though one modern writer who holds with that view reveals its inadequacy in his concluding remarks on the subject: 'However, it must be candidly admitted that, if there was no hereditary nobility, Sparta was unique in the ancient world. To which it might pertinently be retorted that Sparta was unique in more ways than this.'[29] This is surely a non-argument. But even those who do not reject the idea that there was a hereditary aristocracy tend to deny it any political role.[30]

ARISTOCRACY OLD AND NEW

The starting point for any discussion of the question must be Aristotle's explanation of the stability of the Spartan constitution:

> For a constitution to last it is necessary for each section of the state to wish it to continue in the same way. The kings certainly hold this view, on account of the honour accorded them; the nobility [*hoi kaloi k'agathoi*] on account of the *gerousia* (for this office is a prize of excellence [*aretē*]); and the common people on account of the ephorate, which is appointed from the whole population.[31]

It has been denied by some, however, that the terms *kaloi k'agathoi* (literally, 'the handsome and good') and *aretē* (literally, 'goodness') here refer to the aristocracy, and they argue that these terms are rather to be understood 'in a moral sense'.[32] Aristotle's definition of goodness is indeed a moral one, but it does not exclude heredity, as we shall see in a later chapter.[33] His view of the relationship between moral excellence and noble birth is encapsulated in his succinct definition of the latter: 'Noble birth is inherited [literally, 'ancient'] wealth and excellence.'[34] The connection between birth, wealth and the term *kaloi k'agathoi* is made by Aristotle a few lines further back:

> People are accustomed to calling only those mixed constitutions 'polities' which tend towards democracy, and they prefer to call those tending towards oligarchy 'aristocracies', because education and noble birth are more associated with the wealthier elements, and the rich are thought to possess already those things the lack of which drives wrongdoers to crime. The people, therefore, call the rich *kaloi k'agathoi* and 'nobles' [*gnōrimoi*].[35]

There is no reason to believe that Aristotle is using the term *kaloi*

THE REPUBLIC OF DEMIGODS

k'agathoi in any different a sense in the passage on Sparta quoted above, and the whole tone of that passage would tend to corroborate this view. Aristotle has divided the Spartans into three: the kings, the *kaloi k'agathoi* and the *dēmos*. These are not moral but social and political categories. Moreover, it would make no sense for Aristotle to claim that the council (*gerousia*) was the prerogative of the morally superior while the ephorate was open to all. The method of election seems to have been the same for both – the system whereby the candidates accorded the loudest cheers were elected, with a body of men locked in a windowless room acting the part of the applausometer.[36]

It is nonsensical to argue, as a modern writer has done, that 'the very use of the term "equals" (or "peers") shows that every Spartan citizen was as good as his neighbour, and there could not have been an exclusive nobility within the ranks of the peers.'[37] The Spartiates proper did indeed claim to be *homoioi* or 'Equals', but what is the significance of that? This equality among the Spartiates was attributed by Xenophon, and no doubt also by the Spartans of the classical period, to the reforms of Lycurgus, who, we are told, 'made the state equally the property of all those who fulfilled their legal obligations, and he took no account of either their physical or financial disabilities.' Cowardice, however, deprived a man of his status as an 'Equal'.[38] Though Xenophon here emphasizes that there were differences of wealth among the 'Equals', the concept of Spartiate equality is also connected with the tradition, related by Plutarch in his life of Lycurgus, that the lawgiver had redistributed the land into 39,000 equal lots (*klēroi* or, in Doric, *klaroi*), assigning one to each of the *perioikoi* (30,000) and Spartiates (9,000).[39] The system was then continued by granting a lot to each new-born healthy Spartiate boy.[40] This tradition of equal lots has come under attack from modern scholars, some of whom dismiss it out of hand as 'a myth created in the later fourth century'.[41] But it is too persistent a tradition to be so airily waved aside, and we already have a reference to it in Plato's *Laws*, written in the mid-fourth century. Talking about Argos, pre-conquest Messenia and Sparta, he says:

> In establishing equality of property their lawgivers were free from that most serious reproach which often occurs in states governed by laws of a different type, if anyone attempts a disruption of the ownership of land or the cancellation of debts, seeing as he does that without these measures equality could never be effectively achieved. The lawgiver who attempts to disturb any such institutions is greeted

with the universal cry, 'Leave well alone', and he is cursed for introducing the redistribution of land and the abolition of debts, the result being in each case that he is at a loss. But in this regard too there was harmony among the Dorians and no stigma attached. The land could be divided up without opposition, and there were no large outstanding debts.[42]

Unlike Xenophon and Plutarch, Plato here attributes the equality of land distribution to the founders of Dorian Sparta rather than to Lycurgus, but that is a problem to which we shall have to return later.

In practice there was almost certainly never any real economic equality among Spartan citizens. Several Spartans are known to have been extraordinarily rich, with resources comparable to those of the wealthiest inhabitants of more 'normal' Greek states. Pausanias gives a list of Spartan horse-breeders – no profession for a pauper, and one, moreover, which we are told became especially fashionable in Sparta after the Persian Wars.[44] Several of them won chariot races, notably Arcesilaus and his son Lichas, who together won three times at Olympia, Lichas' victory in 420 causing quite a stir because Sparta was not then allowed to participate officially. Lichas' generosity to strangers attending the Spartan annual gymnastic festival of the Gymnopaedia was famous throughout Greece, or so both Xenophon and Plutarch tell us – a further indication of his great wealth.[45] Another Spartan, Evagoras, is said by Herodotus to have been the only person to equal the feat of Cimon son of Stesagoras, a member of the great Athenian aristocratic house of the Philaids, in winning an Olympic chariot race three times with the same team.[46] These victories are probably to be dated to the third quarter of the sixth century, but time did nothing to close the gap between rich Spartiates and poor. One of the reasons given by Xenophon for the disastrous Spartan defeat at the hands of Thebes at the battle of Leuctra in 371 was the inferiority of the Spartan cavalry, which he attributes to the fact that horse-breeding was in the hands of the richest men, who handed the horses over to the soldiers only minutes before they took the field.[47] After the battle the gap between rich and poor widened even further. Aristotle, writing in the mid-fourth century, says baldly that 'it has happened that some Spartans own too much property and others very little, so that the countryside has fallen into the hands of a few.'[48] What particularly grieved Aristotle was the fact that nearly two-fifths of the land was in the hands of women.[49]

But the fact that there had always been inequalities of wealth among the Spartiates does not mean that there had never been any attempt to check such inequalities. Of all the ancient authors who write about Spartan social and economic conditions Aristotle is the only one who does not express the explicit belief that there was a time in Spartan history when there was economic equality among the Spartiates, yet even in his case we cannot infer, as some modern scholars do, that 'Aristotle knew of no Lycurgan land distribution'.[50] The whole tenor of Aristotle's argument is that the inequalities in wealth in Sparta had become intensified in his own day. What he says about Lycurgus' economic programme is worth studying a little more closely. Lycurgus, says Aristotle, 'acted rightly in making it dishonourable to buy or sell existing property, but he also made it permissible for anyone who wished to give away or bequeath his property.'[51] What does this mean? Aristotle is clearly opposed to the growing concentration of property in the hands of a few. So, if he commends Lycurgus' ban on the sale of property we must surely assume that this ban was intended to prevent such concentration. In other words, Aristotle clearly believed that Lycurgus' legislation was intended to have an egalitarian bias but that it was unsuccessful because the freedom to dispose of property by methods other than by sale in the long run counteracted the ban on sale and purchase. Whether Aristotle is right in attributing to Lycurgus the permission to give away or bequeath property at will must still be discussed. Nevertheless, a ban on the sale of land is not at all the same as a redistribution of land, even though they may both be motivated by the same egalitarian concern. In this connection we must now consider whether the tradition of equal land allotments in Sparta derived from the division of the land among the Dorian conquerors at the very beginning of Spartan history or whether it derived from a subsequent revolutionary redistribution.

Plato, as we have seen, and also Isocrates believed that equality in Spartiate landholdings was to be dated to the earliest days of the Dorian state, but Xenophon, Ephorus, Polybius, Plutarch and Justin attribute it to the reforms of Lycurgus.[52] Of the two theories the latter is the more attractive, largely because economic equality would fit into what we know of the Lycurgan reforms much better than into the most likely picture of the original Dorian conquest. In its early days and for several centuries thereafter, as we have already pointed out, Sparta shows every sign of being a normal aristocratic Greek state, and in this setting there would not be a place for the concept of equal allotments. The tenor of the Lycurgan reforms, on the other hand, was egalitarian. That is not to say, of course, that there was no allotment at all after the initial conquest of Laconia. Each of the conquering Dorians would have received a share of the land, but hardly an equal one.

It is noteworthy too that the equal distribution of 'public land' (*politikē chōra*) is singled out by Polybius, the second-century historian, as one of the three differences between Sparta and Crete, the others being the Spartan scorn of money and the retention of hereditary monarchy and life-tenure for councillors.[53] 'Among the Cretans', says Polybius, 'in all these respects the situation is quite the opposite. The laws there allow them to acquire as much land as they can *ad infinitum*, as the saying goes, and money is esteemed among them to such a degree that its acquisition is thought to be not only necessary but also most honourable.'[54]

In these economic matters, it is worth stressing, Spartan institutions differ from Cretan ones in being more egalitarian. Plato, similarly, writing two centuries earlier, makes a very clear distinction between Argos and Messenia on the one hand and Sparta on the other, in believing that, though economic equality was established early on in all three states, it had survived only in Sparta.[55] Xenophon, writing shortly before the battle of Leuctra, is equally explicit: 'Now it is clear that these laws are of great antiquity, for Lycurgus is said to have lived at the time of the Heraclids. But though they are as old as that they are quite new to the other Greeks even now. And, what is most surprising of all is that everyone praises institutions such as these but no state wishes to imitate them.'[56]

We certainly cannot push this evidence into the realm of myth, as some scholars have tried to do.[57] Xenophon, Plato and Polybius obviously believed not only that there had been some sort of economic equality among Spartan citizens in the distant past but also that it still existed in the classical period. How can this be squared with the very decisive evidence already cited that at no time was there genuine Spartiate economic equality. The clue probably lies in Polybius' phrase, 'an equal share of civic land'. What is meant by 'civic land'? Despite a good deal of scholarly airing there is no very clear answer.[58] All that can be said is that not all the land was divided up into equal allotments. There was presumably land other than 'civic land'. Hence the inequalities already noticed. This interpretation ties in with passages in Plato and Plutarch. Upon the birth of a boy, according to the latter author, the child was taken to a place called Lesche, where it was officially examined by the elders of the tribe. If declared healthy it was assigned one of the nine thousand lots and handed back to its father to bring up.[59] It was presumably this lot (*klēros* or, in Doric, *klāros*) which could not be sold. Plato's *Laws* advocates an ideal system which is in many respects Spartan in inspiration, so it is worth looking at its provisions on land tenure, which are specifically aimed at correcting the defect, as Plato saw it, of the Spartan system, namely the permission to Spartiates to bequeath their property at will. Plato's law therefore lays down that the 'ancestral allotment' (*patrōos klēros*) must be left to one of the testator's sons, with freedom to distribute the rest of his property among his other sons as he pleases. The main point of the very elaborate 'law' proposed by Plato – which includes detailed provisions for childlessness and intestacy and careful instructions as to how the husband of a female heir is to be selected – is to keep the ancestral allotment in the family.[60] But, it is important to note, the fact that a testator can be assumed to have property other than his ancestral estate shows that Plato did not consider all the land of his ideal state as being divided into ancestral allotments.[61] Could this not be a reflection of the reality of the Spartan land system? Only if we accept this view, namely that the ancestral allotments did not account for all Spartan land, can we make sense of Plutarch's statement that every healthy male Spartiate was given an allotment at birth. If all the land was already taken up, where did the new-born infant get his land from? There is no strain imposed on our credulity or on the credibility of the evidence if we explain it in this way, and it seems infinitely preferable to dismissing Plutarch's evidence out of hand or to trying to explain it away – a favourite scholarly pastime.[62]

Once we realize that not all the land was taken up in allotments we can easily see how both the egalitarian and the inegalitarian traditions about Spartan landholding can be true at the same time. The system of allotments – presumably all roughly equal – was obviously designed to allow all holders a certain independence, but the possibility of amassing additional landed property clearly led to serious inequalities in wealth. But, though it was illegal only to sell one's allotment, it was considered disgraceful to sell land of any kind.[63] The indivisibility of the allotments, which is undoubtedly to be assumed, explains the polyandry mentioned by Polybius:

> Among the Spartans it was both traditional and customary for three or four men to share a wife, or even more if they were brothers, and

the children would be common to all. And when a man had begotten enough children it was quite proper and customary for him to lend his wife to one of his friends.[64]

The wife shared among three or four men would presumably be an heiress and it is possibly a reflection of the shortage of ancestral allotments. Anyone without an allotment of his own (or at least a share in one) would probably not be a full citizen. Certainly, anyone unable to pay his share of the common mess meals, or *phiditia*, lost his rights of citizenship, and, according to Aristotle, there were in his day some Spartiates who were unable to afford the expense entailed.[65]

One reason for Aristotle's emphasis on the economic inequalities among Spartiates is undoubtedly that the gap between rich and poor had widened not long before his time. According to Plutarch there had actually been a change in the law. Until the change every Spartiate had to leave his allotment to his son, but an ephor called Epitadeus, 'a powerful man, arrogant and intractable', wishing to debar his own son from his inheritance, passed a *rhetra*, or bill, making it permissible for a Spartiate to give or bequeath his 'estate and allotment' (*oikon kai klēron*) to anyone he liked.[66] This event is placed by Plutarch in the aftermath of the defeat of Athens (i.e. after the end of the Peloponnesian War, 404) and as a precursor of the revolutionary situation of the mid-third century. The law has sometimes been dismissed as a fictitious aetiological anecdote, and, as we have seen, both Plato and Aristotle believed that, since the time of Lycurgus, it had always been permissible for a Spartiate to give away or bequeath his property to whomever he wished, and that only sale was disallowed. Aristotle's statement is sometimes misinterpreted, however, as referring to Epitadeus' law, but, for one thing, the whole context of his remark is concerned with Lycurgus, and, for another, he clearly regards the ruling that it was permissible for a Spartiate to give away or bequeath his land as deriving from the same lawgiver as did the ban on its sale, that is, from Lycurgus himself. But who is right, Plato and Aristotle, or Plutarch? It would seem unlikely that Phylarchus, upon whom Plutarch is probably relying in the relevant passage and who wrote in the second century, would be a more reliable source on events of the turn of the fifth and fourth centuries than Plato or Aristotle. Yet the very concept of testamentary inheritance without adoption, which is implicit in what Plato and Aristotle say as well as in Epitadeus' supposed law, was quite unknown anywhere in Greece before the fourth century, when it appears in Athens for the first time. This may give us a clue as to how we may reconcile Plato and Aristotle with Plutarch and Phylarchus. Since testamentary inheritance was unknown to the framers of the Lycurgan code they would obviously have made no mention of it, considering it sufficient to place a ban on sale. But this omission could later be used by a skilful debater as an argument showing that the freedom to bequeath land at will was sanctioned by the Lycurgan laws. There is no way of knowing whether this is the argument actually used by Epitadeus in favour of his bill, but it would seem the best way to gain support without appearing too revolutionary, and, more important for our purpose, it would enable us to accept Plato and Aristotle's version without rejecting the historicity of Epitadeus' law. Seen in this light Epitadeus' law was really a loophole in the Lycurgan code: technically, as we have seen, it is probably quite true to say that the Lycurgan code had not outlawed the bequest of land. Plato and Aristotle may therefore be forgiven for believing that it allowed it.[67]

There are, however, those who hold that the new law went further than Plutarch seems to think. As a result of the law, says Plutarch, 'the powerful [*hoi dunatoi*] unscrupulously gained possession of property, displacing the rightful heirs. And with wealth flowing into the hands of a few, poverty gripped the state.'[68] This statement, it has been held, 'points unmistakably to purchase'.[69] There is no evidence, though, that the sale of allotments was ever legalized, but it certainly is clear that in the fourth and third centuries there was a growing gap between rich Spartiates and poor. We do not know who the people were in whose hands property accumulated except that Plutarch calls them 'powerful men', the same epithet as he applies to Epitadeus and a term that usually refers to influence as well as to wealth.

But when were these egalitarian reforms enacted? Their association with the name of Lycurgus does not help, because, in point of time, Lycurgus is one of the best travelled figures in antiquity. Dates proposed for him span more than three centuries, from about 900 to about 550, and, to complicate matters still further, there are also attempts to dissociate some or all of the 'Lycurgan' reforms from Lycurgus and to regard them as gradual developments.[70] Both Herodotus and Thucydides offer dates for Lycurgus at the early end of the spectrum, with Aristotle not very much behind them at 776, and these eminent authorities have not been without their modern followers, but modern opinion seems to tend more towards the other end of the spectrum.[71] In itself the question of date is of very little importance, but it is essential to date the reforms in order to understand their causes.

There was a demand for a redistribution of land during the Second Messenian War, according to Aristotle, who based this conclusion upon a poem by Tyrtaeus on *Eunomia* or 'Orderly Government'.[72] This passage occurs in Aristotle's *Politics* as an example of how revolution can result from serious inequalities in wealth. If Aristotle is right in believing that the situation in Sparta in the time of Tyrtaeus was revolutionary, then we must believe that a redistribution of land was not only called for but also effected, and that it was done not too long after the poem was written, because the revolutionary situation was certainly defused – and no similar demand is heard again until the third century, more than four hundred years later. Tyrtaeus himself fought in the Second Messenian War, as has already been mentioned, but it is not quite certain to which of the two Messenian Wars the passage mentioned by Aristotle referred.[73] If the first war is meant, Jones may be right in suggesting that the institution of the Carneian festival, traditionally placed in the 26th Olympiad, 676–673, celebrated 'the end of civil strife'.[74] It is more generally assumed, however, that it is the Second Messenian War that Aristotle had in mind, which is generally placed in the middle of the seventh century. This date accords better with the association often made between the Lycurgan reforms and the introduction of the hoplite phalanx, which, it is now accepted, cannot be dated much before the middle of the seventh century.[75] That the fighting described by Tyrtaeus in the Second Messenian War was conducted in phalanx formation can hardly be doubted, as there are several injunctions to the men to fight shoulder to shoulder.[76] The idea that the Lycurgan reforms were introduced as the result of the victory of a 'hoplite revolution' has had some supporters but must be handled with care.[77] A phalanx needs a good deal of organizing, so, as has been well said, 'hoplites were an instrument before they became a force'.[78] The introduction of hoplite formation fighting was probably not therefore directly causally linked with the Lycurgan reforms, but the connection was probably at one remove, thus: the new combat technique gave Sparta great military power, which she used to her advantage by conquering Messenia in order to find additional land to satisfy the poorer Spartiates. Hence the strangely pessimistic key of Tyrtaeus' poetry already remarked upon. Though the war was indeed a war of conquest, it was a necessity in terms of Spartan internal affairs. Only victory over the Messenians could ensure domestic peace.

But, according to a persistent tradition, the Lycurgan reforms were not concerned solely with land and property. Indeed, the whole fabric of Spartan social and political life was thought to have been revolutionized by him. The whole militarization and communalization of life which characterized classical Sparta was thought to owe its origin to Lycurgus, but even within this tradition there was room for doubt. In his usual open manner Herodotus offers two accounts of the origin of the Lycurgan system, one being that it was revealed to Lycurgus by the Pythia, the priestess of Apollo at Delphi, and the other that he imported it from Crete.[79] That there were marked similarities between the social systems of Crete and Sparta was well known in classical times and much discussed, notably by Polybius, Ephorus and Aristotle.[80] But, it is sometimes said, do not such similarities point to a common Dorian heritage rather than to direct borrowing from one to the other? When held, this view tends to be a bald assertion and not a fully argued case, its holders no doubt regarding it as almost a self-evident truth.[81] The *agōgē*, the name given to the system of military discipline to which all Spartiate boys were subjected, with its peer group communal barracks and messes, may bear a passing resemblance to the practices of some societies in Africa and Oceania, but, whatever the ultimate origins of the *agōgē*, there can be no doubt that in its classical form it was very remote from any tribal roots it may have had. Furthermore, it is worth noting, in no Dorian area other than Sparta and Crete were there, so far as we know, even the most vestigial traces of any similar system. According to Aristotle, Lycurgus got his ideas from a visit to the Cretan city of Lyctus (Lyttus), which he says was a Spartan colony which had adopted the local institutions.[82] It is now generally believed, however, that Sparta had no overseas colonies besides Tarentum,[83] but that is not to deny that the Lycurgan institutions could have had Cretan origins. Indeed, the men's messes, called in Sparta *phiditia*, *philitia*, *sussitia* or *suskeniai*, were originally called by their Cretan name, *andreia*, when first introduced into Sparta.[84] As both Ephorus and Aristotle argue, the Spartan institutions were by and large more finished versions of the Cretan ones, another reason for believing that they moved from Crete to Sparta.[85] But we are still left with the nagging question of how they had originated in Crete in the first place. Though both Ephorus and Aristotle again maintain that the institutions were survivals from Minoan Crete, what little we know about society in that period lends no positive support to this view, though, as we have already seen, Mycenaean society certainly was both hierarchical and aristocratic.[86] In any case it cannot be assumed that, if Ephorus and Aristotle are right, the 'Minoan' institutions would have remained static, and it would not appear impossible for the communalized system of classical times to have developed out of the society of Mycenaean Crete, in which military considerations played an extremely important part, if the subject-matter of the Cnossos tablets are anything to go on. It is, finally, no more surprising that reformers and constitution-makers in antiquity should have borrowed foreign models than that their modern counterparts should do so. The idea is also found elsewhere in antiquity besides the case of Sparta and Crete, notably in Livy's story about the Roman embassy to Athens at the time of the drafting of the Twelve Tables, which, even if untrue, at least shows that the idea was not intrinsically implausible to the ancient mind.[87]

There is certainly no difficulty in explaining the purpose of the Lycurgan reforms. Their main aim was clearly to knit the Spartan citizen body together and to inculcate a spirit of solidarity among the Spartiate. The various reforms collectively known as Lycurgan each reflect a different facet of this: the levelling down of the position of the kings and aristocracy, the nationalization of education, the communalization and militarization of the life of the boys and men, the breaking down of family ties in favour of peer group ties, and the introduction of a certain amount of economic as well as political equality. As can be seen from this list, the Lycurgan reforms were nothing short of a revolution. The privileged group had been widened to include all Spartiates, not just the old aristocracy, who were now no more than their fellow 'Equals'. Equality among the citizens proper became the keynote of Spartan government, though vestigial traces of inequality persisted, such as the exclusive access of the aristocracy to the *gerousia*, which has already been mentioned.

According to both Herodotus and Thucydides Sparta was in a state of turmoil and revolution from its foundation as a Dorian state until the reforms of Lycurgus.[88] Classical post-Lycurgan Sparta, on the other hand, was characterized by internal harmony and tranquillity. But that is not of course to say that there was no opposition to the reforms. On the contrary, there is evidence of hostile aristocratic reactions both initially and later. We read in Plutarch, for example, that the introduction of common meals especially incensed the wealthy, who assembled together in the agora and threw stones at Lycurgus. The reformer took to his heels closely pursued by his attackers, one of whom was so close behind him that when Lycurgus turned round to see who it was, he was struck in the eye by his pursuer's staff and blinded.[89] The story itself looks credible enough on its own, until we read that in commemoration of the incident Lycurgus built a temple dedicated to Athena Optiletis, the word *optilos* being the Doric for *ophthalmos*, or 'eye', and also that no weapons were permitted at the Spartan assembly. This ending might make us suspect the story as an aetiological concoction of the sort so familiar in classical mythology. But, if we accept the institution of the *agōgē* and *sussitia* as deliberate reforms, as is argued above that we should, rather than as survivals from a tribal past, then there is every reason to accept the likelihood of aristocratic opposition, or, what must have amounted to the same thing, the opposition of the rich. This particular reform is interpreted by Plutarch, and not without reason, as a sumptuary law:

> With a view to an even severer attack upon luxury and the passion for the acquisition of wealth, Lycurgus enacted his third and most admirable measure, the institution of the *sussitia*, the result being that they all come together for meals and dine on the same bread and meat of specified types. They are not allowed to stay at home and recline on sumptuous couches at ornate tables in the shade, with attendants and cooks to look after them, fatten them up like voracious brutes and ruin not only their minds but also their bodies, which, permitted the indulgence of every passion to excess, require long hours of sleep, warm baths, plenty of leisure, and, in a manner of speaking, daily nursing.[90]

This is not the only evidence of aristocratic opposition to the Lycurgan programme. The last clause of the great *Rhetra* itself, the document summarizing some of the constitutional and military reforms, is relevant here. Plutarch was undoubtedly right in holding that its last clause was a later addition, and we may be justified in regarding it as a concession to an aristocratic backlash against the egalitarian tenor of the rest of the document. Whether the *Rhetra* was an oracle or an enactment of the Spartan assembly is of no consequence to our present discussion. But there can be no doubt that it was a genuinely ancient document reflecting the Spartan constitution after the Lycurgan reforms. The rider to the *Rhetra* reads as follows: 'But if the people should make a crooked decision, the elders and kings shall set it aside.'[91] The interpretation of this clause is nothing if not controversial, and the translation of the last two words (*apostatēras ēmen* literally, 'to be standers aside' or 'to be setters aside') is particularly in dispute and has been variously interpreted, Plutarch himself interpreting it to mean that the council had the right not only to refuse to ratify a 'crooked' proposal but also to reject it and dissolve the assembly.[92] But, however interpreted, the basic sense of the clause is not in doubt – and is directly contrary to the tenor of the main body of the *Rhetra*, which, after defining the powers of the kings and council, ends with the words: 'But sovereignty and power are to belong to the people.'[93] The original Lycurgan constitution was, therefore, democratic in the sense that it vested power in the hands of the assembly of all citizens, but the amendment seems to have shifted the balance back to some degree in favour of the aristocratic council.[94] To hold, as some modern scholars do, that the *Rhetra* had included the rider from the start and that Plutarch is mistaken in regarding it as a later amendment, is insupportable.[95] The question as to whether sovereignty lay in the assembly or in the aristocratic council was one which exercised the Spartans themselves, as can be seen from the two versions of a poem by Tyrtaeus. As quoted by Plutarch, the lines place the emphasis squarely on kings and council, but the slightly extended version quoted by Diodorus Siculus stresses the sovereignty of the assembly: here is Plutarch's version:

> Initiative in counsel belongs to the god-honoured kings,
> Whose care is the lovely city of Sparta,
> And to the elders of the council. Next come the men of the people,
> responding with straight enactments.[96]

The interpretation of the last line is particularly disputed, but the picture here is clearly one of aristocratic government: kings and council come first, and only then the people. The kings, it should be noted, were just ordinary members of the council, though *ex officio* and not elective. To what are substantially the same lines Diodorus' version has added four more, which give the whole thing a completely new twist:

> (The men of the people) are to speak what is proper and act rightly
> in everything;
> And not to plot against the city,
> But victory and power are to follow the mass of the people.
> For so has Apollo revealed to the city.[97]

Whether Plutarch's or Diodorus' version is the more likely to be the original is not relevant to the present discussion. What is noteworthy, though, is that the two versions reflect diametrically opposed political tendencies.

COUNCIL AND ASSEMBLY

But where did the real seat of power lie in practice? According to Aristotle, the assembly had 'no power other than to ratify the decisions of the elders'.[98] Did this include the power to reject such decisions? Another passage in Aristotle has often been thought to indicate that in Sparta, by contrast to Carthage, the assembly had no right to debate the proposals put before it by the council.[99] But it is by no means easy to disentangle what refers to Carthage alone from what refers also to Sparta and the Cretan cities. Of far more weight is the evidence we have of actual political proceedings, and here, both in Thucydides and Xenophon, it is the assembly rather than the council which appears to have the final say. There is not a single reference in the whole of Thucydides to the Spartan council, but the assembly puts in an appearance on three occasions, the best known and most important being 432, when, after a heated debate, the assembly decides to go to war with Athens.[100] In the thirty-odd years covered by Xenophon's *Hellenica* there are eight reports of meetings of the assembly, in all but two of which definite decisions, all on matters of considerable moment, are recorded – and again usually only after genuine debate.[101] It is unjustifiable, however, to conclude from this, as is sometimes done, that the council played a less important role in decision-making than the assembly.[102] Even the rider to the *Rhetra* recognizes the decision-making powers of the assembly but allows the council to set aside such decisions when they are 'crooked'. But how, it may be asked, could the assembly make 'crooked' decisions if, as Aristotle says, it had no initiating powers? Plutarch answers this thorny question by maintaining that the assembly had the right of amendment, for which, however, there is no evidence.[103] An attractive modern suggestion is that it was permissible for the ephors to put their own proposals before the assembly and that in this way the people could make a crooked decision.[104] It is certainly true that in all the examples we have it is always an ephor, and never a king or elder, who summons, presides over or makes proposals to the assembly, and decisions of the assembly are expressed in the formula, 'It was resolved by the ephors and the assembly'.[105] There also are one or two cases in which a debate seems to be going on in the assembly at the same time as one on the same subject in the council, and quite independently of it.[106] In one case, indeed, recorded as happening in the year 242, the assembly was evidently called in to resolve a deadlock in the council on the question of the radical reform programme of King Agis IV. After a very emotional debate in the assembly, Plutarch tells us, 'the masses followed Agis, but the rich begged Leonidas (the other king) not to forsake them, and, entreating and persuading the elders, who had the power of proposing legislation, they managed so well that those voting against the bill were in a majority of one.'[107] From this account it seems unlikely that the assembly had taken a formal vote by the time the council decided to reject the reforms, as has been suggested by some.[108] But there are several cases in which it is clear that a decision was taken by the assembly without any motion before them from the council. The famous debate of 432 leading to the outbreak of the Peloponnesian War is one such case. Before the Spartans began debating amongst themselves the assembly was addressed by various envoys of allied states and then by an Athenian envoy. It would seem highly unlikely that all this was simply a repeat performance of what had already happened before the council. What is especially significant is not so much that the envoys addressed the assembly but rather that that body deliberated upon the addresses straight away:

> And when the Spartans had heard the accusations of their allies against the Athenians and also what the Athenians had said, they dismissed them all and deliberated by themselves upon the current situation. And the opinion of the majority concurred in holding that the Athenians were already in the wrong and that they should at once go to war.[109]

King Archidamus then gets up in the assembly and tries to exercise a restraining influence, but the rousing speech of the ephor Sthenelaidas, agreeing with the original consensus, carries the day. Not only, therefore, is the final decision taken in the assembly, but it is there and there alone, so far as we know, that the question is discussed from the beginning. Several similar examples are to be found in Xenophon, such as the settlement of internal divisions in Athens in 403, the decision to send aid to Acanthus and Apollonia in 383, the Spartan intervention in Thebes in the same year, and the disastrous decision to march on Thebes in 371.[110] In all these cases the decisions were reached in direct reaction to speeches which were made before the assembly in the first instance.

How does all this square with the statements of Aristotle and Plutarch to the effect that the council had the sole right to initiate legislation – or with that haunting rider to the great *Rhetra*? In fact these cases can be easily explained in terms of the constitutional proprieties. In practice the relations between council and assembly do not appear to have been too dissimilar to those subsisting between the two chambers in a modern bicameral legislature in which bills may originate in either house but require the approval of both. In cases such as the ones we have been considering, in which both the initial proposal and the final decision were made in the assembly, it is likely that it was only when the decision was confirmed by the council that it was considered legally 'proposed', and it may then have had to return to the assembly for final formal ratification. In such circumstances we can easily understand what is meant in the rider to the *Rhetra* by the term 'crooked' decisions. Even though the whole decision-making process may in cases like these actually have taken place on the floor of the assembly, the elders could be 'standers aside' or 'setters aside' by refusing to formulate an unwelcome proposal as a motion, thereby effectively vetoing it. This is the way in which the tension evident in the early documents between the aristocratic council and the 'democratic' assembly was resolved in practice.

In other respects too the equality among Spartiates that Lycurgus had attempted to introduce was modified.

THE EPHORS

Probably the most important manifestation of the struggle against the original Spartan aristocracy was the institution of the ephorate, an office aptly compared by Cicero to the Roman tribunate of the plebs.[111] The Roman tribunes were of course originally the champions of the plebeians against the aristocratic patricians in the so-called Struggle of the Orders in the early Roman Republic. But this picture of the role of the ephorate is not universally shared. Some claim for the ephorate an antiquity going back to the very beginnings of Dorian history, probably as priests, but this seems unlikely.[112] There certainly were ephors in several other Greek cities, including Thera, which claimed to be a Spartan colony, as well as the cities of the *perioikoi* and Messenia, but these may all have borrowed the institution from the classical Spartan model.[113] There was, moreover, no trace of any religious function attaching to the ephorate in classical times.

The majority of ancient writers attributed the institution of the ephorate to Lycurgus. They include Herodotus, Xenophon, Plato, Ephorus, Isocrates and Justin.[114] Aristotle, however, does not share this view but assigns the introduction of the new office to King Theopompus, who was traditionally associated with the First Messenian War.[115] The date of the holding of office of the first board of ephors was computed in different ways by various ancient authors, but all converge on the year 754, which does indeed tally with the generally accepted period of the First Messenian War.[116] Whether the new institution was the work of Lycurgus, Theopompus or someone else is irrelevant, but the new office certainly fits well into the 'Lycurgan' scheme of things. Every month the kings and ephors met and swore a mutual oath, the ephors agreeing to preserve the kingship provided the kings respected the laws of the state.[117] There was never any doubt in anyone's mind as to which party to this agreement had the upper hand. The ephors alone had the right to remain seated in the presence of a king, and if summoned by the ephors the king was obliged to obey.[118] He was allowed to refuse the summons twice, but the third time he had to go.[119] The ephors were able to fine a king – the best known example being Archidamus' fine for marrying too short a wife – arrest him, impeach him, and even depose him, though the last mentioned power could be exercised only if the ephors saw a shooting star on a specific night set aside for the watching of the heavens every ninth year.[120] In all these respects the ephors are clearly to be seen as a counterweight to the kings, and also in the fact that, though in all other regards the power to declare war was held by the kings, the annual declaration of war on the helots was made by the ephors.[121] But, we may well ask, what power did the kings have that needed so strong a counterbalance? The answer of course is 'none'. The kings were nothing more than the noblest members of the aristocracy, as is well indicated by the fact that in the absence of a king from the *gerousia*, his nearest relation among the councillors acted as his substitute, casting two votes for the missing king in addition to one for himself.[122] The institution of the ephorate, like the rest of the Lycurgan reforms, must be seen as an anti-aristocratic, not as an anti-monarchical, measure.

In this connection it is worth noting that the ephors were five in number. But why five? The number which underlies the structure of several Spartan institutions is not five but three, based no doubt on the three Dorian tribes, the Hylleis, Dymanes and Pamphyli, which were to be found throughout Doric Greece. There were of course thirty councillors (including the two kings), but it is particularly in the fields of religion and warfare that the threefold division is most noticeable. Even in the Carneian festival, whose traditional date of foundation was only 676/3, the participants were divided into 27 phratries, nine from each tribe.[123] The Spartan 'cavalry' (which in classical times was really an élite corps of hoplites) was commanded by three *hippagretai*, each with a hundred *hippeis* under him.[124] Herodotus' brief catalogue of the Lycurgan reforms includes a military institution called the *triecas*, which, though its meaning remains obscure, was clearly based on the number three.[125] In a much discussed passage in a fragment of Tyrtaeus the Spartans are described as fighting in three separate divisions bearing the names of the Dorian tribes.[126] This has caused a fair degree of scholarly puzzlement, because the Spartan army appears elsewhere to be organized not on a tribal basis but on the basis of *lochoi* of which there were five.[127] This presupposes a change in the organization of the Spartan army. But when did it take place and to what purpose? Tyrtaeus' lines turn out to be less helpful than we might have expected, because they come from a fragmentary poem and it has been suggested that the tribal army mentioned by Tyrtaeus was not intended as a description of the army of his own day in the Second Messenian War but rather by way of contrast with it.[128] The importance of this question has been exaggerated out of all proportion and it has received far more attention than it deserves, especially since it is entirely a matter of conjecture whether Tyrtaeus was referring to his own day or to some previous generation. The purpose of the army reform is, however, a really important problem, and we may perhaps find a clue by comparing the two types of military organization. The tribal arrangement was undoubtedly based on a family structure, or, in other words, it was an aristocratic military system. What we would expect of an anti-aristocratic programme such as the Lycurgan reforms were is a shift from family-based to regional organization, as we shall find in Cleisthenic Athens. But does the Spartan army reform fall into this category? That very much depends upon the precise meaning of the term *lochos*. The names of the five *lochoi* were Messoatas (or Messoages), Hedolus (or Haedolius), Sinis, Arimas (or Sarinas) and Ploas.[129] Of these names only one tallies with anything else, and that is Messoatas or Messoages, which may be connected with the ōba of Mesoa.[130] A further connection between *lochoi* and obes is indicated by Thucydides' objection to Herodotus' mention of a Pitanate *lochos*.[131] Pitane, like Mesoa, was the name of an obe, but there was no military *lochos* named after it, so Thucydides was strictly correct if somewhat pedantic in his criticism of Herodotus, who was probably thinking of a *lochos* which, even though it was not named after Pitane, was made up of Pitanates. Now, we know Pitane not only as an obe but also as a Spartan village,[132] from which the conclusion follows that 'obe' means 'village' and that there was some connection between these villages and the *lochoi* or regiments, in other words, the replacement of a tribe-based military system with one based upon geography, as we expected. This view is not accepted by those who regard the obes not as geographical areas but rather as tribal divisions.[133] An ingenious etymological association has been suggested between the word *ōba*, the Latin word *avus* ('grandfather') and the reconstructed Indo-European word *owos* ('kinship group'),[134] but even if we accept this rather strained link we are no better equipped to understand the meaning of the word *ōba* in practice than, for example, is the man who knows that 'villain' comes from 'villa' able to determine the sense of the former word. Another objection to the connection between *ōbai* and *lochoi* is numerical. Estimates as to the number of obes vary from four to seven. Pausanias mentions only four, Limnae, Cynosura, Mesoa and Pitane, which correspond to the names of four of the six divisions known from Roman times, the additional ones being Amyclae and Neapolis.[135] It is fairly certain that Neapolis was a Hellenistic foundation, so we are left with five obes, the four mentioned by Pausanias, which were wards of the city of Sparta itself, and Amyclae, a village about three miles away. The so-called obe is a recent 'discovery' and depends upon a conjectural reconstruction of an inscription.[136] If, therefore, as seems most likely, there were five obes in classical Sparta, there can be little doubt that there was some connection between them and the five military *lochoi*. If every Spartan citizen was assigned to one of these local districts, we must assume that each was legally regarded as domiciled in the city of Sparta itself or Amyclae, however far afield his estate might be.[137] This would probably not be a legal fiction, since citizens under the age of sixty probably spent more time in their barracks in Sparta than on their estates, which were worked by helots.

Is it too much to infer some connection between the number of obes and the number of ephors? It is also worth noting that the number five crops up elsewhere in Spartan institutions. Though, as we have seen, the 'cavalry' was divided into three sections, the five oldest *hippeis* to retire each year were given the title of *agathoergoi* ('benefactors') and were entrusted with various special assignments on behalf of the state.[138]

The most probable explanation of this discrepancy is that the threefold division derived from the earliest days of the Spartan state, whereas the *agathoergoi* were instituted after the 'Lycurgan' reforms. This view is corroborated by the other occurrences of the number five in Spartan institutions, all of them being *ad hoc* bodies in the classical period. In about 570, for example, when the Spartans were called in to mediate in the quarrel between Athens and Megara over Salamis they appointed five arbitrators.[139] Similarly, there were fifteen Spartan signatories (in addition to the two kings) to the Peace of Nicias in 421 and either ten or fifteen Spartan negotiators to arrange Athens' surrender at the end of the Peloponnesian War in 404.[140] All this shows that, as we were expecting to find, institutions were placed upon a geographical basis, presumably to counteract the family-based system of early aristocratic Sparta. Whatever its exact date, the change must surely be part of the 'Lycurgan' reform programme, and the ephorate must be seen as an important element in the shift. The ephors were the most important Spartan magistrates: they presided over the assembly and probably also over the council; they supervised the activities of all other officials and had the power to fine or imprison them or even to depose them while in office; they controlled the *krupteia*, or secret police; they acted as judges in all civil suits and homicide cases and they had control of the day-to-day management of foreign affairs and of finance.[141] But the power of any individual ephor was limited by the fact that the five were expected to function as a college, by majority vote, and new ephors were elected each year, no ex-ephor being eligible for re-election.[142] In contrast to the members of the *gerousia* the ephors were often poor, so much so, according to Aristotle, that they were open to bribery.[143] It was the lowly origins of the ephors that made Aristotle regard the ephorate as the popular element in the Spartan constitution, as against the *gerousia*, which he regarded as being the aristocratic component.[144]

The name Lycurgus was a convenient personalized peg upon which to hang a variety of Spartan institutions. But, though we are well advised to remain sceptical about Lycurgus' own part in the establishment of the reform programme that bears his name, it is worth noticing how high a proportion of these reforms share a common tenor. This comes home particularly forcefully if we consider the oldest extant list of 'Lycurgan' reforms, namely Herodotus' brief catalogue, which is made up of three categories: military institutions, the ephorate and the *gerousia*.[145] Of these the last is obviously out of place as part of the

'Lycurgan' reform, but, as we have already seen, the institution of the ephorate fits into the anti-aristocratic pattern to which also belongs the whole system of military discipline, including the *agōgē* and the *sussitia* and the constant emphasis upon the equality of the *homoioi* ('Equals'). Sparta was the only Greek state to have a nationalized educational system, under a magistrate called the *paidonomos* or 'pastor' (literally, 'boy-herd'), but state control over a Spartan covered almost his whole life. The new-born Spartiate boy was already thought of as state property and, as has already been mentioned, had to be inspected by the elders of his tribe for physical deformities. If he failed this test he was exposed, and if he passed he was entrusted to the care of his parents until he turned six. From then until the age of thirty he lived in barracks together with others of the same age and was subjected to strict discipline and regimentation. Only after this period of training was he allowed to set up house on his own.[146] But this by no means marked the end of his public service. Until the age of sixty he could be called upon to lay down his life for the state in battle and he would remain a member of his *sussition*, which was more like a mess than a dining club, until the day he died.[147] The older men seem also to have acted as unofficial supervisors of the exercises of the young boys.[148]

ATHENS AND SPARTA COMPARED

Sparta was uniquely successful in supplanting the old aristocracy and reconciling it to the new 'Lycurgan' regime in which social, political and military institutions were based upon age-group and geographical divisions, which cut across and replaced the older divisions according to family and clan. But, though the 'Lycurgan' revolution was directed against the old Spartan aristocracy, it was not opposed to the concept of aristocracy as such. In this respect the Spartan political outlook was in marked contrast to that of Athens in the fifth and fourth centuries, as we shall see in a later chapter. Yet the constitutional differences between the two states were far less marked than is usually assumed. Both limited participation in politics to the citizen body, and in each case citizens made up a small minority of the total population, though this proportion was probably higher in Athens than in Sparta. Ancient population statistics are a notoriously controversial area, since evidence tends to be both scanty and unreliable. The best comparative figures for Sparta are probably the numbers of combatants at the battle of Plataea in 479 as recorded by Herodotus, who puts the Spartiates at

THE REPUBLIC OF DEMIGODS

5,000, each with seven light-armed helots to attend him, and the *perioikoi* at the same strength as the Spartiates.[149] This yields a ratio of one Spartiate to eight non-Spartiates, which may reflect the ratio in the population at large. In Athens the ratio was probably more like one citizen to two non-citizens.[150] More important than this difference in ratio, however, is the difference in absolute numerical terms between the total citizen population of Sparta and that of Athens. Estimates of the Athenian citizen population show a wide range depending on source and date, but for the fifth and fourth centuries are within the limits of 20,000 to 45,000. For Sparta no estimate has ever gone above 10,000 and 5,000, the number of Spartiates at the battle of Plataea in 479, is generally thought to be nearer the mark, though even this figure is high by comparison with all later figures: about 3,500 at the battle of Mantinea in 418: 1,050 in 371 (700 at Leuctra and the remainder in Sparta). These battle figures will obviously need supplementing in order to reach the full number of adult male Spartiates: the figure for Mantinea represents a thirty-two-year call-up, i.e., men aged between eighteen and fifty, and the figure for Leuctra (as well probably as that for Plataea) represents a thirty-five-year call-up.[151] But, even with the necessary supplementation of these combat figures, one cannot but be struck by the diminutive size of the Spartiate population, considering that it was not only able to keep in check a subject population eight times its own size but also to be the leading land power in Greece for close on two hundred years, from the mid-sixth century to the defeat at the hands of Thebes in 371.

But these numerical differences do not explain the constitutional and political differences between Athens and Sparta. The key factor is to be found in the nature of the subject population controlled by the citizen body of each. In Athens the great bulk of the non-citizen population was made up of slaves, who were evidently not particularly well disposed towards the state of Athens, as can be seen, for example, from the fact that more than 20,000 of them, according to Thucydides, deserted to the Spartans at Decelea in 413 – a quarter of the total number of adult slaves, including women, regarded as the maximum possible by a generally accepted modern estimate.[152] But, though evidently not exactly devoted to their Athenian masters, the slaves were also not in the habit of rising in revolt and the citizens of Athens do not appear to have regarded them as a threat to their security. This is precisely the difference between Athens and Sparta, because the Spartiates were in a permanent state of insecurity, living as they did in perpetual fear of a Messenian rising. It was undoubtedly this common fear which impelled the rich Spartiate to sink his differences with his poor neighbour and the nobleman to fraternize with the commoner. It was this siege mentality which underlay Spartiate solidarity. That is also why the Spartiates had an ambivalent political attitude. They regarded themselves as the freest of the free – a paradoxical position, since they were in fact slaves of their own insecurity – and their equality was the wonder of their neighbours, yet they spurned the concept of democracy.[153] To someone requesting the establishment of a democracy in Sparta came the curt reply, inevitably attributed to Lycurgus: 'Set up a democracy in your own household first.'[154] Though the attribution of this remark to Lycurgus is hopelessly anachronistic, there is no reason to doubt that it reflects the traditional Spartan reaction to democracy. But why was it so? After all, as pointed out above, in Athens no less than in Sparta non-citizens were excluded from participation in politics.

To the modern mind the question of the nature of Spartan government seems much more clear-cut than it did to the ancients, none of whom could have penned this verdict, for example:

> It is quite certain that the form of government was purely oligarchical, the oligarchy in this case being the privileged body of Spartan peers. That there were obviously 'democratic' aspects within the oligarchy makes no difference whatever; no oligarchy could function at all without them, since all the members of the privileged caste must have equal rights.[155]

The last statement is misleading. It is true that there is a tendency towards equality within the ruling group of aristocracies and oligarchies, but Sparta differed from more typical examples by including all citizens within the privileged circle. One might quarrel with the Spartan definition of citizenship, but is the Athenian definition any more in keeping with modern tastes? Ancient authors were less reluctant to admit their puzzlement, and so we find Spartan government defined in a variety of ways in their writings. Plato was not sure whether it should be classified as a democracy or a tyranny – the ephors being the tyrants – but it did not cross his mind that it could be regarded as an aristocracy or an oligarchy.[156] Isocrates, that long-lived Athenian conservative, declared it unequivocally a democracy – indeed he regarded the Spartans as the most democratic of peoples.[157] Cicero, hedging his bets as was his wont, described the Spartan constitution simply as 'mixed'.[158] Of the ancient authorities Aristotle is the only one who considered the possibility of Sparta's being an oligarchy, but his criteria of oligarchy might seem curious to the modern reader. As oligarchical features in the Spartan constitution he singles out the fact that all offices were elective and none filled by lot, and also that the right to pronounce sentences of death or exile was in the hands of a small number of men.[159] But Aristotle himself preferred to regard the Spartan constitution as a harmonious blend of both oligarchy and democracy.[160]

This survey of ancient opinion does not help us, though, to put our finger upon the main factor differentiating the Athenian from the Spartan form of government. Probably more important than anything else was the psychological difference between the situations in which the two states found themselves. Whereas Athens was never subjected to any political pressure by her slaves or metics (*metoikoi*, 'resident aliens'), the Messenian helots – unlike their Laconian counterparts – always regarded themselves as a nation of free men held in bondage, a claim which was readily accepted by Sparta's enemies. A body of literature even developed tracing the history or pseudo-history of the Messenian nation, and when Sparta was forced to give up Messenia after her defeat by Thebes in 371, the Theban general Epaminondas proudly announced the re-establishment of the state of Messenia, much in the same way as modern statesmen hailed, for example, the rebirth of Poland after World War I.[161] But, by referring to the Messenian helots simply as Messenians the Spartans themselves were tacitly admitting the Messenian claim. That the Spartans did so refer to the Messenians is indicated by the treaty with Tegea as quoted by Plutarch, in which it was agreed that Tegeates were to 'throw the Messenians out of the land and that it was not permitted to make them good' – this last phrase presumably meaning that the Tegeates should not grant the Messenians citizenship. Clauses of this kind were a standard feature of Spartan treaties.[162] The constant reiteration of the Messenian claim forced the Spartiates into an aristocratic position. Though the 'Lycurgan' revolution attacked the old aristocracy, the concept of aristocracy could not be abandoned, but it could be modified. The new aristocracy comprised all Spartiates, so, like the old one, it too was an aristocracy of birth. To the modern mind there might appear to be a greater degree of difference between the old and new Spartan concepts of aristocracy than is actually the case. Modern definition might plausibly label the old concept as a class-based one and the new concept as a racialist one, but the difference is more apparent than real. The chasm which divides nobleman from commoner in the 'class-based' aristocratic world of the Homeric epics is hardly narrower than may be found between 'superior' and 'inferior' races in the most thorough-going of racialist theories. In the epics, to all intents and purposes, the aristocracy was a breed apart.[163] Nobility today is dismissed as an 'accident of birth', but the Greeks did not see it in that way. In Homer, as has already been noted, nobility or its absence is immediately apparent not only from a man's actions but even from his physical appearance. In the ancient concept of aristocracy are combined the modern concepts of 'accident of birth' and merit: the aristocrat is not only born into a wealthy and privileged stratum of society; he is also thought to deserve to be: he is literally one of 'the best'. A very similar attitude permeates the Spartan outlook on life. Elevating as they did the military virtues above all else the Spartiates were by definition the 'best men', for they and they alone devoted their whole lives to military discipline.[164] That, in short, is how an anti-aristocratic revolution gave birth to an aristocratic state, a 'republic of demi-gods'.

DISAFFECTION

It cannot be sufficiently stressed that of the three elements which made up the subject population of Sparta it was only the Messenian helots who were troublesome. If their Laconian counterparts were disaffected they did not show it, and the *perioikoi* were consistently loyal to their Spartiate rulers. The explanation for this perioecic loyalty might plausibly be sought in the internal autonomy which the *perioikoi* enjoyed. But that still leaves the puzzle of the docility of the Laconian helots unsolved, and it is a puzzle which tends generally to be glossed over, perhaps because it does not fit into the modern framework of thought. The modern mind generally regards it as almost axiomatic that any class or group of people in a subordinate position in any society is bound to feel rebellious and that revolution is inevitable if the situation persists.[165] A much deeper understanding of the causes of revolutions is demonstrated in this passage from the pen of that great student of revolutions, Alexis de Tocqueville:

> It is not always by going from bad to worse that a state falls into revolution. What happens most often is that a people which has endured the most oppressive laws without complaint throws them off violently once their weight is lightened. The regime destroyed

by a revolution is almost always better than the one which immediately preceded it, and experience teaches that the most dangerous moment for a bad government is when it begins to reform itself.[166]

Oppression *per se*, however defined, is not the cause of revolution. The cause is what in modern sociological jargon is called 'relative deprivation'. In other words, a man in an inferior social position, be he an Untouchable in the Indian caste system or a serf in medieval Europe, will not necessarily revolt against his masters or even feel disaffected. If his father, grandfather and great-grandfather before him were in the same inferior position as he is, he will probably accept his lot as inevitable and will not expect anything better for his children or grandchildren. This is especially the case where religion or some other form of indoctrination has been brought to bear on the situation and reconciled those of inferior status to their position – as happened in both the examples given above. In this kind of unchanging and, to all appearances, unchangeable, atmosphere it would be as unrealistic for a member of the lower orders to envy the life of an aristocrat as it would for a cabbage to envy that of a king. And, in a static social and political situation, the thought would probably hardly cross the minds of those in the lower orders. Comparisons would rather be made with others in a similar position and with their own circumstances in previous years or previous generations. If, however, something happened which enabled members of an inferior class to compare their lot with that of their 'betters', then they might indeed feel aggrieved.

This theory is well illustrated by Spartan history, especially in regard to the subjected elements of the population other than the Messenian helots, the Messenians being something of an exception because they never accepted the role of a subordinate class, but, as has already been mentioned, always regarded themselves as a nation of free men defeated in battle and unjustly reduced to subjection. In other words, the Messenians were beset by a feeling of 'relative deprivation' from the very moment of their defeat at the hands of the Spartans. Unlike most subject classes, they were never reconciled to their lowly status. But even in this exceptional case it is possible to trace the cause of rebellion to the hope for change, which in turn was prompted by what may have appeared to be a realistic possibility of change.

The first example in this connection is the somewhat dubious case of the helot rising of the turn of the sixth/fifth centuries. It is not my intention to enter into the argument on whether there was such a rising.[167] As in so many other similar debates there is not enough evidence to resolve the problem conclusively one way or the other. All one can honestly say is that there is a fair possibility that there was such a rising. Plato is the only ancient author to mention it specifically, and he does so in a passage explaining the Spartans' absence from the battle of Marathon in 490 as being due to their involvement in a Messenian war at the time.[168] Those who believe Plato generally link this rising with the name of the Messenian hero Aristomenes, who is mentioned by Pausanias, though he attaches the Messenian hero to the Second Messenian War, pointing out at the same time that there was disagreement among his sources as to the correct dating of the legendary hero.[169] None of them dated him to the period of the Persian Wars, but Pausanias betrays his own dating by saying that, after the end of the Second Messenian War, the Messenians were invited to Italy by Anaxilas (or Anaxilaus), tyrant of Rhegium – because Anaxilas lived at the turn of the sixth/fifth centuries, at the time of Marathon.[170]

If, therefore, combining Pausanias with Plato, we accept that there was a Messenian rising in about 490, how do we explain it? The Messenians were permanently disaffected, so we are not in need of any other general explanation, but it would still be interesting to know what precipitated it. It has been suggested by some scholars that King Cleomenes I, whose reign extended from about 520 to 491, 'attempted to stir up the helots against the Spartan government.'[171] Though this view is shared by several modern writers it is pure conjecture and has no basis in ancient evidence. But that is not to say that we must dismiss out of hand the possibility of any connection between Cleomenes and the helot rising. We do not know anything about Cleomenes' attitude to the helots, but we do know that he was instrumental in arranging the deposition of his colleague, Demaratus, and also that, when his machinations were revealed, he fled to Arcadia and tried to organize the Arcadians for an attack upon Sparta.[172] This unprecedented display of discord at the very highest levels of Spartan government may indeed have sparked off the helot revolt by encouraging the Messenians in the belief that the hitherto adamantine solidarity of the Spartiates had finally cracked.

The connection between the prospect of change and the outbreak of a rebellion was demonstrated again about two decades later. This time the story focuses on Pausanias, who was regent for his nephew, the infant King Pleistarchus, from 480 to about 467. Pausanias, the hero of

Plataea, developed a domineering manner as a result of his great successes, was eventually charged with treason and was allowed to starve to death in a temple where he had taken refuge from his pursuers. But he was also suspected of another offence: the Spartans, as Thucydides tells us, 'learnt that he was also plotting something with the helots. And this indeed was so, for he promised them freedom and citizenship if they rose up in revolt and helped him achieve power.'[173] Pausanias' death occurred at some time between 473 and 466, and it was probably in 464 that Sparta was convulsed by a severe earthquake which, if we can believe Diodorus Siculus, killed nearly 20,000 people and left only five houses standing.[174] The helot revolt which followed (sometimes called the Third Messenian War) is usually regarded as being triggered off by the earthquake alone, but perhaps Pausanias' conspiracy is not entirely irrelevant.[175] Pausanias had raised false hopes in the breasts of the Messenians and it is not difficult to understand how the dashing of these hopes might rouse the Messenians to militancy. The general prostration occasioned by the earthquake gave the Messenians their opportunity and they attacked Sparta, but King Archidamus II rallied the Spartan army and the rebels retreated to Messenia.[176] This fact, together with Thucydides' description of the composition of the rebel forces, may indicate that the rising was essentially a Messenian revolt and not a general uprising as may be inferred from Diodorus' and Plutarch's description of the rebels as a combination of 'helots and Messenians'.[177] Thucydides, however, regards it as a Messenian revolt with the adhesion of only two perioecic towns, Thouria and Aethaea. 'Most of the helots', he continues, 'were the descendants of the ancient Messenians who had been enslaved long before, as a result of which they were all called Messenians.'[178] Whatever the exact make-up of the rebellion, it would seem to have been Messenian in inspiration and control.

If even the Messenians needed the spur of the dashing of recently raised expectations to impel them to revolt, it may be imagined how much more difficult it was to drive the other inferior classes to violence. In fact, it is true to say that the Spartiates were never faced with a general rising, the only known attempt at one being Cinadon's abortive conspiracy of 398. Word reached the ephors in time and the attempt was smartly nipped in the bud.[179] Cinadon was a young man who, significantly enough, was not one of the 'Equals' and who, according to the ephors' informant, was counting upon the support of all the inferior classes: helots, *neodamōdeis*, *hupomeiones* and *perioikoi*. Yet, when asked how many men were involved in the plot the informer revealed that there was only a small coterie.[180]

This episode introduces us to two elements among the inferior classes that we have not previously encountered, namely the *neodamōdeis* and the *hupomeiones*. The latter term appears nowhere else in classical literature and its meaning is not quite certain. Literally *hupomeiones* simply means 'inferiors', and, when Cinadon was finally captured and asked why he had organized his conspiracy, his reply was: 'I wished to be inferior to no one in Sparta'.[181] From this it would appear that Cinadon was himself one of the *hupomeiones*. *Hupomeiones* are generally regarded by modern scholars as Spartiates of an inferior rank to the 'Equals', either because, according to one school of thought, they were unable to gain admission to a *sussition*, or else, according to another school, because they were deprived of their membership of a *sussition* through being unable to afford their mess dues.[182] Again, as so often, the verdict must be 'not proven'. There is, in fact, no evidence whatsoever one way or the other. All we know is that *hupomeiones* were not 'Equals'. We do not even know for certain that they were Spartiates by origin, as is generally assumed. But, if they were, it is easy to understand why they should feel aggrieved. The loss of a right or status which one previously enjoyed is resented far more than the failure to be offered some new privilege hitherto always confined to others. Such a feeling of resentment would be all the stronger if, after a war in which one was accorded equal rights with one's 'betters', there was an attempt suddenly to reimpose the pre-war social pattern. That this is exactly what happened in Sparta after the Peloponnesian War is well demonstrated in the case of Cinadon, in which the ephors employed a ruse to capture the conspirator, sending him at the head of a military contingent of six or seven men with the ostensible purpose of apprehending certain evil-doers. Cinadon's suspicions were not aroused, however, because, as Xenophon explicitly tells us, it was not the first mission of the sort on which Cinadon had been employed by the ephors.[183] What is equally significant is the fact that the half-dozen young men supposedly under Cinadon's command on his 'mission' must all have been Spartiate 'Equals', since they came from the ranks of the three hundred 'knights', the élite corps of the Spartan army.

The *neodamōdeis* are less of a mystery to us than are the *hupomeiones*. There is ample evidence to show that the *neodamōdeis* were freed helots, but there has been a fair amount of scholarly speculation as to whether they were regarded as citizens.[184] Those in favour of so regarding them rest their argument upon the assumption that the literal meaning of the word *neodamōdeis* is 'new citizens', but unfortunately this too is in dispute, it being held by others that the word *damōdēs* was not equivalent to the word *damotas*, which *does* mean 'citizen' – and this in the face of Hesychius' gloss on *damōdēs* as meaning 'citizen with full rights'.[185] But, whether they were technically regarded as citizens or not, there can be no doubt that their status was greatly inferior to that of the 'Equals'. They fought in separate companies from the 'Equals' and, as we have already seen, they were counted by Cinadon among their natural foes.[186] *Neodamōdeis* are unknown before the Peloponnesian War, their *raison d'être* undoubtedly being the Spartan shortage of manpower.[187] The earliest known case of the promise of freedom to helots was made in 425 during the Athenian blockade of the island of Sphacteria. Breaking the blockade, which was what the helots were required to do, was a hazardous task, to say the least, but there was no shortage of volunteers nevertheless.[188] In the following year Brasidas' army was made up partly of mercenaries and partly of helot hoplites, of whom there were seven hundred.[189] Four years later these Brasideii, as they were called, were freed and settled as a garrison in Lepreum, on territory which had previously belonged to Elis.[190] Here they were joined by some *neodamōdeis* properly so called, though the difference between *neodamōdeis* and Brasideii is not at all clear: perhaps the *neodamōdeis* proper had already been freed upon enlistment, whereas the Brasideii were freed only when settled in Lepreum. A force made up of the same two elements reappears at the battle of Mantinea in 418.[191] The decision to allow helots to gain their freedom in this way was clearly prompted only by the critical military situation, and the Spartiates' misgivings about that decision are well demonstrated by an episode related by Thucydides. At some unspecified date during the Peloponnesian War the Spartan government announced its intention to free those helots whom they considered had fought most bravely against the enemy. As a result about two thousand helots were selected and anticipated their new-found freedom by crowning themselves with garlands and parading around the temples. 'But not long afterwards the Spartans made them disappear and no one knew how each of them had met his death.'[192]

Cinadon's conspiracy is not important in itself but it is probably to be understood as a symptom of dissatisfaction with the Lycurgan system which was not confined to the inferior classes but is to be found even in the highest echelons of Spartan political life. Both Lysander, the famous naval commander and victor of Aegospotami, and his arch-foe King Pausanias (who reigned from 408 to 394) are thought to have attacked the Lycurgan constitution in one way or another. Lysander's contribution, contained in a tract discovered only after his death, was the suggestion that the monarchy should cease to be hereditary in the Eurypontid and Agiad families and be thrown open to election with all citizens eligible.[193] Lysander was not content, however, to vent his spleen in an inanimate and unpublished document, and, according to Plutarch, he also took more active steps to change the constitution. He first tried swaying public opinion by means of oratory, but, 'realizing that the novelty and magnitude of his proposed revolution called for more daring aid', he resorted to divine assistance. His attempts to bribe the oracles, first of Delphi and then of Ammon in Egypt, were singularly unsuccessful, however, despite the lengths to which he went, including the use of a supposed 'son of Apollo'.[194]

It is perhaps not surprising that opposition to the Lycurgan constitution should be couched in literary form, upon which the Lycurgan spirit frowned so deeply. For Lysander was not alone in lambasting time-honoured traditions with his pen. King Pausanias was also said to have done so, in his case in a treatise attacking the Lycurgan constitution and aiming to abolish the ephorate. The Agiad king is said to have opposed the Lycurgan enactments on the grounds that Lycurgus was a member of the rival royal house of the Eurypontids.[195] But Pausanias' anti-establishment behaviour probably dates only from the period after he fled into exile to avoid suffering the death sentence which had been passed on him for alleged disloyalty.[196]

While in office Pausanias gave no sign of any revolutionary tendencies and was closely associated with the ephors in their attacks upon Lysander. One such attack which is relevant to our theme is the prosecution and subsequent execution of a friend of Lysander and one of his fellow generals, a man with the good military name of Thorax, who was convicted of being in possession of some silver, a crime against the Lycurgan code.[197] The timing of his prosecution – just after a complaint had been lodged against Lysander by the Persian satrap in Asia Minor, Pharnabazus – shows against whom the attack was really aimed. Lysander himself was never guilty of rapacity; on the contrary, he even gave over to his fellow citizens the presents which had been given to him personally.[198] It was he, nevertheless, who was held responsible for the new mercenary spirit which had so recently begun to sully the moral purity of Lycurgan austerity – and not without reason, for his swashbuckling valour had filled the Spartan coffers with foreign silver and gold.[199] Perhaps the best known incident in this connection is the story of Gylippus, a Spartan general entrusted by Lysander with the transportation of sacks of precious metals to Sparta, but who, lacking his commander's scrupulousness, helped himself to some of the treasure and hid it under the roof of his house. Gylippus' guilty secret was revealed to the ephors by his own servant by means of the celebrated riddle, 'There are many owls lurking beneath the tiles', the owl being the familiar spirit of the goddess Athena and was therefore the standard reverse design on Athenian coins, which dominated Greek commerce.[200] It was this incident in particular, according to Plutarch, that caused Spartan heads to shake sagely, to denounce the influx of gold and silver as a 'pestilential decoy' and to call for its removal — a call which was foiled by Lysander's friends, who managed to arrange a compromise whereby the money was to stay in Sparta and was to be used for public purposes only while private possession of it remained a capital offence.[201] It was at this time that the old saying, 'the love of money, and nothing else, will be the ruin of Sparta', seemed particularly apt.[202] A new mercenary spirit had certainly struck Sparta, though it must be regarded as a symptom rather than a cause. But a symptom of what? It suits the currently fashionable highly moralistic teleological approach to Greek history to pin the blame almost as a matter of course on the Lycurgan system.[203] So 'immoral' a system, it is commonly assumed, based as it was upon the domination of the majority of the population of Sparta by a minority, was doomed to inevitable destruction. The facts of the matter do not substantiate this view, however. It was not the persistence of the Lycurgan system which destroyed Sparta, nor was it the system's 'inflexibility' or 'rigidity', as adduced by some, that caused her harm.[204] For one thing, the system was not inflexible. On the contrary, it was easily modified when Spartans began rejecting its values, as we have already seen in regard to the ban on money and in the even more important matter of land and inheritance. The really important question is: why did the change in attitude occur? The answer, in a word, is the Peloponnesian War, which severely jolted Sparta's whole social system. Not only did the war arouse unfulfilled expectations in the breasts of some members of the inferior classes, as we have already seen; it also loosened the bonds uniting the Spartiate community. The war had destroyed — in the minds of some Spartans at least — the whole *raison d'être* of the Lycurgan system. The Lycurgan system was built upon fear, largely the fear of a

Messenian revolution, and this fear was still felt in the more traditional circles of Spartiate society, as can be seen from the prompt and elaborate plan devised by the ephors to foil Cinadon's conspiracy. But others, notably Lysander and his ilk, were blind to what must now have appeared as petty domestic worries in the euphoria of Sparta's victory over Athens. New vistas hitherto undreamed of had suddenly opened up for the ambitious Spartan, thus threatening to dislodge the keystone of the Lycurgan construction, the concept of the equality of all Spartiates. But, as was not sufficiently appreciated, it was precisely that Spartiate solidarity which had brought Sparta to this pinnacle of her power. The removal of this keystone caused the collapse of the Lycurgan system and also of Sparta's pre-eminent position in Greece.

THE BREAKDOWN OF THE LYCURGAN SYSTEM

The concentration of land in fewer and fewer hands was a marked feature of this period, as has already been shown, and one which made no slight contribution to the debacle of Leuctra in 371.[205] The most direct effect was the poor form shown by the Spartan cavalry in that battle.[206] The free disposal of property, which was now permitted by the law bearing the name of Epitadeus, not only concentrated land in the hands of an ever-diminishing number of owners, but also had the further effect of depleting the number of full Spartan citizens, both in absolute numerical terms and relative to the number of inhabitants who were not 'Equals'. One of the conditions of full citizenship was membership of a *sussition*, which in turn depended upon the payment of a subscription. Failure to pay resulted in the loss of one's political rights, and we know from Aristotle that there were some Spartiates in his own day who were unable to afford their mess-dues. It is precisely this concentration of wealth, and particularly the consolidation of the estates of heiresses and the increase in the size of dowries that Aristotle singles out as the cause of the decline of the citizen population. 'It is for this reason that, though the country is able to support fifteen hundred cavalrymen and thirty thousand hoplites, they totalled less than a thousand.'[207] This latter figure presumably refers to the battle of Leuctra, at which, according to Xenophon, the number of Spartiates was seven hundred, of whom four hundred were killed.[208] The minuteness of these figures is stunning not only when set against Aristotle's hypothetical targets, but also when contrasted with previous battle figures. The number of Spartiates at the battle of Plataea, a century

THE REPUBLIC OF DEMIGODS

before Leuctra, was five thousand.[209] At Plataea, moreover, there was one Spartiate for every non-Spartiate hoplite, whereas calculations for Leuctra show the Spartiates as making up only a tenth of the hoplite strength of the Spartan army.[210]

The shock of Leuctra did nothing to arrest the pace of the concentration of wealth. By the middle of the third century, we read in Plutarch, 'there were no more than seven hundred Spartiates left, and of these there were perhaps a hundred who possessed land and an allotment. The remaining masses (*ochlos*) dallied in the city destitute and of no standing, warding off foreign enemies sluggishly and without enthusiasm while constantly on the look-out for an opportunity for internal change and revolution.'[211] This passage has caused a fair degree of puzzlement. For one thing, does Plutarch mean to say that there were only a hundred Spartiates with any land at all, or does he mean that one hundred had more than just an allotment and the remaining six hundred had only that? If the former, then there could only have been a hundred 'Equals', because citizenship depended upon a modicum of wealth. Scholarly opinion on the subject is essentially divided into three schools of thought. There are those who accept that there were only a hundred Spartan citizens. Others prefer to believe that all seven hundred were full citizens. The third school is made up, inevitably, of sceptics who regard Plutarch's figures as an underestimate.[212] But, as is so often the case, there is no way of knowing, and as all too frequently, it is of little importance: what we do know without any doubt is that the Spartan citizen-body had dwindled to a minute fraction of its fifth-century size.

There is also another problem connected with the above passage, and that is: to whom is Plutarch referring when he speaks of the idle and disaffected 'masses' (*ochlos*)? Is he still talking about the six hundred poorer Spartiates, or does he mean the non-Spartiate population? Here again scholarly opinion is divided, but the word *ochlos*, which is usually used in a pejorative sense, clearly settles the issue. It is unlikely that the philo-Laconian Plutarch would use such a word to refer to Spartiates.[213]

A SECOND LYCURGAN REVOLUTION

The social situation in mid-third-century Sparta was essentially, therefore, not dissimilar to the state of affairs at the time of the original 'Lycurgan' revolution. At both junctures wealth and power were concentrated in the hands of a small minority of the population and there was a cry for the redistribution of land. As in the earlier crisis, so now, the solution was seen to lie in enlarging the privileged circle so as to ensure continued domination over the helots. If anything, the revolutionary ferment among the propertyless Spartiates was probably more intense than it had been in the days of the original revolution, when the concept of Spartiate equality was something new. The followers of Agis, Cleomenes and Nabis, on the other hand, were fighting for what they must have seen as the restoration of rights to which they were not only entitled by legislation hallowed by tradition but which their ancestors had actually possessed. The response of the new ascendancy was in keeping with the spirit of their challengers. The aristocracy of Lycurgus' day acquiesced in the sinking of their privileges into the common pool of Spartiate unity, but their third-century counterparts were less amenable. As a result, the internal history of Sparta in this period is a chequered alternation of revolution and counter-revolution.

Three names stand out in this period as protagonists in the struggle for a new Lycurgan dispensation. All were kings, Agis IV (244–241), Cleomenes III (236–222) and Nabis (206–192) and they all met violent ends. Their programmes were basically the same, their aim being to solve the internal social and political crisis and at the same time enhance Sparta's international standing, which had sunk into insignificance since Leuctra.

Agis' programme was embodied in a *rhetra*, or bill, which not surprisingly met with fierce opposition when put before the *gerousia*, but, equally predictably, was acclaimed by the assembly. The bill was in two parts according to Plutarch. First, there was to be a cancellation of debts and, secondly, a redistribution of land. The land which was to be divided into equal allotments (*klēron*) was in two areas, the one evidently being the Eurotas valley, which was 'civic land' (*politikē chōra*), and the other being in perioecic territory. The land in the valley of the Eurotas was to provide 4,500 lots, which were to be distributed among the Spartiates themselves, whose numbers were to be supplemented by the flower of the young manhood of the *perioikoi* and foreigners. The remaining 15,000 allotments were to go to *perioikoi* 'able to bear arms'. Perhaps the most significant statement in this section on Agis' *rhetra*, however, is the concluding remark that the 4,500 Spartiates and promoted *perioikoi* and foreigners were to be enrolled in fifteen *phiditia*, some comprising four hundred members and others two hundred, organized according to 'the system which their ancestors had

had'.²¹⁴ From this two conclusions may be drawn: first, that the selected *perioikoi* and foreigners whose allotments were within the 4,500 were to be made full Spartan citizens; and secondly, that the strict organization of the *phiditia* or *sussitia*, one of the main pillars of the Lycurgan system, had been allowed to lapse.²¹⁵

In the event only the cancellation of debts was enacted, but not before the deposition of Agis' fellow-king, Leonidas, and the forcible replacement of the college of ephors with more amenable members.²¹⁶ The cancellation of debts seems to have been confined to mortgages, since the term used by the Spartans for the documents publicly burnt in great heaps in the agora was *klaria*, a word which is obviously connected with the word *klēros*, or, in the Doric dialect, *klāros*. If so, it makes it all the easier to understand why this part of Agis' programme was the only one to be put into effect. Even the largest of landed estates may be heavily mortgaged, but there is little prospect that those in possession of estates of any size would welcome the redistribution of land. Events seem to have reached an impasse, with the masses (*hoi polloi* or, elsewhere, *to plēthos*), clamouring for the immediate division of the land, but with some of the king's erstwhile aristocratic supporters, notably his uncle Agesilaus, managing to stall.²¹⁷ Just then, fortunately for those opposed to further reform, Spartan aid was sought by their ally, the Achaean League, against the rival Aetolian League. Placed in command of the expedition by the ephors, the king 'was elated by the courage and enthusiasm of his fellow soldiers. They were largely poor young men, who, being now freed from the fear of debt and placing their hopes upon a grant of land if they returned alive from the campaign, made a most striking impression upon Agis.'²¹⁸ But, as we have seen before, there is no sharper goad towards disaffection than frustrated anticipation, and so, since the eagerly expected redistribution of land did not take place, 'even the common people (*hoi polloi*) watched with delight' as the deposed King Leonidas was restored to his throne.²¹⁹ Popular feeling, however, had evidently not turned completely against Agis, who took refuge in a temple when the counter-revolution triumphed. When he was apprehended and sentenced to death by the ephors and *gerousia* in a summary trial, an angry crowd shouting support for Agis gathered brandishing lights and torches outside the prison gates, but, by frightening his enemies, they succeeded only in hastening his execution.²²⁰ He was hanged, together with his mother and grandmother, 'at an age when men's mistakes generally meet with an easy pardon.'²²¹ The seriousness of the situation may be gauged from the fact that Agis IV was the first, and indeed the only, Spartan king ever to be put to death.

Leonidas remained king until his death in 235 and the small band of the rich and powerful made the most of their opportunity.[222] His son and successor, who came to the throne as Cleomenes III, surprised everyone by espousing the principles of his father's late foe. Learning from Agis' mistakes, Cleomenes decided it was best to forestall his enemies. Four of the five ephors were killed while at supper and the fifth was wounded and crept to safety in the Temple of Fear.[223] On the following day Cleomenes removed the ephors' seats, leaving only one for himself, and he justified his action to the assembled citizens by claiming that the ephorate was a late accretion to the Lycurgan constitution and that the early ephors had been nothing more than the kings' appointed servants.[224] He was now able to proceed to enact the social programme of Agis IV, and this time not only were debts annulled, but land-lots were also distributed, though only four thousand are mentioned, these being given to Spartiates and 'the most accomplished *perioikoi*', all of whom were to serve as hoplites.[225] At the same time the traditional *agōgē* was restored and the *sussitia* reorganized according to the Lycurgan pattern.[226] According to Pausanias, who wrote in the mid-second century of the Roman Principate, Cleomenes 'dissolved the power of the *gerousia* and instituted *patronomoi* instead of them' (i.e., presumably, the members of the *gerousia*).[227] Pausanias' language here is somewhat ambiguous. If he means to say that the *gerousia* was abolished and replaced by the board of *patronomoi*, then he is mistaken, because the *gerousia* was in existence side by side with the *patronomoi* in Roman times.[228] Many scholars have thought that Pausanias had mistaken the *gerousia* for the ephorate and that it was this latter institution, which we know was abolished by Cleomenes, that was replaced by the *patronomoi*.[229] What Pausanias actually says, however, is not that Cleomenes abolished the *gerousia* but that he took away its power. The function of the new officials as reflected in their title, *patronomoi*, was to safeguard the 'ancestral laws' as re-established by Cleomenes.

But Cleomenes' revolution did not take place in a vacuum. On the contrary, Sparta was embroiled in war throughout this period. When confronted by the united forces of Macedon and the Achaean League Cleomenes was forced to devise some means of strengthening his own resources. So 'he freed those helots who paid five Attic minas and (in this way) raised five hundred talents; and, arming two thousand in the Macedonian fashion as a counter-offensive to Antigonus' *leukaspides*, he planned a great and altogether unexpected enterprise.'[230] It has generally been assumed that the two thousand men enrolled in the Spartan army came from among the six thousand freed helots. But, as has recently been pointed out, Plutarch does not say so explicitly.[231] The main argument directed against the normal interpretation is linguistic, but the further objection has been urged that Cleomenes' general policy would not lead us to expect him to favour the enlistment of freed helots because that would give these ex-helots political rights.[232] There is, however, no reason to believe that freed helots, either now or at any other time, joined the ranks of the 'Equals'. Those who were freed during the Peloponnesian War, as we have seen, were designated as a specific social element under the name of *neodamōdeis*. Much has been made of the distinction between being freed after serving in the army, as seems to have been the case during the Peloponnesian War, and being freed beforehand, as was now the case, but there is no reason why helots freed before joining up should have enjoyed any higher a status than those freed after demobilization or than those who had paid their 5 minas without going into the army.[233] But, whether the two thousand soldiers were ex-helots or not, the important thing to note is that Cleomenes freed helots only when under attack by foreign powers. The liberation of the helots formed no part of his reform programme, as has sometimes mistakenly been suggested.[234]

Despite these emergency preparations, however, the decisive clash between Sparta and her foes, which came at Sellasia in 222, was a disastrous defeat, with the loss, according to Plutarch, of all but two hundred of the six thousand Lacedaemonians, i.e. Spartiates, *perioikoi* and presumably freed helots or *neodamōdeis*, in Cleomenes' army of about 20,000.[235] Cleomenes himself fled to Egypt, where he later committed suicide.[236]

Antigonus Doson, the Macedonian king, now imposed upon Sparta what Polybius is pleased to call 'the ancestral constitution' (*to politeuma to patrion*)[237] and in a sense he is not wrong, for Sparta had two incompatible political genealogies: the Lycurgan line, with heirs such as Agis IV, Cleomenes III and Nabis; and the pre-Lycurgan aristocratic line, which took every available opportunity to recover its position. Both of these could justifiably claim to be implementing that most precious of Greek constitutional ideals, the 'ancestral constitution'.[238] There has been considerable discussion as to the precise nature of Antigonus' settlement, the main question being, how far did Cleomenes' reforms survive?[239] In view of the death of the majority of Cleomenes' army on the battlefields it would seem unlikely that his land reform persisted, and, moreover, the extremely lenient treatment accorded Sparta by Antigonus points to the conclusion that an important part in the government of Sparta was now played by Cleomenes' enemies, the eighty leading men whom he had exiled.[240] This view is corroborated by a passage in Polybius in which Antigonus is portrayed as a liberator and benefactor of Sparta: 'Far from maltreating those who had become subject to him, on the contrary he restored their ancestral constitution and their liberty and became the source of the greatest benefits to the Spartans both generally and individually, and thus returned home. Not only, therefore, was he judged a benefactor at that time but, after his death, also a saviour – and, it was on account of this action of his that he won undying honour and esteem not only among Spartans but amongst all Greeks.'[241] Both Antigonus' conferring of benefits upon individual Spartans and the great acclaim with which his actions were greeted at Sparta would be difficult to understand unless Cleomenes' old foes had returned.

This interpretation is strengthened yet further by the events which followed the death of Antigonus Doson in 220, when those opposed to the regime which he had set up made overtures to the Aetolian League. By this time the ephorate, now restored, was itself divided, three ephors favouring the Aetolian connection and two favouring the continuance of the Macedonian and Achaean alliance. One of the latter, together with a good number of supporters, was killed by a hostile mob when he tried to persuade them of the merits of the Macedonians.[242] New elections returned a solidly pro-Macedonian college of ephors, all of whom were, however, assassinated together with some members of the *gerousia* in the temple of Athena of the Brazen House. The next election reversed the verdict of the previous one, and Sparta duly joined the Aetolian alliance.[243]

It might seem surprising that in this very anti-Macedonian climate an attempt to re-enact the programme of Cleomenes III gained little support. This attempt was set on foot by Chilon, evidently a member of the Eurypontid royal house, who, to support his claim to the throne against his kinsman, Lycurgus, raised the familiar banner of land redistribution, but, contrary to his hopes for a mass rising in his favour, he gained only about two hundred adherents and was eventually forced to flee to Achaea.[244] This fact alone is a good explanation of Chilon's failure. For Lycurgus, the man against whom his move was aimed, was at that very time fighting an offensive war against the

Macedonians and their Achaean allies and it was probably he who had been responsible for the anti-Macedonian revolution which aligned Sparta with the Aetolians.[245] It is quite mistaken to explain Chilon's failure, as has recently been done, on the grounds that Cleomenes' social and economic reforms were still in force.[246] If that were so, not only would Chilon have had little support but he could also not have entertained any hopes of mass support, as he reportedly did, and would probably not have raised Cleomenes' banner in the first place.

This particularly unsettled period of Spartan history ends in 206 with the accession of Nabis, who, though always called a tyrant by Polybius and Livy, was a Eurypontid king.[247] The third of our radical trio, he far outstripped both his models. It is hardly surprising, therefore, that he should have raised the blood-pressure not only of the writers of antiquity but also of more recent times. Polybius, our main source for Nabis' reign and himself a native of Megalopolis, a city at which Sparta had long leered with greedy eyes, can hardly be expected to see Nabis in a flattering light, and we ought not to be surprised by Livy's lack of sympathy for a social revolutionary.[248] It is difficult to know how much credence to give to Polybius' descriptions of Nabis' reforms. For one thing, he gives two accounts which are not easily compatible. In the first we are told how, after banishing the richest and noblest Spartans, Nabis gave their wives and land to the most distinguished of his own supporters and to his mercenaries. We are then treated to a long list of the professions from which Nabis' adherents were largely drawn: murderers, burglars, footpads and housebreakers.[249] Polybius' second account makes Nabis free the 'slaves' of the exiled men and marry them to their erstwhile masters' wives and daughters.[250] The two accounts are united by Livy, according to whom Nabis freed slaves and gave land to the landless 'plebs'.[251] But who were these 'slaves'? It is maintained by some that they were just that, not helots but conventional slaves, who were no longer totally unknown in Sparta.[252] Support for this assertion may be derived from Livy, who here uses the word *servi*, but generally refers to helots by the cumbersome designation *castellani agrestes* ('rural serfs').[253] We also read, however, that, in 188, four years after Nabis' death, Philopoemen, the Achaean general, decreed 'that all foreign auxiliaries who had served the tyrants as mercenaries should leave Spartan territory; and next, that those slaves whom the tyrants had freed – and there was a large number of them – were to depart before a specified date. Those who remained it would be permissible for the Achaeans to capture, sell and transport.'²⁵⁴ Those who remained after the deadline and were sold into slavery numbered three thousand according to Plutarch, and the same figure is given by Pausanias, who specifically calls them helots.²⁵⁵ From this we may safely conclude that Nabis did free helots. But what was their status after liberation? Plutarch's description of Philopoemen's banning order, which is very much briefer than Livy's version quoted above, lumps together all those who were affected by the order as men 'who had been made citizens by the tyrants'.²⁵⁶ This description undoubtedly fits some of the men banished, such as, for example, the mercenaries and foreign supporters granted land by Nabis in Polybius' account,²⁵⁷ but it is difficult to believe that freed helots became full citizens. This doubt is confirmed by Livy, who, a few lines further down from the passage already quoted, again mentions the two classes of banished people, but this time refers to them as 'the foreign auxiliaries' and *Lacedaemoniis adscripti*, which, he explains parenthetically, 'is what they call those freed by the tyrants'.²⁵⁸ The term 'Lacedaemoniis adscripti' is, therefore, to be taken as referring to freed helots. It obviously represents a Greek technical term, but not *politēs* ('citizens'): the Latin for *politēs* is *civis*, not *adscriptus*. The nearest Greek word to Livy's *Lacedaemoniis adscripti* would appear to be *neodamōdeis*, which we have already had reason to believe was the normal status of freed helots.²⁵⁹

It must be stressed that however many helots Nabis might have freed, he did so under pressure of foreign invasion and not as part of his reform programme. Nabis' death in 192 or Philopoemen's decree of 188 may be taken as the end of the history of an independent Sparta, but the helots remained a subordinate class. We have the testimony of Strabo, who wrote in the early Principate, that helotry survived until the Roman domination, which dates from 146.²⁶⁰ Helotry was probably never formally abolished, but, as Spartan society became increasingly aristocratic, and wealth was concentrated in the hands of a small number, the descendants of 'Equals' were reduced to the status of subjects whose social position was probably hardly distinguishable from that of the helots, who had long been able to improve their economic lot – presumably by selling their excess crops – as we can see from the fact that there were six thousand helots who were able to afford the considerable outlay of five Attic minas (or five hundred drachmas) in order to buy their freedom in the reign of Cleomenes III.²⁶¹ In the reign of Augustus Sparta was almost the personal patrimony of the emperor's friend C. Julius Eurycles.²⁶² Membership of the college of six *patronomoi*, one of whom was eponymous, was closed to all but an inner circle of aristocratic families and other offices were reserved for the slightly wider circle made up of nobles and those commoners who were adopted by them.[263]

* * *

Sparta's ultimate defeat at the hands of the Achaeans in 192 resulted in her loss of the perioecic towns, which were placed under the 'protection' of the Achaean League.[264] It is important to note that this loss, like that of Messenia in 371, was the result not of internal revolution but of defeat in war. Spartan history is too often treated as an Aeschylean tragedy, with *hubris* – in this case Spartiate domination over the inferior classes – inevitably leading to nemesis. This mistaken construction rests squarely on the common liberal axiom that a subjected people is an oppressed people and that an oppressed people is bound sooner or later to rebel against its oppressors.[265] There is more than a dash of moralistic wishful thinking in that sort of approach, and the error is compounded by the commonly held tacit assumption that change is inevitable. In Sparta the Messenians did rebel on several occasions, but not in protest against oppression. The risings occurred at a time when the level of their expectations had been raised only to be dashed to the ground. Not subjection, therefore, but reform is the spur to revolution. Change itself is the best inducement to further change, and stability, at whatever level, is the best guarantee of future stability. The initial changes that led to the Messenian revolts were necessitated by the exigencies of foreign war, yet even these changes were not able to impel the other subject peoples of Sparta into revolt, only the Messenians, who had never wholly accepted the role of an inferior class but kept their national tradition alive. In Crete, the similarity of whose social system to that of Sparta was a standard topic in classical literature, revolution was as unknown as foreign war – until the mid-fourth century, when, as in Sparta, the impact of war shook the system.[266] In the absence of the pressures of foreign war there was no need for the ruling elements in the Cretan cities to alter the traditional social relations or to compromise with their *perioikoi* (as the Cretan counterparts of the Spartan helots were known) in any way. Local wars among the various Cretan cities were not a threat to the social system, because all the Cretan states were in the same boat and none would therefore be prepared to take the part of rebellious *perioikoi*, as Aristotle points out, contrasting this situation with that of Sparta, surrounded by hostile neighbours only too glad to take advantage of internal upheavals.[267]

The moral of the story is that war is the greatest threat to an aristocratic regime, and it is a lesson of which the Spartans were by no means ignorant.[268] For, it is important to note, at no time was the Spartan system of government anything but aristocratic. Spartan history is essentially a story of conflict not between aristocratic and anti-aristocratic forces but between elements representing two different types of aristocracy: the 'conventional' type, with power and wealth concentrated in the hands of a small number of families; and the 'Lycurgan' type, a citizen-aristocracy. Equality within the ruling element, as Aristotle recognized,[269] is a valuable contributory factor to the survival of oligarchical and aristocratic regimes, and no system of government has ever placed more emphasis upon such equality than the one that bears the name of Lycurgus. It was the destruction of that spirit of equality, not surprisingly, that doomed the Lycurgan system as a whole to destruction, but while it lasted it kept the Spartiate 'Equals' immune alike to overthrow from below and to internal dissension within their own ranks. Not all Greek states were quite so fortunate.

CHAPTER IV

ALTERNATIVE TO ARISTOCRACY

It was fear that had knit Spartiate society together and guaranteed the stability of the state. But not all Greek states were fortunate enough to have a helot problem. In the absence of such a threat there was no curb, such as was exercised by the Lycurgan system in Sparta, upon changes in the social and economic relations of society, and, as we have seen, it was precisely such changes that threatened the survival of aristocratic government.

In the period between 650 and 550 BC aristocratic governments were overthrown in many Greek states and replaced by tyrannies. Today the word 'tyranny' has pejorative connotations, but these bad associations date only from the fifth century BC. Before that the word had simply been a neutral synonym for 'king' and there is strong evidence that in their own day the tyrants were genuinely popular leaders of anti-aristocratic revolutionary movements.

Yet, despite the abundance of the evidence, this view of the tyrants has never been fashionable among modern scholars. Which is hardly surprising, in view of the revulsion felt at the name of a modern dictator such as Adolf Hitler. The fact remains, however, that, like Napoleon Bonaparte or Benito Mussolini, Hitler had a tremendous popular following. In an age like the present when the will of 'the people' is invested with an aura of sanctity it may be uncomfortable to realize that what 'the people' want is not always in accord with the liberal principles that they are meant to hold so dear.

Plato and Aristotle shared a hearty dislike of tyranny – though not for the same reasons as modern writers – yet they were honest enough to admit its popularity.[1] 'The majority of tyrants', says Aristotle, 'have generally developed out of demagogues who have gained the confidence of the people through their attacks upon the nobles.'[2] A study of the evidence corroborates this interpretation.

Cypselus of Corinth, for example, the earliest tyrant of whom we know, is said to have held the position of polemarch before seizing power from the ruling Bacchiad aristocratic clan in about 655. This is often disbelieved by modern scholars, who argue that Cypselus could hardly have held office in so narrowly aristocratic a regime as Bacchiad Corinth since he himself was at best only half a Bacchiad – his mother Labda was a lame Bacchiad who had been unable to find a husband within the clan as she was meant to do and so had to marry outside it. But Cypselus may well have been accepted as a Bacchiad nevertheless, just as Pericles, who was only an Alcmaeonid on his mother's side, could be considered subject to the Alcmaeonid family curse. During his tenure of the polemarchy, we are told, Cypselus 'endeared himself very much to the common people' through his humane treatment of convicted criminals, who were placed in his custody until they paid their fine. Normally the polemarch had been in the habit of taking part of the fine for himself, but not only did Cypselus not do so: 'he neither imprisoned nor bound any citizen, but some he released on security and for others he himself stood surety.'[3] The fact that Cypselus did not need a bodyguard may be an indication that the army supported him, and this is the way in which it is generally interpreted by modern scholars. But both Aristotle and Nicholas of Damascus mention it in the same sentence as his popularity. Thus Aristotle: 'Cypselus was a demagogue and he went right through his reign without a bodyguard.'[4] This was no mean feat considering that Cypselus' reign lasted for thirty years. The point Aristotle is making is that he could rely upon his popularity to protect him.

But how exactly did Cypselus reach power? Nicholas of Damascus tells us:

> Seeing that the Corinthians were hostilely disposed to the Bacchiads but without a champion whom they could employ to overthrow them, he offered his own services and curried favour among the masses . . . Then finally, getting together a band of supporters he killed the reigning Bacchiad, Patroclides, a violent and unpleasant character. The people quickly made him king in his place.[5]

This picture of Cypselus' rise to power accords well with what we know about tyranny in other Greek states. In Sicyon, for example, the advent of tyranny seems to have followed a very similar pattern to the Corinthian one. According to one tradition Orthagoras, the first Sicyonian tyrant, was the son of a cook or butcher, but the imputation of low birth was so standard an insult in ancient Greek politics that it must always be viewed with healthy scepticism. And in this case, as it happens, we have evidence which is incompatible with low birth. Like Cypselus of Corinth Orthagoras is said to have been polemarch before becoming tyrant, and his respectability is corroborated by the fact that his brother Myron was an Olympic chariot-race victor – not the sort of honour to which any but the very rich could ordinarily aspire. More important, Orthagoras is said to have secured the position of polemarch through his popularity with the mass of the citizens.

Cypselus of Corinth's lack of bodyguard was fairly unusual for a tyrant. Plato regarded the request for a personal bodyguard as typical of tyrants or aspirants to tyranny. What is particularly noteworthy is the fact that this bodyguard was requested of – and, more important, granted by – the masses. Aristotle in his *Rhetoric* names three tyrants who reached power in this way: Theagenes of Megara, Peisistratus of Athens and Dionysius of Syracuse.[7] The same three names occur in the *Politics* as tyrants who were 'the champions of the people' (*hoi prostatai tou dēmou*) a significant phrase which we shall encounter again in the next chapter in the setting of fifth-century Athens.[8] The three tyrants are said to have won the confidence of the people by their 'enmity towards the rich'.

In the case of Theagenes this consisted in slaughtering the cattle of the rich while they were grazing on the river bank.[9] Peisistratus, who was tyrant of Athens on and off for a total of about twenty years between 565 and 527, came to power as the leader of a party known as 'the hillmen' (*diakrioi*) or 'the men from beyond the hills' (*hyperakrioi*), but it would undoubtedly be wrong to take this as a purely geographical description. Both in his *Athenian Constitution* and in his *Politics* Aristotle sees the party as an expression of social, political and economic forces and Plutarch explicitly includes among Peisistratus' supporters 'the masses of thetes, who were extremely hostile to the rich'.[10] It was, says Aristotle, precisely because he appeared particularly favourably inclined towards the commonalty (*dēmotikōtatos*) that Peisistratus was made the leader of the 'hillmen', and elsewhere Peisistratus is listed together with Panaetius of Leontini, Cypselus of Corinth and Dionysius of Syracuse as rising to the position of tyrant through demagogy.[11]

The story of Peisistratus' struggle for power illustrates his popularity very well, even in the version given by Herodotus, who was certainly anything but an admirer of the Peisistratids. Peisistratus' first tyranny was won by the capture of the Acropolis by his bodyguard of club bearers or *korunephoroi*. But what is particularly noteworthy is that this bodyguard had been voted to him by the Athenian assembly in response to his claim – disbelieved by both Herodotus and Aristotle – that he had been physically assaulted by his enemies. Both Herodotus and Aristotle state quite baldly that the wounds which Peisistratus used to persuade his fellow citizens to vote him a bodyguard were self-inflicted, but that does not seem to have been the view of the majority in the assembly. Whatever the assembly thought about the wounds, the majority must have been supporters of Peisistratus. They would certainly not otherwise have armed him against the two other factions. And Peisistratus must have continued to enjoy popular support, because he retained power for five or six years before being ousted for the first time, the other two parties uniting against him for this purpose. But, with this objective achieved, the uneasy alliance fell apart and Megacles, leader of the party of 'the coast', made a pact with Peisistratus and cemented it by giving him his daughter in marriage. It was then that the well-known procession took place in which Peisistratus appeared in a chariot side by side with a tall woman dressed up as the goddess Athene. It is hard to believe that the people of Athens were sufficiently gullible to accept this woman as the goddess, in spite of her remarkable height – unless they wanted to accept her as such for some other reason, namely, once again, their support for Peisistratus.[12]

In his third and final return to power Peisistratus received military or financial assistance from a number of Greek cities, but he could still rely on popular support in Athens as well. The first town in Attica that he took was, not surprisingly, Marathon, near the family home in Brauron: 'and while they were encamped there partisans of theirs arrived from the city and others flocked to them from the demes, men to whom tyranny was more welcome than liberty.'[13] It is significant that, despite the hostility reflected in this last phrase, Herodotus does not try to disguise the fact that Peisistratus had popular support.

Dionysius of Syracuse came to power in Syracuse in 406, over a century after the expulsion of the Peisistratids from Athens, but a glance at his career will show how right Aristotle was to bracket him together with the popular tyrannies of the archaic period. Dionysius is one of the very few Greek tyrants who really do seem to have been of humble birth. He is said to have started life as a secretary or scribe but was nevertheless used by oligarchical leaders to act as their spokesman. His sponsors had probably not bargained for the speech that Dionysius gave before the Syracusan assembly, an impassioned outburst against the rich. He even went so far as to advise the assembled citizens to choose as generals 'not the most influential men but rather those who were most favourably disposed towards and popular among the common people.'[14] Needless to say, this resulted in Dionysius' own appointment as a general.

The popular nature of tyranny is corroborated by the policies adopted by the tyrants once in power. Dionysius went further than any of his forerunners by redistributing property among the masses.[15] But probably the greatest tribute of all to Dionysius' popularity is the fact that, after a reign of thirty-nine years, his throne could pass peacefully to his son.

Peisistratus' popularity was obviously not confined to his regional base in north-east Attica. As we have already seen, Peisistratus first seized power with the aid of the bodyguard voted him by the assembly – and it is highly unlikely that there were many present there from the remote hill country of the north-east. In the light of this realization, it is not surprising to find that Peisistratus' economic policy generally favoured the city of Athens, though he also helped the small farmers. He extended loans to the poor, for example, so as to help them set up as farmers, but also with a view to easing the overcrowding of the city, and he levied a ten per cent tax on agricultural produce, probably the first direct tax in Athenian history. A story related by Aristotle tells of Peisistratus' compassion for a poor farmer who complained that, since his stony soil produced nothing but troubles and miseries, Peisistratus would have to take a tenth of those as well. The tyrant exempted the farmer from all taxes, and this may be a reflection of a general policy of tax relief for the rural poor.[16] The introduction of itinerant judges is another indication of Peisistratus' concern to protect the small man against the influence of the rich and noble. Furthermore, the immense programme of public works initiated by Peisistratus cannot but have benefitted the poor.

Public works were a standard feature of the rule of Greek tyrants, and no wonder. They provided employment in a time of rising urban populations and they also acted as a focus of national loyalty to counteract the decentralized localistic focuses upon which the traditional aristocracies depended for their authority. Besides, they served a very real practical need.

The policies regarded as most typical of tyranny were thought by Aristotle to have been invented by Periander of Corinth, Cypselus' son and successor. These measures include:

... The cutting down of the illustrious and the destruction of the proud, and also the prohibition of dining clubs, social clubs, education or anything of that sort; the close surveillance of every activity which normally gives rise to the two emotions of high spirits and mutual trust; a ban on the establishment of schools or other cultural societies; the adoption of every means whereby everyone will be as unknown to everyone else as possible (for familiarity breeds mutual trust).[17]

It will be noticed that all these measures are directed against the activities of the rich. The poor were not much given to joining dining clubs or cultural societies. A few lines further down we read of another tyrannical device: 'setting men by the ears and stirring up friction between friend and friend, between the people and the aristocracy and within the ranks of the rich.' But why, one may ask, should the government bother to set friends against one another – except amongst the rich and influential? The one type of dissension missing from Aristotle's list, significantly enough, is dissension within the ranks of the masses, and we can be sure that the omission is not accidental. The solidarity of the poor was the mainstay of the tyrant's support.

Though Periander has a uniformly bad press among extant writings, vestigial traces remain of a more appreciative attitude. Above all, we know that Periander was enrolled as one of the Seven Wise Men of Ancient Greece.[18] Judging by Aristotle's *Politics* he does indeed seem to have dispensed his advice freely, though it is not the sort of advice to endear him to a fourth-century writer. His best known piece of advice occurs in an anecdote about an exchange between him and his friend Thrasybulus, tyrant of Miletus, though in its most familiar form, in Herodotus, the roles are reversed, with Thrasybulus advising him. The story as told by Herodotus is that Periander sent a herald to Miletus to ask Thrasybulus' advice on the conduct of government. His advice was lost on the messenger because it was conveyed not by words but by actions and amounted in fact to a graphic demonstration of the policy he was recommending:

> Thrasybulus led the man who had come from Periander outside the city and, entering a sown field, he walked through the corn questioning and interrogating the herald about his voyage from Corinth, and all the time he was lopping off any ears of corn that he saw projecting above the others, and he cast them aside as he cut them

down until he had destroyed the best and richest portion of the crop by this means.¹⁹

This charade may have been wasted on the servant, but, if we can believe Herodotus, it certainly was not lost on his master. This graphic demonstration epitomizes in itself the role of the tyrant as the enemy of the rich and noble and as a leveller.

It is worth noting that the states where tyranny sprang into existence were the most economically advanced in Greece. The chief centres of revolution were also the chief centres of commerce and industry. But there are two notable exceptions, Aegina and Chios. At no time do we hear of an Aeginetan tyranny, yet Aegina was undoubtedly the leading commercial centre of Greece proper in the sixth century. But two key factors in the rise of tyranny were missing in Aegina: industry and over-population. Though it was so major a trading power, Aegina founded not a single colony. Significantly, Aristotle remarks that the most numerous class in Aegina and Chios was the merchant-class.²⁰ This 'middle-class' character of the bulk of the population may explain why both Aegina and Chios had comparatively tranquil political histories. Thucydides in fact singles Chios out for special commendation:

> Of all the peoples with whom I am familiar the Chians alone, second only to the Spartans, have combined moderation with prosperity, and, as their state increased in stature, so did the stability with which they governed it.²¹

The cohesiveness of Chian society is reflected in the fact that as early as the sixth century there was a 'popular council' (*boulē dēmosiē*) in an otherwise aristocratic or oligarchical constitution.²² The fact that this mixed constitution could continue to function smoothly over an extended period of time is clearly indicative of harmonious social integration.

We do not know what the aristocrats of the seventh and sixth centuries thought of the newly enriched commercial nabobs, but it would not be at all surprising if these proud nobles utterly scorned and despised them. Merchants and aristocrats nevertheless seem to have exercised a certain strange attraction upon each other. A partnership of convenience grew up – and not for the last time in history – between the wealth of the one and the social respectability and political standing of the other. Not all aristocrats were prepared to dilute the purity of their noble blood with inferior corpuscles – be they even of solid silver or gold – and such men were outraged at the materialism of their fellow aristocrats. Thus Theognis:

> When it comes to rams and asses and horses, Cyrnus, we seek out the thoroughbred, and one is intent upon breeding from good stock. But a nobleman does not worry about marrying the common daughter of a common man if he gives him plenty of money. Nor does the wife of a base man scorn to be the spouse of a rich man, but she prefers wealth to quality. For it is money that they value, and a good man marries into a base family while a base man marries into a good family. Wealth has bastardized the breed. So do not be surprised, son of Polypaus, if the descendants of our fellow citizens fade into obscurity, for the good is mixed with the bad.[23]

This fusion explains not only why Chios and Aegina were freer from revolutionary upheavals than the other leading commercial and maritime states, but also why the rise of tyrants cannot be interpreted solely in terms of the interests of the 'new class of wealthy traders and financiers', despite the strenuous attempts on the part of some modern scholars to do so.[24] The natural tendency for the *nouveaux riches* was to try to blend into the old aristocracy. With the prudence of at least a portion of the aristocracy overcoming their initial repugnance, this indeed is what happened, and, in the absence of any permanent distinguishing marks such as racial differences, it was impossible for the outsider to tell who had started life as a nobleman and who as a commoner. In those states, notably Chios and Aegina, where the old aristocracy and the increasingly prosperous merchant class were the only two sizeable social classes, this process of fusion served to relax social tensions and to check conflict. In the majority of Greek states, however, there was in addition a numerous – and ever-growing – class of impoverished small men whose expectations were increasingly raised by the sight of growing prosperity all around them while they themselves were being dashed to the ground by the realities of the situation, which enriched the rich more and more at the expense of the poor. The amelioration of their lot seemed constantly within reach – for, after all, did they not see all around them men with backgrounds as humble as their own rising to great wealth and living in the lap of luxury and ease? – and yet it always eluded their grasp. This simultaneous combination of growing hope and growing frustration only embittered these people yet further and turned them into a potentially revolutionary force.

In order to become an actual revolutionary force this amorphous mass of embittered people had to find a leader – and who better than an able, ambitious and disaffected aristocrat who already had a foothold in the government? Here was the formula for tyranny. In the circumstances it can be seen that tyranny was not only an alternative to aristocracy. It was *the* alternative to aristocracy.

CHAPTER V

ARISTOCRATS AGAINST ARISTOCRACY

There is scarcely a government in the world today which does not claim to be a democracy. However defined democracy is now generally regarded as the sole criterion of the merit of a political constitution or form of government. This is all the more remarkable because it has not always been so. The vogue of democracy dates only from the mid-nineteenth century, and it was then, too, that Greek history first came to be seen as a gradual progression towards the ideal of democracy. Before that time it would not have occurred to anyone to write books about 'the mission of Greece and Rome to defend and promote freedom and the rule of law', and it was not Athens but Sparta which received most sympathy from the community of the learned. This is worth stressing now that the fashion has changed.[1]

The unspoken argument that pervades so many modern books runs something like this: Democracy is by definition the highest form of political life, and Athenian democracy is democracy par excellence. Therefore, if not absolutely flawless, Athenian democracy must be seen as at least highly commendable. After all, the argument continues, if this paradigm of democracy is to be deemed a failure, what hope can there be for its latter-day counterparts in the contemporary world?

This sort of identification of modern parliamentary democracy with the Athenian variety is more than a little paradoxical. For, not only is there the obvious difference between a direct and an indirect type of democracy, but there is the even more striking fact that the two varieties stem from diametrically opposite origins. What goes by the name of democracy in the contemporary West, and especially in the English-speaking world, is a form of government which has grown essentially from an extension of oligarchical privileges to wider and wider circles, whereas, as we shall see presently, Athenian democracy was essentially anti-aristocratic. But there is a double paradox here, because whereas modern liberal democracy, derived though it is from aristocracy, has developed a solid body of theory, anti-aristocratic Athenian democracy never did. In practice, however, the emphasis of Athenian democracy was strongly on equality rather than on liberty, whereas modern parliamentary democracy has tended to lay stress on liberty rather than equality. This is not only a difference in emphasis but again reflects an opposite tendency, because liberty and equality are at least potentially mutually antagonistic. Concern for individual liberty has generally been interpreted to mean less interference by government in the daily affairs of its subjects, whereas equality cannot be attempted without the most strenuous government efforts, whether in raising the humble or in lowering the proud.

But there is yet a third paradox in the identification of modern parliamentary government and Athenian democracy. For, though parliamentary democracy is a development of aristocratic government and Athenian democracy was an essentially anti-aristocratic form of government, yet, though the Athenian system of government went to great lengths to ensure the political equality of its citizens, the accepted scale of values remained aristocratic throughout, whereas the scale of values prevalent in the world today is undoubtedly egalitarian and anti-aristocratic. This aristocratic ethos, as we may call it, that persisted throughout classical times and beyond, will be the subject of the next chapter.

ARISTOCRATS IN ATHENIAN DEMOCRACY

A yet further paradox exists in Athenian democracy, and that is that despite its much vaunted egalitarianism its history is largely dominated by high-born aristocrats. How can this be explained? There are essentially two schools of thought among modern writers on Greek history in this matter. There are those, probably the majority, who either regard this prevalence of aristocrats in fifth-century Athenian politics as a matter of little consequence or else ignore it altogether; and there are those who try to use it to show that there was no basic conflict in fifth-century Athens.[2] 'In fact,' writes A. H. M. Jones, who belongs to our first category, 'the Athenian people were rather snobbish in their choice of leaders,' but this is not seen as detracting in any way from 'the equality of citizens in formulating and deciding public policy.'[3] On the other hand, we read that the aristocracy was 'the Establishment' of fifth-century Athens, an age of consensus politics: 'There is more than enough evidence to show that the extraordinary success of Pericles was based on a union of hearts – a system of loyalty to persons rather than to ideas. The political machine of Pericles in fact drew from all elements of Athenian society, but predominantly from those very *chrestoi* in whom we are supposed to see a party of the opposition.'[4] Each of these views contains a grain of truth, but both are demonstrably false in essentials.

It is of course incontrovertible, to tackle the second 'school' first, that the political leaders of fifth-century Athens were overwhelmingly of noble descent, but some of them were nevertheless popular leaders opposed to aristocracy. The fact that Cleisthenes, Pericles or Alcibiades was a nobleman does not necessarily mean, as is sometimes assumed, that he identified himself with the aristocracy as a whole or wished to advance their interests – any more than, say, Julius Caesar in Republican Rome or Lord John Russell in Victorian England.

But it also does not follow that because such illustrious nobles as Cleisthenes, Pericles or Alcibiades did not uphold the cause of aristocracy there was no such cause. Indeed, the ancient authors were in no doubt whatsoever on the subject, though it is no longer fashionable to agree with them.

'From the beginning', says Plutarch, 'there had been a sort of hidden seam, as in iron, marking the difference between the popular and aristocratic parties.'[5] Aristotle similarly singles out two politicians in every generation, one billed as 'the people's champion' (*prostatēs tou dēmou*), and the other as leader of the 'notables' (*gnōrimoi*), or aristocracy. After listing Solon, Peisistratus and Cleisthenes as the first three people's champions, with Isagoras as Cleisthenes' short-lived aristocratic opponent, we find Xanthippus as popular leader confronted by Miltiades, then both Themistocles and Aristeides as contemporary popular champions, followed by the three opposing pairs (with the popular leader first in each case) of Ephialtes and Cimon, Pericles and Thucydides son of Melesias, Cleon and Nicias, and finally Cleophon together with Callicrates on the popular side and Theramenes on the other.[6] There is no reason to believe that there were two organized 'parties' – not that Aristotle says there were, though his analysis is probably a little too schematic and simplistic. But it probably gives a more accurate picture of the workings of politics in fifth-century Athens than the bland descriptions which have become so fashionable of late and which do their best to play down, or even to gloss over altogether, the role of political organization behind the scenes and the very real divisions and disagreements in Athenian politics.

SOLON AND THE ARISTOCRACY

Even Solon, whose name is still a byword for wisdom, does not seem to have realized quite how unbridgeable the political gulf was that separated the common people of Athens from the aristocracy in his own day. He is listed by Aristotle as the first of the Athenian popular champions, but he ought perhaps more accurately to be seen as the prototype of the modern politician who earnestly sets about attempting conciliation and compromise between two extremes which share no common ground.

The same sort of economic crisis which had already brought tyranny to several Greek states occurred in Athens at the beginning of the sixth century:

> At that time the disparity between rich and poor reached its culmination and the whole city was in an altogether critical situation. Tyranny seemed the only way to stabilize matters and to put an end to the disorder. For the whole of the commonalty was in debt to the rich. For they either cultivated their land for them and paid them a sixth of the proceeds, being therefore referred to as hectemorians ['sixth-parters'] or *thētes*, or else they incurred debts upon the security of their own bodies and were liable to seizure by their creditors, some becoming slaves at home and others being sold into slavery abroad. Many were compelled even to sell their own children [for no law prevented it] and to go into exile because of the cruelty of the creditors. But the majority of them, who were also the sturdiest, would meet together and urge one another not to ignore their plight but to choose one trusty man as their champion, to set free the overdue debtors, redistribute the land and make a radical change in the form of government.[7]

As we are told by Aristotle, 'Solon was of the first rank in birth and esteem, but in wealth and occupation of the middle class.'[8] Like the typical tyrant of whom we met some examples in the last chapter Solon was a maverick nobleman: sufficient of an aristocrat to have a foothold in government but at the same time courting popular support and succeeding in avoiding being tarred with the same brush as those in power. He blamed the rich for the conflict and identified himself with the poor and, not surprisingly, the masses called on him to become tyrant. They were naturally very disappointed when he demurred and they began to express doubts about his wisdom and sagacity, so much so indeed that he felt obliged to write verses justifying his refusal to become tyrant.[9] But, if Solon's failure to assume the position of tyrant and institute a wholly popular regime offended the poor, his reforms at the same time went too far not to arouse the anger of the ruling Eupatrid aristocracy, who had at least been prepared, in view of the critical nature of the situation, to entrust him with a great deal of power by electing him archon in 594.[10] The simultaneous attack on him from both sides was met by Solon with a somewhat shiny apologia:

> If it is necessary to rebuke the commonalty openly, it must be said that what they now have they would never have seen even in their dreams. As for those who are superior in rank and power, they might well praise me and regard me as their friend, for if anyone else had obtained this honour, he would not have restrained the people or checked them until he had churned up the state and taken the cream from the milk. But I stood as a boundary stone in the midst of disputed territory.[11]

Solon has been placed at various points on the political spectrum, though there is no reason at all to doubt the characterization of his position which he himself spells out so painstakingly and laboriously in his poems:

> I gave the common people such rights and privileges as are sufficient, neither adding to it nor subtracting from it. As for those who had power and whose wealth was the envy of all, I saw to it that they should suffer no wrong. I stood casting a strong shield over both and did not allow either to win an unjust victory.[12]

Solon's economic measures alone are evidence enough that he was a reformer, but a moderate reformer, as he claimed to be. Thus, for example, he relieved the plight of debtors without a redistribution of land. It was undoubtedly precisely this moderation that was the main cause of Solon's failure to stem the tide of revolution for any length of time, but, paradoxically perhaps, it also explains his high posthumous reputation: being a moderate he could be claimed in the fifth and fourth centuries as the founder equally of democracy and of oligarchy.

In his political as in his economic reforms Solon plays the role of the avuncular moderate arbitrator. He enfranchises the *thētes* but at the same time limits the magistracies to members of the upper classes. Two sources tell us that he reserved the archonship for the *pentakosiomedimnoi*, the richest class, and, despite some modern reservations, there is no point in rejecting this evidence.[13]

This attempt to placate the poor while keeping power in the hands of the rich must be seen as one of the main motifs, probably the main motif, of Solon's reforms altogether. His reforms in the interests of the poor were essentially designed to defuse a potentially revolutionary situation, but what he was doing at the same time, whether deliberately or unintentionally, was to get the rich to gang up and close their ranks. This was the effect of the shift from birth to wealth as the basis of politics.

Like Lycurgus in Sparta, Solon created a new type of ruling élite. In both cases the élite was extended from a small hereditary aristocracy to a wider circle, but there the similarity ends. Lycurgus' system lasted for three centuries; but five years after Solon's archonship an anarchy was declared in Athens (in the literal sense of their being no archon elected).

The reasons for the difference are obvious but instructive. First, the attitude of the aristocracy itself was different in the two cases. In Lycurgan Sparta the aristocracy was much more co-operative than were the Eupatrids in Solonian Athens, this being at least partly explicable in terms of the relative danger confronting them. The sacrifice of aristocratic privilege to the cause of Spartiate supremacy was one which the Spartan aristocracy was evidently prepared to make, especially no doubt since at the time when they made it, namely at the time of the Second Messenian War, Spartiate supremacy was in very real danger.

Secondly, the new Athenian élite, based as it was merely upon wealth, lacked the organic unity which welded the Spartiates together so effectively. This disunity in the new Athenian élite is reflected in the appearance soon after the Solonian reforms of two upper-class parties, the 'men of the plain' (*pediakoi*) under Lycurgus and the 'men of the coast' (*paralioi*) under Megacles. This division played into the hands of Peisistratus and his new party of 'hillmen' (*diakrioi*) or 'men from beyond the hills' (*hyperakrioi*). The rich plains round Athens and Eleusis would probably have attracted more than their fair share of aristocratic investment, and it is hardly surprising therefore that, as

Aristotle tells us, the 'men of the plain' should be the name given to the oligarchical party.[14] The geographical term 'coast' seems to have included the Peiraeus, so the 'men of the coast' may well have included the new commercial and trading interests, which fits Aristotle's description of the party as supporting a moderate constitution: the new rich had, after all, probably been the chief political (as against economic) beneficiaries of Solon's constitutional reforms.[15] It is sometimes argued that this interpretation is contradicted by Aristotle's explicit statement, over and above his political interpretation of the differences between the parties, that the parties 'took their names from the places in which they farmed.'[16] There is no reason to doubt that those who supported Megacles were concentrated along the coast, but, if that was the only difference between them and the party of Lycurgus it is hard to understand why Peisistratus could forge a temporary alliance with Megacles but never with Lycurgus. Another pointer in the same direction is the very fact that this party was under the leadership of Megacles, son of Alcmaeon, a member of what was undoubtedly the most illustrious of the noble families of Athens and the only one able to boast the distinction of having its own family curse.[17] Like the leading noble houses in many other societies the Alcmaeonids were never satisfied to be just another aristocratic house.

NOBLES AND TYRANTS

It was in this setting that Peisistratus attained power with the support of the poor, as we saw in the last chapter. Solon had been the first hope of the impoverished masses, but when he failed them they found a more reliable champion. Peisistratus did not let them down.

It is worth comparing the ease with which Peisistratus managed to gain power on three separate occasions with the total lack of success attending the enemies of the tyranny in trying to oust Peisistratus' son and successor, Hippias. After the assassination of his brother Hipparchus in 514 Hippias is portrayed as displaying all the conventional tyrannical vices of the fourth-century stereotypes, yet, if his rule did become harsher and more repressive after his brother's death it does not appear to have made any sizable body of citizens go over to his enemies. His aristocratic opponents, under the leadership of the Alcmaeonids, now living in exile, made several attempts to overthrow the tyranny, but to no avail. Even when they managed to capture and fortify Leipsydrium on the slopes of Mount Parnes in north-east Attica and were joined there by some supporters from the city, Hippias had no difficulty in dislodging them.[18] This dismal failure on the part of the aristocratic opposition stands in striking contrast to the success attending the very similar move made by Peisistratus when he used Marathon as the base for his second return. The Leipsydrium episode further confirms the view that the Peisistratids did not rely only on regional support. For, as a glance at a map will show, Leipsydrium is itself within the hill country which gave the Peisistratid party its name. The aristocratic opposition would appear to have been very ill-advised to choose a place within the local sphere of influence of the tyrant as their headquarters for operations against him – unless it did not matter; unless, that is, it was realized that the popularity of the tyranny was so widespread that no area would give a very enthusiastic welcome to its enemies.

In 510 the tyranny was finally overthrown, but only with the aid of a Spartan army.[19] In Athens, therefore, as in Rome at roughly the same time, the aristocracy was triumphant. But the histories of the two states very soon diverge. No sooner were the Athenian aristocracy back in power than they began to fall out. Herodotus' account is terse in the extreme:

> Athens, which had previously been a great city, was now freed from her tyrants and became even greater. In this city two men held sway, Cleisthenes, an Alcmaeonid, who is said to have induced the Pythian priestess [to persuade Sparta to overthrow the tyranny], and Isagoras son of Tisander, a member of a noble house, though I cannot say what his ancestry was; his kinsmen sacrifice to Carian Zeus. These men engaged in a party struggle for power; Cleisthenes was defeated and added the common people to his faction.[20]

The whole account of this episode in Aristotle's *Athenian Constitution* is somewhat distorted by additions made in the spirit of the fourth century, which was generally very hostile to tyranny. Cleisthenes' popularity with the masses is therefore attributed to his hostility to the tyranny and Isagoras is described as 'a friend of the tyrants'.[21] A few lines further down, however, we read that King Cleomenes of Sparta was a guest-friend (*xenos*) of Isagoras, which, if true, indicates a very close connection between the two men and their families.[22] These two associations of Isagoras can hardly have co-existed at the same time. We gain a clue to the puzzle from Herodotus, who lets slip the remark that Cleomenes had been a guest-friend of Isagoras 'since the siege of the Peisistratids', which presumably refers to the Spartan siege of Hippias and his adherents who had been driven to take refuge within the so-called Pelasgic Wall, in 511/10.[23] If the friendship between Cleomenes and Isagoras was of such recent vintage it is indeed likely that Isagoras had been a friend of the tyrants at some time before that, but certainly not at the time of his struggle for power with Cleisthenes.

Despite Herodotus' ignorance of Isagoras' ancestry it seems reasonably certain that he belonged, directly or indirectly, to the noble house of the Philaids, a family which, like that of the tyrants themselves, originated from the vicinity of Brauron, 'beyond the hills', and claimed descent from non-Athenian stock. The Philaids had a close association with the Peisistratids, and the two families also seem to have married into each other, but that of course does not necessarily mean that they were always allied politically.[24]

A similar fluctuating relationship existed between the Peisistratids and the Alcmaeonids. Cleisthenes himself appears as archon in 525/24, which does not necessarily mean, as has been a little too easily assumed by some modern scholars, that the persistent tradition which portrayed the Alcmaeonids as opponents of the tyrants must be altogether set aside.[25] The relations between Cleisthenes' father, Megacles, and Peisistratus were anything but static, and even marriage was not able to cement a permanent political alliance between the two houses. It is quite conceivable, therefore, that after a period in exile the Alcmaeonids once again made up their quarrel with the Peisistratids, as Cleisthenes' archonship in 525/24 would appear to indicate, and it is not at all surprising to find that the two families fell out again later and that the Alcmaeonids were instrumental in inducing the Spartans to oust Hippias from power. It is equally unsurprising to find the Alcmaeonids in collusion with the Persians – and the exiled Hippias – at the time of Marathon, flashing a shield at them from the top of Mount Pentelieus as a prearranged signal.[26]

AFTERMATH OF TYRANNY

It was, therefore, the two aristocratic families most closely associated with the tyrants – in alternate bouts of friendship and hostility – who were the main contenders for power after the Peisistratids had been deposed by foreign military might. The Spartans may well have been hoping to see the restoration of aristocratic government in Athens, but this does not appear to have been Cleisthenes' plan.

It is significant that when King Cleomenes together with Isagoras and his supporters took the Acropolis, 'the rest of the Athenians united and besieged them for two days', the result being the surrender of the Spartan army.[27] This remarkable achievement, the overpowering of the mighty Spartan army by a motley host of Athenians, is yet further testimony to the tremendous popularity of the tyrants. It does not necessarily indicate any popular support for Cleisthenes and the Alcmaeonids as such, who, as we have seen, had been unable to make any headway against Hippias before 510. The point is that now, with Hippias out of the way, Cleisthenes could move into the position of anti-aristocratic leader of the masses, a position left vacant by the removal of Hippias. It is this that Herodotus is referring to when he says that Cleisthenes 'added the commonalty to his *hetaireia*'.[28]

CLEISTHENES' REFORMS

This interpretation of Cleisthenes' position is corroborated by a glance at his reforms. The most important of these was probably his reform of the tribal system, which he used as the basis for his new Council of Five Hundred. The four old Ionian tribes were replaced by ten new tribes, each of which was made up of all citizens resident in three quite separate geographical areas called *trittues* ('thirds'), one being in the city of Athens itself or its environs, one on the coast and the other inland. The *trittues* were themselves made up of varying numbers of demes, or local areas.[29] Fifty members were supplied to the new council by each tribe and there seems to have been something like a fixed quota for each deme.[30]

What was the point of all this reorganization? Clearly, to use Aristotle's phrase, it was designed 'to mix up the masses'.[31] But why? The fact that each of the three *trittues* which made up a tribe was geographically separate from the others indicates both a positive and a negative purpose. Athenian unity was clearly intended here, but also the breakdown of traditional regional sentiment – and regional sentiment was bound up with phratry-cults, which served as the basis of aristocratic power and prestige.

But how could such a reform benefit Cleisthenes himself, for were the Alcmaeonids not aristocrats too? Or are we to assume that Cleisthenes was simply a selfless democrat? In fact, Cleisthenes' reforms could do nothing but good to the interests of his family, which, being of Phylian origin, was therefore a comparative newcomer amongst the aristocratic houses of Attica and which therefore, unlike more normal Athenian aristocratic houses such as the Boutadae, the Bouzygae or the Praxiergidae, lacked any regional power-base stemming from a local religious cult.[32]

The disruption of these traditional associations, therefore, benefited the Alcmaeonids as much as it harmed the other aristocratic houses. At the same time this process gave a fillip to Athenian unity, which had already been greatly fostered by the tyrants in their struggle against aristocratic control over the localities. The Peisistratids had expanded the Panathenaic festival, introduced the four-yearly Great Panathenaea, instituted or at least reorganized the city Dionysia (thus providing the new literary genre of drama with a venue), built a second temple at Eleusis more than twice as big as the original one and turned the Eleusinian mysteries into a national cult.[33] Cleisthenes' political reforms were in a sense the secular counterpart to these religious measures in fostering national unity.

TWO POLITICAL TYPES

We cannot, therefore, but agree with Aristotle in lumping Cleisthenes together with Peisistratus as 'champions of the people'.[34] But, though the traditional aristocratic brand of politics was dished by Cleisthenes' reforms, it continued to put up a doughty struggle.

The most successful of the conservative aristocratic politicians in fifth-century Athens was undoubtedly Cimon, though his success is sometimes misunderstood. His period of influence extended for more than fifteen years after the Persian War, from about 478 to 462, during which time he is known to have been elected a *stratēgos*, or general, no less than six times.[35] But how did he achieve this, considering that he was opposed to the reform of 462 instituted by Ephialtes which increased the power of the Council of Five Hundred, the Assembly and the jury courts at the expense of the old Areopagus Council? There can be little doubt of the popularity of Ephialtes' reform, which was passed while Cimon was away in command of an army sent to help Sparta put down a helot revolt. Cimon had no hesitation in coming out against the reform upon his return, which only let loose a barrage of vituperative abuse against him, including verses making insinuations about his relationship with his sister and lambasting him for his fondness for wine and Sparta.[36] That was after he had been rudely rebuffed by the Spartans, who refused the proffered aid and sent the Athenian army packing. It was a blow to Athenian pride. But that alone cannot be the explanation for the sudden reversal of Cimon's political fortunes, which culminated in his ostracism in 461. Cimon's pro-Spartan policy had long been manifest, and, coupled as it was with an anti-Persian outlook, was probably not unpopular in itself, given the fact that Athens still regarded herself as at war with Persia. What seems to have happened in 462 is that Ephialtes' political faction, which probably included Pericles, managed to outbid Cimon for popular support. This was in a sense a repeat performance of what Cleisthenes, Pericles' great-uncle, had done half a century previously. But how had Cimon built up the popular support which he had undoubtedly had before 462?

Both Aristotle and Theopompus tell us of Cimon's generous beneficence and open-handedness.[37] Cimon, we are told, allowed any citizen to enter his fields and gardens and help himself, offered free meals in his own house to the poor and was generally accompanied by two or three young men who would disburse small change to anyone who asked for alms. If he saw a citizen who was particularly shabbily dressed he would ask one of the youths to change clothes with him. That is essentially Theopompus' account. There is one main difference between it and Aristotle's, which is that whereas Theopompus talks of Cimon's generosity to 'citizens', Aristotle speaks specifically of Laciadae, Cimon's fellow demesmen, at least in regard to his hospitality in his own house. It is likely in any event that those who availed themselves of Cimon's bounty would have been people who knew him and lived near him. The picture here is one of an old-fashioned traditional aristocratic politician whose ties are of a personal and local nature. To lump this generosity of Cimon's together with the very different sort of generosity displayed by Pericles and other democratic politicians is to ignore the very significant difference between what were not only two quite distinct political styles but also two distinct political tendencies.[38]

Aristotle specifically contrasts Pericles' beneficence with that of Cimon and maintains that Pericles deliberately set out to rival Cimon in this regard; but, lacking Cimon's great fortune, he took the advice of a friend and introduced pay for jury service, juries being chosen by lot from among volunteers.[39] There can indeed be scarcely any doubt that the introduction of pay for jury service was not merely 'a purely administrative measure', as a modern scholar has recently maintained.[40] But this was only one of several ways in which Pericles lavished money on the masses. He is said by Plutarch to have arranged pageants and processions for them and to have sent out sixty triremes for eight months each year with citizens on board who were to be trained as seamen and were paid a wage all the while. He is also credited with a lavish colonization programme, 2,750 colonists being sent out to the Chersonese, Naxos, Andros and Thrace and a further unspecified number to Thurii in southern Italy. Above all, he was the author of a massive building programme, including the Parthenon.[41] The contrast between the two types of largess, Cimon's and Pericles', could hardly be more striking. Where the former was personal and regional and, above all, was a private benefaction paid out of the pocket of the benefactor himself, the latter was the wholesale disbursement of public money. Cimon's bounty might well attract to him the political support of individuals and localities without regard to policy, but Pericles' was clearly aimed at a much wider constituency, namely the mass of the poor. All his benefactions clearly pandered to the interests of the poor, and not least his building programme. The numerous colonies and cleruchies are a good indication of the unemployment which Plutarch specifically mentions as a motivating factor for Pericles' programme.[42] But the remark about the sixty triremes is even more striking. If it is true, it means that about 12,000 men of military age were employed in this way for the greater part of the year.

But this was not the only difference between popular and aristocratic politicians. It is sometimes said that, just as Cimon or Nicias would have belonged to a *hetaireia*, so would Pericles or Cleon.[43] The evidence adduced to prove this will not, however, bear scrutiny. There is absolutely no reason at all why we should regard Cleon's 'hundred flatterers' referred to by Aristophanes as members of a *hetaireia* or of any formal club or association whatsoever, and the fact that Cleon is once addressed by a supporter in Aristophanes' *Wasps* as '*hetaire*', or 'comrade', proves exactly nothing.[44] In fact the line in question is actually a parody of a line of Alcaeus, as the scholiast remarks.[45] We have already noticed that in 411 Peisander, a belated convert from democratic politics, does not appear to have been a member of any of the clubs to which he appeals for support. Even so early a popular politician as Aristeides is said by Plutarch not to have been a member of a *hetaireia*, though not everyone believes him and some even deny that Aristeides was a popular politician.[46] Ephialtes was a member of a *hetaireia*, but, even though he is said to have been poor, he turned down the offer of ten talents (a large sum of money) from his colleagues, on the ground that he would have to contravene the dictates of justice in order to repay his debt of gratitude, but that if he failed to reciprocate the favour he would be thought an ingrate. If his friends had financed Ephialtes in this way they would no doubt have expected political favours in return. This *quid pro quo* would not have troubled a more traditional politician. Indeed, it would have been quite a normal occurrence, not because traditional aristocratic politicians were less honest than democratic politicians, but simply because their definition of honesty or justice (*dikaiosune*) was different from that of their democratic counterparts. It is said by Plutarch that Themistocles replied to someone who had maintained that impartiality was the mark of good government by pointing to the archon's throne and saying, 'May I never sit on that throne without my friends gaining more from me than strangers.'[47] Plutarch did not approve of this attitude, and upbraids Themistocles for 'placing the government under an obligation to friendship and yielding public and national interests to private favours and concerns.'[48] But he goes on to quote another remark which shows that favouring one's friends in politics up to a certain point (which is unfortunately not specified) was regarded by Themistocles as perfectly in keeping with his concept of justice. The remark in question was made in reply to a request from the poet Simonides which his friend Themistocles considered not quite proper. We are not told what the request was, but it was obviously connected with Themistocles' political position. 'Just as a poet is not competent if he sings out of tune,' said Themistocles, 'so a man is not fit to be an archon if he grants favours repugnant to the law.'[49] Whether these two anecdotes are true or not, there can be no doubt that the political attitude here attributed to Themistocles was quite widely held as late as the end of the fifth century, the best known formulation of it being that to be found in Plato's *Republic*, where it is put into the mouth of Polemarchus, who, interestingly enough, rests it upon the authority of none other than Simonides. Polemarchus' attitude is succinctly summarized in the phrase that defines justice, or, as we should rather term it, right conduct, as 'doing good to one's friends and harm to one's enemies.'[50] The same attitude is referred to, not always favourably, by such diverse authors as Aeschylus, Pindar, Xenophon and Isocrates.[51]

If Plutarch is critical of this attitude to politics and morality, he is no less critical of the opposite attitude which he juxtaposes with it, namely the attitude personified by Cleon, who, when he first decided to take up a political career, 'gathered his friends together and dissolved his friendship with them on the grounds that it tended generally to deflect and divert government from right and honourable policies.'[52] Plutarch is quite mystified by this, saying that what a city required was not 'men without friends or associates but righteous and self-disciplined men.'[53] This betrays his lack of understanding of the fifth-century situation. Friendship automatically entailed mutual obligation, and mutual obligation necessarily entailed favouritism in the exercise of power. Polemarchus derives this from Simonides' dictum that it is right to give everyone his due, the point being that the due of a friend was very different, both in quantity and in quality, from that of a foe.[54] In order, therefore, to avoid being caught up in the toils of mutual obligation, as Cleon rightly realized, one would have to sever the Gordian knot and renounce friendship altogether. Only by being nobody's friend could he hope to be everybody's friend – or at least the friend of everybody who was not himself involved in political friendships and coteries; in other words, the friend of the common masses. And Cleon certainly reached that position. Cleon is one of the main butts of the humour of Aristophanes and we meet him either in person but more often in the dialogue of others in several plays. In the *Wasps* the two main characters are a father and son named Philocleon ('friend of Cleon') and Bdelycleon ('Cleon-hater') respectively. The names are very significant, because Philocleon and his fellow-jurors, the wasps of the title, were precisely the sort of poor Athenians who undoubtedly supported Cleon in real life as well. The 'friendship' that existed between Cleon and his supporters was of quite a different kind from what is normally meant by the term, because it was essentially an impersonal relationship and not a personal one like that of traditional aristocratic politics. Cleon was the leader of a mass movement and his adherents looked to him for guidance and protection. A term used of him by the chorus of jurors in the *Wasps* is *kēdemōn*, or 'protector'.[55] In the *Knights*, a slightly earlier play, the relationship of Cleon to Demos – a kindly old man meant to personify the people, and particularly the common people, of Athens – is constantly described as that of an *erastes*, or lover.[56] The character in the play identified as Cleon is given the name Paphlagon – probably in order to insinuate that he was of foreign extraction – who, together with Nicias and Demosthenes (no relation of the fourth-century orator of that name), is portrayed as a slave of old Demos competing with his fellow slaves for his master's favour.

Cleon is credited by several ancient authors with introducing a new style of oratory into Athenian political life, a brash, vulgar style of loud harangues, angry outbursts and vituperative abuse, accompanied by dramatic gestures and with his *himation*, or cloak, hitched up to reveal an expanse of thigh.[57] The object of the exercise was presumably in order to pose as a man of the people. For, despite Aristophanes' constant jibes at Cleon's low origins and his description of him as a tanner, or leather-seller, in fact he was no such thing, but the son of a well-to-do manufacturer of leather.[58] Which brings us back to the anecdote about his renunciation of his friends, because his friends would undoubtedly have been influential men of standing and wealth like himself.

It is instructive to compare this picture of the demagogue with some more recent counterparts. For the ranting and shouting again one need not look much further back than Hitler, who, interestingly enough, though clearly idolized by large numbers of Germans was himself a friendless man who was not even on familiar terms (i.e. on *Du* terms) with his two main lieutenants. It will be objected that Cleon had nothing like the power that Hitler was to have in Germany, but that is not what we are talking about just now.

The advent of Cleon at the centre of the stage did indeed signalize a change in the style of politics, but its importance should not be exaggerated. Cleon's antics and hysteria may have been new but they represent merely a new interpretation of an old political role – that of the demagogue – rather than a new role in themselves, as some modern writers seem to maintain.[59] The same role had been played before by Pericles, Ephialtes, Cleisthenes and Peisistratus, each imbuing the part with a distinctive character. But it was essentially the same role nevertheless, the role of the people's champion against the main body of the aristocracy. Cleon himself, together probably with Ephialtes, was not a noble, though, as we have seen, he was far from poor. Ephialtes is said to have been poor, but nothing is known about his background except, as already mentioned, that he was a member of a *hetaireia*, which would argue against low-class origins. But, with these two exceptions, all the other politicians mentioned were nobles, as were all the rest of the leading politicians before the Peloponnesian War, such as Miltiades, Aristeides, Themistocles, Cimon and Callias, and several leading figures during the War, including Nicias and Alcibiades.

We have already seen how Pericles differed from Cimon in his general approach to politics. It must now be noticed how similar his outlook was to that of Cleon. There were also very significant differences between these two democratic politicians. Where Cleon displayed *levitas popularis*, Pericles displayed *gravitas*. Cleon hitched his cloak up in an unseemly fashion and harangued the mob with his arms flailing the air, but Pericles, we are told, walked slowly, spoke softly, always showed a composed expression and kept his arm covered by his cloak (in sling fashion, as portrayed in numerous statues).[60] All this conjures up an image of Pericles in a somewhat aloof patrician mould, but, as we have seen in connection with Cleon, aloofness is not necessarily a mark of aristocratic politics. The traditional aristocratic politician would be anything but aloof from his own coterie of friends and associates, though his attitude to those outside his own circle may well be cold and haughty in the extreme. But Plutarch also tells us two other facts about Pericles' general demeanour. For one thing, we are told just before the list of attributes already mentioned that Pericles had 'changed his mien and his way of life', which presumably means that the cool, unruffled Pericles of the standard portrait was a deliberately cultivated image and that Pericles had displayed different characteristics previously. We are also told that Pericles was to be seen walking along only one street, the one leading to the Agora and the council-chamber – a picture of aloofness, perhaps, but aloofness from whom? For, if Pericles had chosen to walk freely about the city, it is more than likely that he would have stopped for a chat with friends and acquaintances every now and again, and this would probably have served to associate him in the public mind with those friends and acquaintances – who would undoubtedly have been nobles and men of substance like himself.[61] We gain a deeper insight into this attitude from another anecdote related by Plutarch, namely that Pericles refused all invitations to dinner and turned down all hospitality, 'so that in the long time that he was engaged in politics he did not go to a single one of his friends for dinner, except that, when his cousin Euryptolemus got married he stayed until the libations were poured and then immediately got up and left.'[62] Here again we can draw a parallel with Cleon's dramatic renunciation of his friendships. How convincing a champion of the poor would Pericles be if he was constantly in the company of the rich, eating their food and quaffing their wine? For the people who invited him to their houses and offered him hospitality would naturally be rich.

One of the favourite pastimes of modern writers on ancient history is to set aside any evidence which does not square with their preconceptions. 'The description of Pericles as a democrat', reads one such attempt, 'was not a contemporary description.'[63] It was, we are urged to believe, concocted by Pericles' enemies shortly after the Peloponnesian War. However, we do have contemporary evidence and, in any case, Pericles' activities were quite within living memory at the end of the War. In the Old Comedy we have plays (or fragments of plays) which were not only written but also performed before mass audiences either during Pericles' lifetime or within a few years of his death, which occurred in 429. The evidence of comedy, like the rest of the evidence about Pericles, can be divided into two broad categories, one which portrays him as a haughty aristocrat and one which portrays him as a demagogue.

Plutarch was very struck by this contrast and automatically concluded that the explanation was to be found in a change in Pericles' policy. He is therefore seen as an initially democratic politician who subsequently became somewhat domineering and overbearing.[64] It is no doubt this same apparent divergence of the sources that has led some modern scholars to reject the tradition that Pericles was a democrat. Yet are there two descriptions? Is not the very haughtiness of this particular haughty aristocrat in itself a sign of his staking a claim to being leader of all the people, and especially of its most numerous element? A closer look at the evidence will certainly support that view.

Pericles is the butt of attack of two plays written during his lifetime, the *Cheirones* ('The Inferiors') of Cratinus, written before the Peloponnesian War, and the *Moirai* of Hermippus, written early on in the war.[65] Unfortunately only fragments survive, but Cratinus' play seems to have had as its theme one familiar from the plays of Aristophanes, namely the decline of moral standards in Periclean Athens by comparison with the good old days. A fragment of another play of Cratinus', the *Ploutoi*, may actually combine the imputation of a Periclean tyranny with democracy in saying, 'Now that tyranny has begun and the *dēmos* rules . . .', but this reading is not quite certain.[66] It is thought that this play dates from not long after the ostracism of Thucydides son of Melesias, which happened in 443.[67] A similar view of Pericles' primacy in the state is to be found in a fragment of another play of roughly the same vintage, by Telecleides, in which the Athenians are said to have entrusted Pericles with absolute power over the allied cities – a description which bears a remarkable resemblance to that which Aristophanes applies to the power of a demagogue in the *Knights*.[68] It was at about this time too, significantly enough, after the putting down of the Samian revolt in 440, that, according to a scholiast, the freedom of speech of the comic poets was curbed, though the ban was lifted three years later.[69]

The very fact that Pericles was attacked by the writers of comedy shows that he was thought of as a democratic politician. For it is noticeable that the butts of Old Comedy include a good number of demagogues but no conservative politicians. The comic playwright Plato (no relation of the philosopher) even went so far as to name three plays after the demagogues that he attacked in them, Hyperbolus, Cleophon and Peisander (in his pre-oligarchical days). Hyperbolus was also attacked in Hermippus' *Artopōlides* ('Breadsellers'), Eupolis' *Marikās* and in another play by Plato entitled *Alliance*.[70] Thucydides son of Melesias, by contrast, who is mentioned only twice by Aristophanes, is accorded very sympathetic treatment indeed and his accusers are attacked in no uncertain way in one of these passages.[71] Like Cleon, therefore, Pericles could be seen as a demagogue, and even as a tyrant. Even Aspasia, a *hetaira*, or lady of the profession, and a close friend of Pericles', could be described as a tyrant by the comic writer Eupolis. It is particularly significant that, as Plutarch tells us, (unnamed) writers of comedy dubbed Pericles and his associates 'new Peisistratids' and called upon him to take an oath not to make himself a tyrant.[72] It is true that if he was still in a position to forswear tyranny Pericles could not have been regarded as having quite reached the position of tyrant, but it is clear that he was thought close to it.

We have now come full circle. In testing the proposition proffered by some modern scholars that Pericles was an aristocrat's aristocrat, we have now reached a very different image of him altogether. But how far in this direction can we travel? Can we, for example, agree with Thucydides' famous description of Periclean Athens as 'in name a democracy, but in fact rule by the first citizen'?[73] In rebutting this interpretation the modern writers belonging to the second 'school' of scholars referred to above hasten to point to the fact, mentioned by Thucydides shortly before the quoted phrase, that in 430 Pericles was fined and deprived of his office, the *strategia* or generalship, which, according to Plutarch, he had held for fifteen years in succession.[74] This, it is averred, shows that even so obviously popular and respected a leader had no independent power of his own but had to persuade the assembly on every issue separately.[75] There is a certain amount of truth in this, though the generals do seem to have had leverage in several important spheres of policy-making. There were ten generals elected each year and there was no limit to the number of times one could be re-elected. The mechanics of the election have been often and heatedly debated in the pages of the scholarly journals, and it is not my present purpose to become embroiled in that lion's den.[76] The *strategia* seems to have been instituted in 501/500, and, though supreme command of the forces was still vested in the hands of the polemarch, one of the archons, at the battle of Marathon in 490, with the introduction of partial sortition (*klērōsis ek prokritōn*) for the archonship in 487/86, the extension of eligibility for it to the Zeugites in 458/57 and the later change of the method of selection to a double sortition, the *strategia* became more and more important.[77] Indeed, it became the most important office in Athens and was held by the leading statesmen. Miltiades, Themistocles, Xanthippus, Aristeides, Cimon, Nicias, Cleon, Demosthenes, and Alcibiades are among the most famous fifth-century generals besides Pericles himself. It is worth noting that all of these except for Cleon, Demosthenes and perhaps Nicias were noblemen, and these three men were anything but poor.[78] (The fourth-century orator Deinarchus does say that there was a property qualification for the *strategia*, but he has generally been disbelieved.)[79]

The power of a general was the product not so much of constitutional enactments as of the fact that the *strategia* was the only important elective office in Athens. Though there were ten generals, one of them tended to be rather more prominent than the rest. This pre-eminence again would not have depended on constitutional prerogatives, though from 460/59 at least it was possible for two or more generals to be elected from the same tribe – an important development, considering that the number ten for the board of generals must obviously have been originally intended to correspond to the ten Cleisthenic tribes.[80] The question of whether one of the ten generals had any legal predominance and whether there was a commander-in-chief at all, perhaps on a rota basis among the ten, has been endlessly discussed, but, as has already been said, that is less important than the actualities of the situation.[81] When in 431 the Spartan army had penetrated to the neighbourhood of Acharnae, only about five miles from the city of Athens itself, and were busy ravaging the land, the Acharnians were anxious to take the field against the invading force. Pericles, however, believed that such action would be folly and so refused to call a meeting of the assembly.[82] By what power could Pericles do this? It is hard to say, but it is not unparalleled. The one-year truce which was concluded between Athens and Sparta in 423, six years after Pericles' death, included a provision that 'the generals and the *prutaneis* were to call an assembly for the Athenians to consider in the first instance the question of peace.'[83] The *prutaneis* were the fifty men from one of the ten tribes who were the 'chairmen', or leading element, in the Council, or *Boulē*, during one-tenth of their year of office, so it is hardly surprising that they should be involved here. But why the generals? We have here inescapable evidence of the power of the generals over the ordinary functioning of government, and in this case a power clearly enshrined in constitutional form. In an inscription generally dated to 430 any business brought before the assembly by the generals is given precedence over other matters,[84] which is perhaps not very surprising in wartime, but what is more significant is the likelihood that the generals were regarded as *ex officio* members of the *Boulē* and the certain fact that they could propose motions in that body, though the earliest known example of that is from the early fourth century.[85] A true realization of the political influence and even, as we have seen, actual constitutional prerogatives, of a popular general like Pericles, coupled with the knowledge that there was political organization, however rudimentary by modern standards, makes the claims that all power resided in the assembly ring rather hollow. 'Did this assembly really rule?' reads one such assertion, 'or were its meetings only an empty show, and all decisions made elsewhere?'

> We can make a simple test [suggests this same author]: when government is by discussion, as it certainly was in Athens, where did the discussion take place, where were the great speeches made? In this country, in the eighteenth and early nineteenth centuries, they were made in parliament, in the Lords or the Commons, with a growing preponderance of the Commons; in the later nineteenth century in the Commons and on the hustings; now over the radio as well; the House of Commons, with some control by the people, rules. In Rome, in the great days of the Republic, the speeches were made in the senate; for the senate ruled. In Athens they were made only in the assembly. [I believe that we have only one mention of speeches in the *Boulē* or Council, in Aristophanes, in that brilliant parody of a debate in the *Knights*.] Government, then, was by the people.[86]

This is a circular argument if ever there was one. Starting from the premise that Athenian government was 'government by discussion' it is hardly surprising that we arrive at the conclusion that the writer wants us to. But was Athenian government 'government by discussion' and, for that matter, what does 'government by discussion' mean? The parallels adduced certainly do not help the argument. It is a moot point whether Parliament rules or has ever ruled Britain. The idea that people's opinions change in accordance with rational argument and discussion flatters our ego, but people's political attitudes and reactions, as has often been demonstrated, are generally a foregone conclusion. Only on matters of indifference to themselves or on points of detail could they be swayed by argument. On the whole their views can be predicted on the basis of their social, economic and psychological make-up.[87] Seen from this point of view the question 'Who has the whip-hand?' becomes rather meaningless when applied to a popular government like that of Periclean Athens. To be a popular leader it is necessary to be a follower as well, and the roles of leader and follower are not clearly differentiated. The general tenor of an ambitious politician's policies must obviously harmonize with popular political attitudes and feelings as a glance at some of the issues decided during the Peloponnesian War will demonstrate. If we accept a modern scholar's choice of 'the Corcyrean alliance, the rejection of the Spartan ultimatum in 431, the fate of Mytilene, the Spartan overtures in 425 and again in 420, the Sicilian expedition' as 'the great issues' of Athenian politics, in the period covered by Thucydides, it will be noticed that the outcome of all the debates was easily predictable, except perhaps for the second decision on Mytilene, which is the only example we have of a change of mind by a majority of voters. The first two cases are straightforward enough and reflect the aggressive imperialistic tendencies of the Athenian masses, as does the initial decision in the Mytilenean debate to put all adult male Mytileneans to death and to enslave the women and children. The change of mind in the second debate on the following day is perhaps equally instructive. It is worth studying the arguments put forward on both sides, and especially those of Diodotus, the main speaker against the harsh treatment of the Mytileneans. For there is not a single word of concern in his speech for the Mytileneans. The whole oration is designed to show his audience that sparing the Mytileneans was in the *Athenian* interest.[88] Since the whole question was rather remote from the members of the *ekklesia*, to whom the fate of the Mytileneans was clearly a matter of no very great import, they could be persuaded. But that was possible only because Diodotus' proposal could be made to square with their own selfish concerns. The double rebuff to Sparta in 425 and 420 is again to be understood as a natural expression of popular imperialism, as is the decision to embark upon the Sicilian expedition in 415. That is not to minimize the part played by such politicians as Cleon,

Hyperbolus and Alcibiades in fanning the imperialist flame, but there can be no doubt that it was there already. Fanning the flame was acceptable to the masses, but any politician trying to put it out would meet with strong opposition, as Nicias did when he urged moderation and caution both in 420 and again in 415. When the Spartans and their allies invaded Attica for the second time in 430, it is true, the Athenians, hard hit by plague as well as by the war, were prepared to sue for peace and blamed Pericles for having persuaded them to go to war. It is very significant, however, that in the speech by which he managed to deflect them from their purpose and to instill greater enthusiasm for the war Pericles played particularly on their imperialistic spirit:

> It is only fair that you should bolster up the esteem which has come to the state through empire, by which the dignity of each of you is enhanced, and not to shun its hardships – or otherwise not to pursue its honours. And you must not think that the fight is concerned with one issue only, namely the question of freedom or slavery; in addition, there is the issue of the loss of the empire and of the danger resulting from the odium surrounding our rule. It is no longer possible for you to withdraw from the empire, in case anyone wishes to play the gentleman by inaction in his fear of the present situation. For the empire that you possess is already a tyranny, which may seem wrong to have taken but which it would be very dangerous to relinquish.[89]

To whom, though, is Pericles referring here as wishing 'to play the gentleman'? The Greek word in question is *andragathizesthai*, which is compounded from the words meaning 'good' and 'man'. Could this have been intended as a reflection of the label assumed by the aristocratic 'smart set', *kaloi k'agathoi*? Whether it was so intended or not, it was certainly the oligarchs who opposed imperialism. The very wording of this speech put by Thucydides into the mouth of Pericles is echoed in the criticisms of Pericles' transference of the common funds of the Delian League (the official name of the Athenian empire) from the holy island of Delos to Athens as quoted by Plutarch: 'Greece appears outraged by a terrible insult and is subjected to naked tyranny'.[90] Whether Plutarch took this from an older account or whether he devised the wording himself is not particularly important, because it accords with what we know, for example, from the 'Old Oligarch', a writer whose brief tract, entitled like the Aristotelian one, the *Athenian Constitution*, claimed to have been written by a certain Xenophon, and

ARISTOCRATS AGAINST ARISTOCRACY

is generally thought to date from some time during the Peloponnesian War.[91] In this fascinating pamphlet the imperialism of the Athenian lower classes is so described as to make it plain that such sentiments were not shared by the author.[92]

But perhaps the best illustration of the two attitudes to the empire and imperialism is to be found in comedy. In the year 426, during the war and at a time, late in April, when there would have been many foreign visitors in Athens, the young Aristophanes put on the stage a play called the *Babylonians*, in which he attacked Cleon for the first time as well as all other Athenian officials, as the scholiast tells us, 'whether elected or chosen by lot'.[93] As often in Aristophanic comedy, the play took its name from the chorus, the allied cities portrayed as branded Babylonian slaves on a treadmill. Unfortunately, only scanty fragments survive. One mentions a man in chains carrying a shield, which may possibly refer again to the allies.[94] Another describes someone as slaughtering an islander's yoke of oxen for beef, probably another reference to Athenian barbarity in the treatment of their so-called allies.[95] And the scholiast specifically tells us that this play was produced 'with the allies present'. On the question of imperialism, as well as on several other questions, Aristophanes clearly was very much opposed to the prevailing attitudes, but he makes it equally plain how very popular imperialism was with the lower classes. Philocleon, or 'Cleon's friend', in the *Wasps* is perhaps the best known personification of this imperialistic spirit, taking delight as he does in his jury service above all because of the sense of importance that it gives him. Here is part of his foppish and oligarchical son Bdelycleon's reply to him:

> To the politicians whose stock in trade it is to say:
> 'Athenian masses I'll never betray! For the common people's sake
> Forever will I fight!' Lulled by such mouthings, Father, you make
> Such fellows to be your kings. Then by threatening every city
> Fifty talents at a clip they extort, and they show no pity:
> 'I'll aim my thunder at your city if you don't fork up'.
> You meanwhile are quite content on dominion's crumbs to sup.
> When the allies perceive the populace, clinging to their franchise,
> Thin and supine, waste and pine with starvation in their eyes,
> You they ignore and lavish their gifts on the powerful politicians.[96]

Like the arguments put forward by Nicias in the speeches attributed to him by Thucydides, so here the appeal is to purely selfish instincts. It has become fashionable to say that Aristophanes' own political views are irrecoverable, but the very forcefulness with which certain views are put forward in his plays – and, moreover, the fact that they are consistently of a conservative and anti-imperialistic nature – makes a nonsense of that assertion, at least in this particular regard.[97] But for our purpose it makes very little difference whether Aristophanes did or did not express his own political opinions in his plays. It is enough to know that there was a division of opinion on the question of imperialism and that this division coincided with the more general one between the two elements referred to by Plutarch as 'the People' and 'the Few', the former being for imperialism and the latter opposed to it.

ARISTOCRATS AGAINST ARISTOCRACY

However many noble leaders democratic Athens may have had its government was anything but in the aristocratic interest. How then can one tell the difference between aristocratic and non-aristocratic government? It would not have seemed necessary to ask this question if it were not for the fact that, as we noted in our discussion on the fifth century, some modern scholars have been rather confused on this very issue. The predominance of a Pericles or an Alcibiades is sufficient for them to conclude that they were part of an aristocratic 'Establishment'.[98] In fact, however, as we have already seen, such leaders, though nobles themselves, were opposed to the general interests of the aristocracy as a whole. In short, they were aristocrats against aristocracy.

But there is an even more serious and much more widespread fallacy found today amongst writers on Greek history who ignore or play down the fact that leaders such as Pericles and Alcibiades were nobles in their emphasis upon the democratic nature of the system of Athenian government. Again, as we have seen, the reality of Athenian democracy was much closer to the Peisistratid tyranny than would generally be accepted in the salons of currently fashionable belief. The two, tyranny and democracy, can be placed in the same general category, a category of what we might call, as suggested above, popular government. For both shared an essentially popular and anti-aristocratic nature. Not only were both based largely upon lower class support, but both were directed towards the interests of the lower classes and against those of the aristocracy. And while the popular basis of tyranny is generally played down, if not dismissed out of hand altogether, the dictatorial element in democracy tends likewise to be underestimated.

Like the term 'aristocratic', the word 'popular' is ambiguous. Thus, Cimon was popular in the sense that he had the support of large numbers of people, but he was certainly not a popular leader in the sense that, say, Pericles was. Cimon was opposed to the reform of the Areopagus proposed by Ephialtes. He was not in favour, therefore, of extending the power of the masses on an institutional basis. In this sense Cimon was essentially an aristocratic politician and his lower-class supporters were probably connected by personal ties of patronage or obligation to him or to one of his aristocratic allies. This is not to deny the genuineness of Cimon's kindness and humanitarianism. It would not be necessary to say so if it were not for the fact that humanitarianism today tends to be associated with general political posturings and the mouthing of fashionable nostrums all too often unaccompanied by acts of kindness to individuals. The contrast between Cimon and Pericles may in a sense be paralleled by that once drawn between Disraeli and Gladstone: Disraeli understood men but not mankind, Gladstone mankind but not men. A working man would find Disraeli much the warmer and the more friendly of the two, but it was Gladstone's picture that he would probably have hanging in his front room. Similarly, Cimon might entertain a humble neighbour to dinner, but it was Pericles who would speak with the voice of the masses as a whole. Seen in this way it is not difficult to understand why it was the Periclean brand of politics that triumphed. However close their personal ties with a Cimon, the poor inevitably found it easier to identify with a Pericles, who offered them more prospects and proposed policies in their interests. It is also not surprising that this type of political role tended to attract the most ambitious nobles.

But, just as it is wrong to assume an association between Pericles and Cimon simply because they were both nobles, so it would be a fallacy to regard Cleon and Pericles as allies simply because they were both popular politicians in the sense explained above. It would not be at all surprising, indeed, if Cleon had been a rival of Pericles' in wooing the masses, though, so far as our records go, he steps on to the stage of history only after Pericles' death. It has even been suggested that the attacks on Pericles' famous friends, Pheidias the sculptor and the philosopher Anaxagoras, were the work not of oligarchical opponents like Thucydides son of Melesias but rather of rival democratic politicians such as Cleon and his ilk.[99] In the absence of any real evidence no firm conclusion can be reached on this point one way or the other. Cleon may well have attacked Pericles, but that certainly does not destroy the twofold division of politics delineated by Aristotle and Plutarch, as some enthusiastic believers in Cleon's anti-Periclean position tend all too automatically to assume. The real divide certainly was between aristocratic family-based politics geared to the supremacy of the aristocracy as a whole and popular politics pandering to the interests, hopes and fears of the masses as a whole. That does not mean that there were two monolithic parties confronting each other across this divide. On each side there undoubtedly were several rival groups and factions in shifting alliances of longer or shorter duration. Sometimes, as for example in the famous case of the ostracism of Hyperbolus in 417 (the last ostracism, incidentally, ever held in Athens), an alliance of this kind could unite two elements from opposite sides of the basic divide, in this case the factions led by Nicias and Alcibiades, but that was probably a very rare phenomenon, and it is significant that the object of the alliance on that occasion was purely negative, the removal of a common rival in a situation where one of the three was bound to be ostracized.

The real paradox lies elsewhere. How the ordinary Athenian citizen chose his political favourite is hard to say, but, as we have seen, even after the ascendancy of rich commoners like Cleon, Hyperbolus and Cleophon, there was still a good number of nobles elected to high posts. The fact is that the masses were not only prepared to choose noble leaders, but they clearly also valued birth as such. An understanding of this phenomenon will probably go far to explain a lot of the confusion of thought surrounding the whole issue of Athenian politics. For, to put it in a nutshell, democratic Athens was simultaneously anti-aristocratic in government and aristocratic in ethos. Why and how this could possibly be so is the subject of the next chapter.

The aristocratic ethos never altogether disappeared in Athens. It certainly was under attack in the fifth and fourth centuries but it subsequently regained strength as oligarchy reverted to aristocracy in government. From 323 Athens was ruled by an oligarchy of wealth, but, since wealth tended to be hereditary, oligarchy soon gave way in practice to aristocracy, with some newer families eventually joining the charmed circle of the surviving Eupatrids. The most vigorous and long-lived of these ancient houses turned out to be the Ceryces, the family of Callias, Conon and Timotheus. It was to this family too that Demetrius of Phalerum is sometimes said to have belonged, the man who was the virtual ruler of Athens between 317 and 307, though his connection with the Ceryces seems rather to have been by marriage.

Thanks to an inscription from the reign of Augustus we know the names of fifty members of the *genos* spanning the period from the third to the first centuries. But that by no means marks the end of the line, and the best known Athenian of Roman times, the millionaire of Marcus Aurelius' reign, Herodes Atticus, was a member of that same house, which by then shared its dominant position in Athens with only three other families.[100]

CHAPTER VI

THE ARISTOCRATIC ETHOS

The aim of this chapter is to show that the dominant ideology amongst the ancient Greeks was an aristocratic one. But what is meant by 'an aristocratic ideology'? It is an ideology which believes not only that some people are superior to others but also that this superiority is innate and hereditary. This point, which is not always fully appreciated, is of the utmost importance. What it means is that the type of society envisaged by the adherents of the aristocratic ideal is a closed society – a society in which there is no social mobility. In other words, the aristocratic ideal is at variance not only with egalitarian ideals but no less so with the modern ideal of 'meritocracy', which is invariably allied to a belief in 'equality of opportunity'.

Egalitarian ideals are essentially of two types: belief in absolute equality (whether political, economic or both) and belief in equality of opportunity. Such beliefs all refer to equal rights, i.e. equal political rights, the right to economic equality or the right to enjoy equal opportunity. But this belief in entitlement to equal rights derives from a more basic belief in equality of worth. Thus, the belief that everyone should enjoy equal political rights rests upon the belief that everyone has equal political worth and that no man's political opinion is worth more than any other's. It is upon this ideological foundation that the sanctity of the modern concept of 'majority rule' is based. Even Gladstone, that great liberal, could regard majority rule with a certain amount of scepticism. 'Decision by majorities', he said, 'is as much an expedient as lighting by gas.' The example is instructive: lighting by gas is now largely obsolete. Decision by majorities has nevertheless become more sacred than ever, because the concept of equality underpinning it has become more widely accepted.

But, however egalitarian one's political ideal may be, it is hard to escape the fact that different people display differing degrees of ability and worth. On the face of it, this might not appear incompatible with equality of rights, but ultimately, consciously or unconsciously, it has to be admitted that rights and worth are inextricably linked and bound up together. Out-and-out egalitarians often try to get around this awkward truth by blaming 'society' for the differences in human ability. Thus, for example, if there is a dearth of famous female poets, this is explained in terms of 'social pressures' rather than in terms of lower female poetic creativity. But – and this is the important point – by arguing in this way the advocates of 'women's liberation' are tacitly – and probably unwittingly – admitting that rights must depend upon worth.

This admission is consciously made by the advocates of 'equality of opportunity' and 'meritocracy'. To boil the doctrine down to its paradoxical essentials it may be summarized as proposing that everyone must have an equal opportunity to become unequal. This inequality would depend upon 'merit', i.e. upon the worth of the individual concerned without any of the advantages or disadvantages of birth, wealth or environment generally.

The ideal of 'equality of opportunity' resulting in 'meritocracy' is very different from that of an ideology of any type of absolute equality, but all these ideologies share a vision of an open society, i.e. of a society in which there is open competition for leadership and decision-making.

In the aristocratic ideal, as I have already mentioned, the aim is exactly the opposite: a static and closed society in which a hereditary ruling class holds eternal sway. It is an ideal which, when fully understood, is repugnant to all that is held dear by most modern political ideologies. If it can be imagined in modern terms at all, it is invariably as a nightmare – as for example in Aldous Huxley's *Brave New World* (Penguin 1955).

In the ancient world, by contrast, the aristocratic ideal was not strange. On the contrary, it often persisted even in societies that operated a deliberately anti-aristocratic form of government.

Today the principle of equality has become so fashionable that probably no government anywhere in the world would underestimate the degree to which equality existed in its own country. On the contrary, it might well be tempted to exaggerate it. So much is plain enough. But until quite recently the opponents of a regime were quite as likely to exaggerate the degree of equality in it as were its supporters. In the early decades of the Soviet state in Russia, for example, the fiercest opponents of the new regime were quite as fully convinced of its egalitarian character as were its most fervent admirers. As a result of this paradoxical conspiracy of opposites the Soviet Union has managed to cultivate an image totally at variance with the true nature of its society – an image that is still quite widely accepted by friend and foe alike. How are we to account for this paradoxical agreement? The answer is simple enough, though it is seldom recognized. It could be stated as a paradox, thus: the more fundamental the disagreement on principle the greater the agreement on the factual situation, and vice versa. Now, the admirers of the Soviet Union have generally professed egalitarian principles while those opposed to it have generally rejected the idea of 'communism' (defined as enforced equality). It is, therefore, in the interests of those in favour of the Soviet regime to exaggerate the degree of equality in it as much as possible, and it is equally in the interests of those opposed to the regime to accept such exaggerated accounts at face value. It suits neither extreme to recognize the regime for what it is, namely, as has become increasingly apparent, a bureaucratic oligarchy which is slowly turning into a bureaucratic aristocracy.

PLATO AGAINST DEMOCRACY

Athenian democracy provides us with a similar agreement between opposites. The egalitarian nature of Athenian politics and society is asserted as fervently by detractors of the system as by its adulators. Indeed, the detractors' picture of democracy is, if anything, even more egalitarian than that painted by its admirers. One of the features of democratic government that particularly annoyed Plato was the unprofessional way, as it seemed to him, in which it treated politics. For Plato politics was a science – the science of knowing what is best for your state and society. Since it is a science it is teachable and only those who have mastered it through training ought to have a say in the running of a government. Only philosophers, therefore, ought to rule – the famous doctrine of the philosopher-king:

> Unless philosophers become kings in our states or those whom we now call kings and rulers become genuine and able philosophers, and there is a combination between political power and philosophy, while the large number of men whose temperaments impel them to seek one without the other are forcibly excluded, there will be no end to the troubles besetting our states, my dear Glaucon, nor, I believe, to those besetting mankind as a whole.[1]

For Plato, then, politics is the profession par excellence. And yet, he complains, democracies treat all men as equally qualified to participate in government and in political decision-making:

> I notice that when we meet together in the assembly, whenever it is necessary for the state to deal with something concerned with building, the builders are sent for as advisers on the subject of building; whenever it is a question of shipbuilding we call for the shipbuilders, and so on in regard to all subjects which are considered capable of being learnt and taught. But if anyone else, whom they do not regard as a craftsman, tries to advise the people, they do not accept his advice, no matter how handsome, rich or well-born he may be; instead they laugh at him and boo until he either gives up the attempt when drowned out or the police drag him away or remove him altogether by order of the prytanes. That is the way they act on matters which they consider to be technical. But when they have to discuss something to do with the administration of the state, a carpenter may stand up to advise them, or equally a smith, a cobbler, a merchant, a shipowner, a rich man, a poor man, a nobleman, a commoner, and no one reproaches him as in the previous example for not having studied the subject anywhere or for not having a teacher to point to when he makes a bid to advise them.[2]

The cult of the amateur in politics is still very strong, and in most states which regard themselves as democracies it is true to say that no professional or technical qualification is required for membership of a parliament or assembly or even for an appointment as a cabinet minister – let alone for the franchise. The basic underlying reason for this is a belief in the principle of equality, the idea that no amount of study or experience gives anyone a better right to make a political decision than anyone else. But, as we have seen, this picture of Athenian democracy as a genuinely egalitarian system of government in which everyone had an equal say is a gross exaggeration. Despite the theory, birth and wealth evidently did give their holders a certain advantage and the one office that continued to require a certain amount of expertise, namely the generalship, became the most important in the state – and was filled largely with the rich and noble. But it would obviously never have done for Plato to admit that. He was against democracy and, therefore, the more extreme a picture of it he drew the more completely he could reject it. His hostility is revealingly coupled with his exaggeratedly egalitarian portrayal of democracy in his description of it as 'distributing a sort of equality to the equal and unequal alike'.³ It is quite clear from this that Plato does not regard everyone as equal. For that reason the charge of levelling is one of the most serious indictments that he can make against any form of government.

THE OLD OLIGARCH

But Plato's exaggeration of the degree of equality in Athenian democracy is as nothing by comparison with the exaggeration of an earlier author, writing at some time in the second half of the fifth century. I refer to the so-called pseudo-Xenophon, the author of a political pamphlet whose political tone has earned its author the designation 'The Old Oligarch'. The tract is a somewhat inelegantly written attack upon Athenian democracy shot through and through, nevertheless, with a shrewd cynicism and a good deal of political sophistication. It seems to have been written by an Athenian oligarch for like-minded men elsewhere and is an attempt to explain the strength of democratic Athens. However distasteful the government of Athens may be, runs the argument, there is no denying that it is in the interests of the Athenian lower classes and that it has their support. If it were not for the emotive language which colours the whole tract there would be no way of distinguishing this oligarchical tract from one in praise of Athenian democracy. 'First of all I want to say that it is right for the poor and the masses generally to have more than the noble and the rich, because it is the masses who man the ships and give the state its strength . . . Since this is so, it seems only fair for everyone to take his share of the magistracies, whether filled by lot or by election, and for any citizen who wishes to do so to be allowed to speak.'⁴ He does go on to admit that the Athenians usually elected their generals and hipparchs from among the upper classes, 'but', he quickly adds, 'those magistracies that have the advantage of carrying a salary or giving an opportunity for private profit are eagerly sought after by the people.'⁵ He makes an attempt to see things through the eyes of the ordinary Athenian citizen, the aim being to explain to his readers the essential nature of Athenian democracy.

> Someone might say that they should not have allowed everyone to speak on an equal footing and to sit on the council but only the ablest and best men. But even in this regard they have taken the best decision in allowing even the base to speak. For if the men of

worth alone spoke and deliberated it would be advantageous to those of their own ilk but disadvantageous to the populace. But as it is any base man who wishes can stand up and achieve something to the advantage of himself and to others like him. 'But what could such a man propose', someone might say, 'that would be advantageous to himself and the people?' The people themselves, however, know that this man's ignorance, baseness and goodwill are more useful to them than the merit, wisdom and hostility of the good man. Such institutions are hardly the basis for the best form of state, but in this way democracy would be most effectively preserved. For what the people want is not to be slaves in a well constituted state but to be free and to rule. A bad constitution matters little to them. For what you regard as a bad constitution is the very bastion of the people's strength and freedom.[6]

The Old Oligarch caps all his other exaggerations of the egalitarianism of Athenian democracy by maintaining that slaves, freedmen and metics were accorded equality with citizens.[7] This was very far from the truth. In fact, in the year 451/50 a Periclean law had limited citizenship to those whose parents were both Athenian citizens.[8] Naturalization of metics, or 'resident aliens', was rare in the extreme and it should also be remembered that, unlike the Roman system, freedmen in Athens ranked only as metics and not as citizens.

The Old Oligarch makes no secret of his own ideal constitution: 'If you are looking for a good constitution you will first notice the most able men making the laws in their own interest. Then the good will punish the base and take decisions about the state. They will not allow madmen on the council nor permit them to speak in public or participate in the assembly. As a result of these good measures the people would quickly sink into slavery.'[9] But it is precisely because his premises and principles are so totally at variance with those of the democrats that the Old Oligarch's portrait of democracy is so similar to theirs.

PERICLES' FUNERAL ORATION

This will immediately be apparent if we turn to what is probably the most famous speech of antiquity, Pericles' funeral oration as relayed by Thucydides:

> Our constitution is accorded the title of democracy, because it is governed not in the interest of the few but in that of the many. All

are on an equal footing before the law in regard to private disputes; and, as regards esteem, as each man is distinguished in any way, so is he preferred in public life, not because of his membership of a particular class but rather because of his merit; again, no man able to do something for the benefit of the state is debarred through poverty or obscurity of rank.[10]

The Old Oligarch's picture of Athens is, if anything, even more egalitarian than this, but this is an exaggerated portrayal of the truth even so, especially in regard to the purely meritocratic nature of Athenian government heedless of wealth or social position that is delineated for us here. As we have already seen, wealth and rank were not quite so irrelevant to political advancement as we are here urged to believe. But at least Pericles does not try to deny that there are differing degrees of human worth and merit – a serious qualification upon what would otherwise be a much more thoroughgoing egalitarian outlook.

Pericles' description of merit is studiously vague. We are not given any clue as to the sources of a man's merit, but the impression is created that merit is somehow independent of birth and wealth alike. This is a denial of the aristocratic principle, but one which was probably not shared by the rank and file of Pericles' fellow citizens. Their preference, for example, for members of his own family, the Alcmaeonid house, is itself a sign that even an anti-aristocratic form of government can co-exist with an aristocratic ethos.

In view of this we should hardly be surprised to find an aristocratic tone dominant in the writings of authors living at a time when aristocratic government was more in vogue. One particularly aristocratic writer was Theognis of Megara, the elegiac poet of the mid-sixth century.

Despite the tone which pervades his poetry, there is one line which has recently been pounced upon as an example of anti-aristocratic feeling:[11] 'All excellence is summed up in justice.'[12] This line is cited by Aristotle as an anonymous and apparently well-known proverb, but the scholiast writing on this passage informs us that it was by Theognis. He goes on to say that it was attributed by Aristotle's pupil and successor, Theophrastus, to Theognis' Milesian contemporary, Phocylides, but that in another of his works Theophrastus had assigned it to Theognis. In collections of Theognis' writings the proverb occurs as the third line of a quatrain reading as follows: 'Prefer to live piously

THE ARISTOCRATIC ETHOS   165

with little wealth rather than to be rich after acquiring wealth unjustly (*adikōs*). All excellence (*aretē*) is summed up in justice (*dikaiosunē*), and every man who is just (*dikaios*), Cyrnus, is good (*agathos*).'[13] The latter half of this passage has been acclaimed by a recent writer as an 'amazing couplet':

> Aristotle cites this couplet as a proverb. At the time of its composition, however, far from being a proverb, it was not even a proposition to which the majority of Greeks would give assent if it were put to them. This is no tame equation of *aretē* and *dikaiosunē*: in view of the connotation of *aretē*, the writer is saying something as startling as did the Stoics when, in a similarly disintegrating society, they claimed that the wise man was the only true king. The writer is not merely claiming that one may only be termed *agathos* if (whatever other conditions may be necessary in addition) one is *dikaios*, which, though far from Homeric, could be fitted into Homeric values. He is claiming that *anyone* who is *dikaios* is *agathos*; and this smashes the whole framework of Homeric values.[14]

The theory underlying this effusion is that there are essentially two sorts of virtues, 'competitive excellences' and 'co-operative excellences', the former including primarily the military qualities of valour, courage and skill and the success which attends them, the latter being the 'quieter' virtues of moderation, prudence and, above all, *dikaiosunē*, or justice. From Homeric times to the time of Plato and Aristotle, runs the theory, the Greeks esteemed the competitive excellences much more highly than the co-operative ones. Throughout this period, we are told, the terms *agathos* ('good') and *aretē* ('excellence') referred only to these competitive virtues, and it required the combined efforts of Plato, Aristotle and the Sophists to introduce the Greeks to the concept of moral responsibility. Only then, we are to believe, was the quality of justice equated with that of excellence.

No wonder the author of this theory proclaims that the quoted passage from Theognis 'smashes the whole framework of Homeric values.' But his attitude to the passage is somewhat ambiguous. After all, Theognis wrote in the mid-sixth century, yet, according to the theory, the Homeric 'competitive' attitude to life still had almost two centuries of life ahead of it. So, despite the fanfare, the Theognis passage has to be swept under the carpet: 'Aristotle calls this couplet a proverb. This might suggest that it sank into the popular consciousness;

but if it did so, it sank without a trace. It is only after much further thought that any change comes over the general sense of *agathos*. Ordinary usage in the fifth century before the period of the sophists is unaffected; and it seems likely that the couplet only appeared as a proverb to Aristotle as a result of the intensive moral speculation of the late fifth and fourth centuries.'[15]

This is special pleading at its worst. Not only does Aristotle quote the adage without any ado as a well-known saying, but it also appears in the works of two sixth-century poets. It is always possible that it was a late intrusion: the collection of poems which has come down to us under the name of Theognis certainly is something of a hotchpotch. But a closer examination of the adage will show that it was far from revolutionary even in the sixth century.[16]

First of all, what is meant by *dikaiosunē*, or 'justice'? The definition of it as 'the quiet co-operation of one citizen with another'[17] is not particularly helpful and may begin to indicate just how meaningless it is to speak of 'competitive' and 'co-operative' excellences. The question begged throughout is, co-operation with whom, and how? For there are different sorts of co-operation. The parlour-maid, for example, may be said to co-operate with the mistress of the household, but not quite in the same way as two equal partners in a business. And every member of a robber-band must co-operate with every other member of the same band, but this brotherly spirit is unlikely to extend beyond the group, and it may co-exist with a certain amount of competition within the group itself as well. This brings us to a passage in Theognis:

> May the great brazen heaven fall on me – that dread fear of earthborn men – if I do not help those who love me and be a vexation and great misery to my enemies.[18]

Is the doctrine enunciated here competitive or co-operative? The answer is that it is both: a co-operative spirit is considered proper in relation to one's friends and a competitive attitude in relation to one's foes. Though the word 'right' or 'just' does not appear in this passage, it is nevertheless quite clear that the doctrine of helping friends and harming enemies is regarded as right. Not only is this sort of behaviour recommended, but the direst of divine punishment is called down upon the head of anyone who does not follow it.

Similar moral attitudes are expressed elsewhere in Greek literature. We have already had occasion to mention the two seemingly contradictory anecdotes related by Plutarch in this connection about Themistocles.[19] Themistocles clearly maintains the traditional view that it is right for a man in authority to help his friends and harm his enemies – an attitude which would nowadays be stamped as intrinsically immoral, or at best amoral. He couples this attitude, however, with one which would be eminently acceptable today: the view that a man in authority should not favour his friends 'unjustly'.[20] Like Theognis, therefore, Themistocles was concerned both to favour his friends and to uphold law and justice.

How can we account for this double standard? Yet, is it a double standard? Recent writings on the subject would certainly regard it as such. Favouring one's friends at the expense of one's enemies is seen as part of the 'competitive' code of conduct, whereas concern for justice is regarded as the hallmark of the 'co-operative' outlook, which is not supposed to have come into fashion until the late fifth century. Fortunately for the believers in the competitive-co-operative schematization, the word *dikaiosunē*, as distinct from the related words *dikē* and *dikaios*, does not appear before the sixth century. In fact, it makes its first appearance in the passage of Theognis quoted above in which virtue is identified with justice. This enables the believers in the competitive-co-operative dichotomy to maintain that the invention of the term *dikaiosunē* is a sign of a new moral outlook on life – except that they cannot allow it to have been invented as early as the mid-sixth century. One of them blithely fathers the new word on Protagoras and tries his best to differentiate the concepts underlying *dikaiosunē* from those underlying *dikē* and *dikaios*.[21]

JUSTICE AND EQUALITY

Throughout the writings of these modern scholars there runs a tacit identification of *dikaiosunē* with a concept of justice which is essentially modern. Now, there is implicit in the modern concept of justice an element of equality. We talk about 'equality before the law' as a fundamental tenet of a just society, and any breach of this principle is loudly denounced. But, as we have already seen, the principle of equality held little attraction for the ancient Greeks. Surprising though it may seem to the modern mind, not even their concept of justice was egalitarian – a fact which seems generally to have escaped scholarly attention. But surely, it may be asked, is not justice without equality a contradiction in terms? What sort of justice can it be if some are treated better than others? The answer is that the underlying principle of Greek justice is not equality but fairness, which is a different thing altogether. Thus, for example, a less able golfer is allowed more free strokes than an abler one, which, though not equal treatment, is regarded as fair.

Only if it is appreciated that the concept of fairness need not include that of equality can one begin to understand Greek concepts of justice. For, though there is a variety of such concepts, none of them is essentially egalitarian.

The doctrine that it is right to help your friends and harm your enemies, which we have already encountered in Theognis and Themistocles, recurs among the arguments attacked by Socrates in Plato's *Republic*. The fact of its existence earlier on, as well as the amount of space devoted to it by Plato, shows that this doctrine was not merely an Aunt Sally set up by Plato in order to shoot down, but that it really was a current view. In any case, Plato was not given to tilting against windmills.

The doctrine recurs in the *Republic* in several slightly different forms, and what is particularly important to note is the fact that they occur in a discussion specifically dedicated to defining the meaning of the term *dikaiosunē*. The first character in the *Republic* to be asked the sense of this term, the rich old man Cephalus, unhesitatingly defines it as meaning 'to speak the truth and to make due return of whatever one may receive.'[22] This is rephrased by Polemarchus in a quotation attributed to none other than Themistocles' friend Simonides: 'It is just [*dikaion*] to render each his due.'[23] In clarification of his position Polemarchus eventually reformulates his view in the classic form, saying that *dikaiosunē* is 'to do good to one's friends and harm to one's enemies',[24] the same formula as we have already encountered in the sayings of Theognis and Themistocles and which is also to be found, for example, in the *Memorabilia* of Xenophon – where, interestingly enough, it is twice placed in the mouth of Socrates himself in the course of a convivial discussion on friendship.[25]

The doctrine is thoroughly aristocratic and closely connected with the aristocratic attitude to politics discussed in the last chapter. The aristocrat sees himself as part of a group of 'friends' to which he owes his first loyalty. This group may embrace the whole of the nobility or it might include the members of only one family or clan, and it may be narrower in certain circumstances than in others. Given this framework of reference, it is easy to see how morality and justice can be identified in the aristocratic mind with 'doing good to one's friends and harm to one's enemies'.

But there is another important side to the aristocratic outlook on life, and that is the belief in inequality. Since men are not all of equal worth, aristocratic belief maintains, one ought not to treat them equally. Fair treatment, i.e. justice, demands that the natural inequalities be respected.

It would be thought nowadays that the doctrine that one should 'help one's friends and harm one's enemies', far from being an acceptable definition of justice or righteousness, is an immoral principle, or at best amoral. But that is largely because the doctrine of fairness upon which it is based is different from the one which is currently fashionable.

Yet it is a doctrine whose existence spans the whole of antiquity from Homer to Justinian. When, for example, Telemachus, accompanied by Pallas Athene disguised as Mentor, visits Pylos, King Nestor's son Peisistratus offers a cup of wine first to the goddess (Mentor being older than Telemachus). This mark of respect impresses Athene and she 'rejoiced in the man's good sense and discernment' (literally, 'rejoiced in the sensible and just [*dikaios*] man'). This is precisely the same concept of justice as that attributed to Simonides by Polemarchus, 'to render each his due', and it is unabashedly inegalitarian.[26] The same concept reappears as the opening sentence of Justinian's *Institutes*, written more than twelve hundred years after Homer: 'Justice is a firm and eternal will allocating to each his own.'[27]

There are three fundamental errors in regard to the concept of justice to be found in the writings of the modern authors referred to above. First, there is the dating fallacy, the assumption that the concept of justice dates only from the late fifth century. Secondly, there is the mistaken belief that the absence of the word *dikaiosunē* indicates the absence of the concept of justice – yet, even when the word does appear it is too early to fit into these writers' preconceived theories. Finally, it is assumed that once the term *dikaiosunē* has been 'invented' its meaning remains unchanged, and that that meaning is 'justice' in the modern, egalitarian sense.[28]

However, Homer's concept of justice is exactly the same as that of Theognis, Themistocles, Simonides and Polemarchus, even though he never uses the word *dikaiosunē*. The adjective 'just', *dikaios*, is a standard Homeric criterion of civilized men as against barbarians, and 'justice', *eudikia*, is a laudable attribute in Homeric rulers.[29]

If we now return to Theognis we shall see that the sentiment that 'all excellence is summed up in justice' is in no way incompatible with the definition of justice as helping one's friends and harming one's enemies, a concept which, as we have seen, is also to be found in Theognis.[30]

The whole of this moral construction, it must constantly be borne in mind, rests upon the bed-rock of aristocracy, the concept of the primacy of birth, which we have also found in the writings of Theognis. But, for all its aura of antiquity, this concept was not without its problems. So long as men of noble birth monopolized all positions of power and distinction it was not difficult to believe that birth alone determined a man's courage, wisdom and moral worth. After all, was it not patently obvious that the well-born were pre-eminent in all species of activity and that men of inferior birth were also inferior in all other respects? But, with the growth of trade new opportunities opened up for the non-noble, and the resultant social mobility made the old equation of birth and worth seem less self-evident than before.

Such doubts did not become current overnight, and there were in any case a good many defences of the aristocratic position ready to hand. One such was Theognis' contention that the decline in political life in his day was the result of the debasement of noble stock through intermarriage. Another, which occurs in the poetry of that champion of aristocracy, Pindar, who wrote in the first half of the fifth century, is taken from agriculture: 'Even now does Alcimidas demonstrate for all to see the inborn merit of his stock, similar to corn-bearing fields, which, with alternating crops, now give men an ample livelihood and now take strength from rest.'[31] A fitting tribute to a noble family to which success in athletic exploits was vouchsafed only every second generation!

But such explanations were not sufficient to allay the increasing doubts about the primacy of birth as the determining factor in human merit. Above all, such explanations could hardly be expected to commend themselves to the philosophical intellect, and signs of scepticism begin to appear in the late fifth century.

EURIPIDES

A good example of this is to be found in Euripides' *Electra*, first produced probably in 413. The setting of Euripides' play is very different from that of his two predecessors, Aeschylus and Sophocles, both of whom wrote plays dealing with the same theme. In Aeschylus' *Oresteia* trilogy, first presented in 458, and in Sophocles' *Electra*, which is roughly contemporary in date with Euripides' play of the same name, Electra is unmarried and lives in the palace together with her mother Clytemnestra and Aegisthus. In Euripides not only is Electra married, but she is married to a humble peasant, outside whose modest abode the action of the play takes place. The introduction of the peasant, who, incidentally, is never named, gives Euripides an opportunity to attack the traditional concepts of aristocracy. Orestes' tribute to the peasant is an eloquent assault on aristocratic notions:

> Ah, there is no accurate test of manliness, for mortal men have confused natures. I have seen before now a worthless son of a noble father and good offspring of base parents; an impoverished spirit in a rich man and greatness of mind in a poor body. How then may one distinguish exactly between these and judge? By wealth? What a wretched standard to use. By a lack of wealth? Yet poverty is a disease and teaches man evil through want. Should I pass on to arms? Yet, who can face the enemy's spears and then testify who the brave one is? Rather leave these things to go their own way at random. For this man is not great among the Argives nor puffed up with the name of a great house; one of the multitude, yet he has been found to be a man of excellence. Do not be foolish, you who are deceived, filled as you are with vain notions; judge men by their behaviour and even the nobles by their characters.[32]

All the traditional criteria of human worth are here unceremoniously rejected: birth, courage, wealth and even poverty, whose great vogue as a criterion of excellence was still in the future. But what Euripides is *not* saying is that all men are equally good. The problem for him is one of criteria and measurement, and, though he suggests some criteria in the last lines quoted, he clearly regards the problem as insoluble, as we can see from the opening lines of the speech.

We should not underestimate the radicalism of the sentiments expressed in these lines. It would be wrong, for example, to follow a modern commentator on them who maintains that 'the general identification of nobility of birth and nobility of character is not here denied by Orestes. You cannot conceive of a "confusion" (*taragmos*) unless you conceive of an order which the confusion disturbs. *Gennaion* (noble) and *kakon* (base) are at once moral and social terms. All Orestes says is that the normal handing down of *gennaiotēs* and *kakia* from father to son is at times surprisingly interrupted.'[33] The whole of this interpretation seems to hinge on the word 'confusion'. Now, the concept of 'confusion' may indeed depend upon 'an order which the confusion disturbs', but that order may be a purely hypothetical or ideal construct. There is certainly no suggestion in the lines quoted above that the confusion is merely a temporary aberration from a norm.

But these lines may nevertheless give an exaggeratedly radical impression of Euripides' social values. It is worth noting, for example, that though Electra is married to the nameless peasant, the marriage has not been consummated: her husband has never 'shamed her bed; she is a virgin still', as he explains at the beginning of the play, the shame being that of his lowly social station: 'for I am ashamed to take the child of rich parents and outrage her, seeing that I am not her equal.'[34] Yet, as we have been told a few lines earlier on, the peasant is actually of noble birth, though impoverished. So close was the traditional bond between birth and wealth that either without the other was accounted a disgrace. It was presumably humiliation enough for Electra to be married to an impoverished peasant. The added indignity of his being of non-noble birth is evidently too much for even Euripides to contemplate. Euripides' attribution of a respectable pedigree to the peasant is reminiscent of Homer's treatment of the swineherd Eumaeus in the *Odyssey*, as was remarked upon in Chapter I.[35] In a sense the nameless peasant is the most heroic figure in Euripides' *Electra*, not a play very replete with heroism of any kind. But, despite Orestes' fulsome tribute to him, his reward at the end of the play is to be deprived of Electra, who is married off to a more suitable husband, Orestes' friend Pylades, and the peasant is given 'plentiful wealth' by way of compensation.[36] Not even Euripides can bring himself to allow a peasant to be his heroine's real husband.

Euripides' ambivalent attitude is a good reflection of the dilemma confronting his age. The traditional aristocratic canons were now unacceptable, but what was there to replace them? The result was a creeping negativism, not only in social and political values but also in moral and ethical matters generally, which is hardly surprising since, as we have seen, all values were traditionally shot through and through with aristocratic principles. It is this sort of scepticism that Aristophanes parodies in his *Frogs*: 'Who knows if life is death, if breath is supper or sleep a sheepskin?'[37] And the sort of amoral negativism that Aristophanes attacks in the *Clouds* is not dissimilar. (For those who maintain that the 'co-operative excellence' of justice was newly fashionable in the late fifth century, it is worth noting in passing that it is to the old traditional morality that Aristophanes gives the name *Dikaios Logos* or 'Just Logic', while the new-fangled clever-clever scepticism that he abhors is called *Adikos Logos* or 'Unjust Logic'.)

JUSTICE IN PLATO'S REPUBLIC

A very different form of assault upon this creeping paralysis of negativism came from another quarter, the philosophical teachings of Socrates, Plato and Aristotle. It is not proposed to enter here into the question of the recoverability of the teachings of the historical Socrates. The views expressed by the character of that name in Plato's Socratic dialogues will be attributed to Plato throughout.

In the political philosophy of Plato we have a double paradox. In the opening book of the *Republic* that arch-foe of democracy launches a concerted attack upon the basic tenets of the aristocratic position, and it is not until later on in the work that it becomes apparent that Plato's own position is equally thoroughly aristocratic. The *Republic* may be said to be an attempt to put aristocracy on a new moral footing.

The book opens, as we have seen, with a discussion of the nature of *dikaiosunē*, or 'justice'. First Cephalus and then his son Polemarchus define it as 'giving each his due', which, as we have seen, is a basic aristocratic tenet. Plato now brings to bear some of his less commendable techniques: schoolboy quibbles, cheap debating tricks, logic chopping and argument by false analogy. In this way he drives Polemarchus into rephrasing his definition in the formula that justice entails helping one's friends and harming one's enemies, which is just a special case of the original definition, for what could possibly be due to friends but mutual assistance and to enemies other than hostility? But, quibbles Plato, what is meant by the terms 'friend' and 'enemy'? Do we mean those we *think* are our friends or enemies, or those who really are? In either case, Polemarchus is in a tight logical corner, and Plato now manages to persuade him that it is wrong to harm anyone at any time. The argument he employs for this purpose is one of the more dubious in his repertoire:

> 'Is it really,' said I, 'fitting for a just man to harm any other person at all?' 'Of course it is,' said he. 'One ought to harm bad men who are one's enemies.' 'When horses are harmed do they become better

or worse?' 'Worse.' 'In regard to the excellence [*aretē*] of dogs, or that of horses?' 'In regard to that of horses.' 'And so, when dogs are harmed, do they become worse in regard to the excellence of dogs and not of horses?' 'Of course.' 'Should we not then speak in the same way of men, my friend, who when harmed become worse in regard to human excellence?' 'Yes, certainly.' 'But is not justice [*dikaiosunē*] the specifically human excellence [*aretē*]?' 'Of course.' 'So it necessarily follows, my friend, that those men who are harmed become more unjust.' 'So it would seem.' 'But, can musicians make people unmusical by means of music?' 'No.' 'And can riding masters make people unskilled in riding by means of horsemanship?' 'Not at all.' 'So, can the just make men unjust through the exercise of justice? Or, in short, can the good make people bad through virtue [*aretē*]?' 'It is impossible.' 'For it is not, I think, the function of heat, but of its opposite, to cool.' 'Indeed.' 'Nor of dryness, but of its opposite, to moisten.' 'Certainly.' 'Nor of the good, but of its opposite, to harm.' 'So it would appear.' 'But the just man is good?' 'Certainly.' 'It is not then the function of a good man to harm anyone, Polemarchus, whether a friend or anyone else, but that is the function of his opposite, the unjust man.' 'I think, Socrates,' said he, 'that what you say is absolutely true.' 'If, therefore, anyone says that it is just to give each man his due and understands by this that what is due to his enemies from the just man is harm and to his friends advantage, he is not a wise man to say so, for he would not be speaking the truth. For it has become clear to us that it is never just to harm anyone.'[38]

This argument purports to have dispatched the aristocratic concept of justice as giving each his due or as helping one's friends and harming one's enemies. As usual in Plato, Socrates' adversary is quickly reduced to a nodding puppet agreeing with every statement made by the great master, however far-fetched or repugnant to good sense it may be. For the sake of clarity it is worth extracting from the quoted passage the essential propositions put forward here by Plato:

1. Harming people makes them bad.
2. A good man cannot make people bad.
3. Therefore, a good man cannot harm people.
4. But, a good man is a just man.
5. A just man cannot make people unjust.
6. Therefore, a just man cannot harm people.

It will be noticed that what we have here are really two linked syllogisms. As a logical structure there is nothing wrong with them; i.e. the conclusions (propositions 3 and 6) follow logically from the premises. But how true are the premises? The first major premise (proposition 1) is dubious in the extreme. Not only is the animal analogy upon which it is based very strained, but even the initial idea that harming a horse or a dog makes it a 'worse' horse or dog than before is by no means self-evident. The first minor premise (proposition 2) is no more convincing. Here again the proposition depends upon an argument by analogy, this time the analogy between the good man and a music master or riding master. But there is a very important difference between the good man and these two supposed parallels and that is that being a music master or riding master is a vocation whose specific function is to teach a particular skill, whereas being a good man is not a vocation and carries with it no specific teaching functions. Plato's picture of the good man is indeed one of a philosophical teacher, but that picture is by no means necessarily implicit in the ordinary definition of the term 'good man'.

Plato's concept of the 'good man' (*agathos*) or of 'goodness', 'excellence' or 'virtue' (*aretē*) was certainly a departure from the traditional aristocratic concept. But the second minor premise of our double set of syllogisms (proposition 4) was not at all new or revolutionary, though it is often considered so by modern writers.[39] For some strange reason, though, such writers are always on the look-out for turning-points in methods of thinking and though they are pleased to recognize a shift in the concept of *aretē*, it never occurs to them that there could have been a matching shift in the meaning of *dikaiosunē*. Indeed, there would have had to be such a shift if the close association between the two concepts – which had always been linked in the Greek mind – was to be maintained. These modern writers deny that this association had always existed, and that is why they can allow the meaning of *aretē* to change radically at the end of the fifth century while that of *dikaiosunē* is considered to have remained unchanged. We have already demonstrated that even in the Homeric epics the attribute of justice is already regarded as highly commendable, and though Plato devotes quite a lot of space to discussing the relationship between *dikaiosunē* and *aretē* no character in any of his dialogues denies that justice is a virtue. The bone of contention in Plato is rather the question whether justice is one of several virtues or whether all virtue is essentially reducible to justice, and it is this latter contention that

Plato himself defends in such dialogues as the *Protagoras* and *Meno*. For the believer in the traditional aristocratic concept of justice, however, it would have made no difference whether all virtue was contained in justice or whether justice was merely one of several virtues – the others being courage, temperance, holiness and wisdom – because there would not have been any conflict in their minds between justice and the other virtues. But the point is that Plato invests 'justice' with a meaning very different from the traditional one – or so it would appear at first sight.

TWO PLATONIC PARADOXES

For here Plato springs his second surprise upon us. The first paradox was that this detractor of democracy should be expending so much time and energy in attacking the aristocratic concept of justice. But no sooner has he apparently trampled aristocratic doctrine underfoot than his argument takes a new turn.

By the end of the argument against Polemarchus it looks as though Plato is on the brink of launching into a defence of some sort of egalitarian view of justice, but nothing could be further from his mind. Instead, after defending justice against the amoral argument that injustice is more profitable than justice, he looks at the whole question from a new angle. Here he introduces the famous analogy between the individual and the state and proposes to discover the nature of justice in the individual through an investigation of its nature in the state. The resulting definition is worth scrutinizing:

> The universal requirement which we posited when we were establishing the foundations of our [ideal] state, it seems to me, or some form of it, is justice. We laid down, and often said, if you remember, that each person ought to engage in whatever service to the state for which his nature is best suited . . . And, as we have often heard people say and have said ourselves, 'justice means doing your own work and not interfering with others.'[40]

And again:

> 'It would then be agreed that justice is the possession of that which is properly one's own and the performance of duties appropriate to oneself.' 'That is so.' 'See now if you agree with me. A carpenter undertaking to perform the work of a cobbler or a cobbler that of a carpenter, the swopping of their tools or rewards, or even the same

man undertaking both jobs – do you think the general interchange of all such jobs would do any great harm to the state?' 'Not really,' said he. 'But, I imagine, if someone who is an artisan or some other kind of tradesman by nature, impelled by either wealth, popularity, physical strength or some other such advantage, tries to enter the ranks of the soldiery; or if one of the soldiers should aspire to be a councillor or Guardian without being worthy of it; and if these men exchange their tools and rewards with one another, or if the same man tries to perform all these functions simultaneously, then I think you will agree that this sort of exchange and meddlesomeness would be the ruin of the state.' 'Most assuredly.' 'Meddlesomeness and interchange one with another among the three orders might well be described as the source of the greatest possible harm and principle mischief to the state.' 'Quite so.' 'And would you not say that whatever causes the greatest mischief to one's own state is injustice?' 'Of course.' 'This, then, is injustice. Again, let us put it in this way: if each of the three orders of tradesmen, Auxiliaries and Guardians minds its own business and performs its own proper function in the state – the opposite of the situation just described – that would be justice and it would make the state just.'[41]

The state referred to here is not of course an actual historical one, but Plato's ideal state as described in the *Republic*, and the three classes mentioned make up the social structure of that state.

Plato's definition of justice in the state is anything but egalitarian. It can only be regarded as a highly aristocratic doctrine, which indeed can easily be accommodated in the formula that Plato had just expended so much energy in repudiating earlier in the same work, namely the definition of justice as 'giving each his due'. What better example of this traditional concept could one hope to find than a situation in which each man attended to his own proper task without presuming to arrogate to himself more than his allotted share of power or esteem, a situation in which each man knew his place in society and kept to it, according his superiors due respect and deference? Yet we find that this is also Plato's picture of justice. But, if Plato's concept of justice was so similar to the traditional aristocratic definition of it, why then was he so hostile to it at the beginning of the *Republic*?

The answer is that there is a certain difference between Plato's ideas on the subject and the traditional doctrines, even though both are of an aristocratic nature. The traditional doctrines had never been fully argued out, and they, therefore, rested on no very solid philosophical foundations. They were taken as axioms whose truth was self-evident. And it *was* self-evident, as was pointed out earlier, so long as nobles had a monopoly of power and prestige. By the late fifth century, however, the sort of sceptical negativism that we have already discerned in Euripides had become fashionable, and in a sense Plato's teachings are a counterblast to it, and an attempt to reassert the traditional values and establish them upon a firm basis of rationality. But, in order to do this, it was necessary to set aside all preconceptions and to start the discussion from scratch. It would not be untrue to say, therefore, that Plato attacked traditional concepts in order to save them. Not that he consciously and deliberately set about this task in this way. That is what he was doing in effect, whether he was aware of it or not.

It might be useful to sketch out the relevant basic steps in Plato's argument. Nowhere does he formulate it in this way, but the propositions enumerated here are distilled from the *Protagoras, Meno* and *Republic*:

1   Virtue (*aretē*) is justice (*dikaiosunē*).
2a Justice entails consideration of the interests of all.
2b Being just is as beneficial to oneself as to others.
3   Therefore, no one acts unjustly voluntarily.
4   Therefore, people act unjustly only through ignorance.
5   Therefore, justice can be taught.
6   Therefore, justice is knowledge.
7   Therefore, virtue is knowledge.
8   Therefore, the salvation of a state depends upon its educational system.

What we have here is essentially an overgrown syllogism, the first two propositions (counting 2a and 2b as a single proposition) being the premises and all the rest being conclusions which follow logically from them. The major premise (proposition 1), as we have already seen, was in itself neither new nor revolutionary. But in conjunction with the minor premise (2a and 2b) it undergoes a radical shift in meaning. We encountered proposition 2a as Plato's answer to the traditional doctrine that justice entailed helping one's friends and harming one's enemies. This forces his adversaries to resort to the argument that, if the doctrine of helping one's friends and harming one's enemies was to be regarded not as justice but rather as injustice, then injustice was preferable to justice. It is to counter this that Plato puts forward proposition 2b, which is really just a single facet of the more general proposition, 2a. So far Plato's argument is essentially at variance with the traditional aristocratic viewpoint. He looks poised to launch into a defence of some sort of moralistic egalitarianism, but, as we have seen, he does nothing of the kind. Yet it is now possible to begin to understand why Plato needed to turn the tables on the traditional aristocratic doctrine. The answer lies particularly in propositions 3 and 7, which are two of the most central of all Plato's teachings. Upon these two doctrines, it would not be an exaggeration to say, hangs the whole structure of Plato's ideal state with its highly stratified society. Yet these two doctrines themselves depend upon propositions 2a and 2b, which appear to be of an egalitarian character. How can we explain this paradox? The answer is that it is not a paradox at all, because propositions 2a and 2b are not in fact egalitarian. Justice may indeed be regarded by Plato as entailing consideration for the interests of all, but that by no means implies equal consideration for all. The faculty of justice, moreover, is one which in Plato's opinion is fully developed only in the philosopher, which is why he believes that only when philosophers become kings or kings philosophers will a perfect system of government come into being.

From all this it should now be clear that the idea canvassed in some modern writings that Plato was responsible for a shift from 'competitive' to 'co-operative' values is meaningless nonsense. Plato's system – whether we call it 'competitive' or 'co-operative' is irrelevant – is as aristocratic as the traditional one. He does not even jettison belief in heredity as the means of perpetuating his aristocracy beyond the first generation, though he does add a qualification. Here by way of illustration is his account of the foundation myth which is to be taught to all citizens of his ideal state:

> Though all of you in the state are brothers, we shall say in our myth, the gods who created you mixed gold into the composition of those fitted to be rulers, and therefore they are the most esteemed, but into the Auxiliaries they put silver and into the farmers and artisans iron and brass. Now, though you will generally beget children of your own type, it is possible, since you are all related, that silver offspring may sometimes be born to golden parents or golden offspring to silver parents, and so on. The gods' principle and most emphatic injunction to the Rulers is therefore that of nothing are they to be such keen observers and watch so scrupulously as the mixture of

metals in the souls of children, and if their offspring is born with an
element of bronze or iron they are not in any way to treat them with
pity but to assign them to the rank appropriate to their nature, and
cast them among artisans and farmers. And again, if a child with an
element of gold or silver is born among these latter classes, they will
honour such children and raise some to be Guardians and others to
be Auxiliaries, on the grounds that an oracle predicted that the state
would be ruined when a man of iron or bronze became a Guardian.[42]

The possibility of the metals not breeding true to type is accepted,
but only as an aberration from the norm. Plato's system is therefore an
aristocracy in the most literal sense: rule by the 'best' men, defined
according to Plato's own criteria of excellence. Plato's ideal state is in
a way an attempt to return to an earlier ideal society in which, as in
the Homeric epics, the aristocracy held sway because they obviously
were the best men. The aristocracy of Plato's own day patently did not
have a monopoly of virtue. So their claim to supremacy had first to be
repudiated in order to establish a new order of aristocracy. 'Aristocracy
is dead, long live aristocracy!' might well be suggested as a somewhat
flippant summary of Plato's political thought.

ARISTOTLE ON 'GOOD BIRTH'

Plato's great pupil, Aristotle, was of a much more practical and down-
to-earth cast of mind. Concerned with analysis of the actual rather
than with construction of the ideal, he approached the main problem
of aristocracy from a somewhat different angle. Aristotle's definition
of goodness, like Plato's, is a moral one, but it does not exclude
heredity. The fullest statement of it is to be found in a fragment of his
separate treatise 'On Good Birth' preserved in an anthology. The
question discussed in the passage is 'What is good birth?'

> A man's own goodness is nearer to him that that of a grandfather, so
> that it would be the good man who is well-born. Some [writers]
> have indeed said this, fancying that they refute the claims of noble
> birth by means of this argument. As Euripides says, good birth is not
> an attribute of those whose ancestors were good long ago but of
> whoever is simply good in himself. But that is not so. Those who
> give pre-eminence to ancient goodness make the correct analysis.
> The reason for this is that good birth is excellence of stock, and

excellence is to be found in good men. And a good stock is one which has produced many good men. Such a thing occurs when the stock has had a good origin, for an origin has the power to produce many offspring like itself. It is the very function of an origin to create many other entities like itself. So, when such a one is produced in the stock and is so good that many generations inherit its excellence, it is inevitable that that stock be good. There will be many good men if the stock is human, or horses if it is equine, and similarly too in the case of the other animals. So it is reasonable to conclude that it is not the rich or the good who are well-born but those descended from ancestors who have long been rich or good.[43]

Being descended from good stock the aristocrat is, therefore, himself good. This naturalistic argument is Aristotle's way of reconciling the traditional aristocratic outlook with the more fashionable view that each individual should be judged on his own merits – a view which, as we have seen, even an iconoclast like Euripides could not altogether bring himself to accept.

The very fact that the concept of aristocracy needed to be defended at all shows that it was under attack. But the attack was launched from a totally negative standpoint and the Greeks never produced a rival theory. The idea that the Greeks were believers in equality must be buried forever.

CONCLUSION

It is now fashionable to condemn oligarchy, or 'minority government', as roundly as dictatorship. As a result, not only is no government particularly anxious to claim the appellation 'oligarchy' for itself, but, more important, oligarchy and dictatorship have tended to become fused in the concept of 'authoritarian', 'autocratic' or 'totalitarian' rule. Both oligarchy and dictatorship are commonly seen to be opposed to 'democracy', which, however defined, is generally considered the only desirable form of government.

It is hardly surprising that this outlook should be reflected in historical studies, and especially in the study of Greek history. Democracy, after all, is the form of government most closely associated with ancient Greece in the popular mind. Any other form of government in Greek history is seen either as a preparation for democracy or else as a lapse or deviation from it. Democracy is seen as the culmination or even the fulfilment of Greek history.

The picture of Greek history drawn in this book is rather different from that. The real dichotomy, it is argued, was between aristocracy and what I have termed 'popular government', which includes both tyranny (or popular dictatorship) and democracy. Aristocracies, whether of the narrow variety as exemplified by Bacchiad Corinth, the more broad-based type as represented by Eupatrid Athens or the racial kind as typified by the specimen from Sparta, all share certain basic characteristics in common (and also have close affinities with the wealth-based oligarchies which generally succeeded the overthrow of tyranny). In all these cases power was vested in a social group which was essentially closed to outsiders and close-knit with a high degree of internal cohesiveness and a common identity. Power tended to be widely distributed within the aristocracy, among the members of which an egalitarian spirit tended to prevail. In addition to purely political power the aristocracy held economic supremacy, mainly through the possession of land, and was also socially pre-eminent. In

CONCLUSION

short, they tended to be politically introspective and introverted, and governed in their own corporate interest. But that is not to say that their subjects always resented their rule, either actively or even passively, especially where, as was often the case, the belief had been inculcated from time immemorial that the aristocracy were superior beings endowed with qualities which set them off from lesser mortals.

Aristocracies are already the order of the day when the mists of the so-called Dark Age begin to lift in the eighth century. In a good number of the more rural states aristocracy persisted into Hellenistic times and beyond, but in nearly all the leading commercial states revolution struck at some time between the mid-seventh and mid-sixth centuries. The revolutions were largely the product of the impoverishment and consequent disaffection of the lowest classes in society, who found a champion in an ambitious and dissident noble, who duly became tyrant. But this form of popular dictatorship did not generally survive for more than two or three generations, if that, and was overthrown by a counter-revolution of its victims, the rich and noble, with or without the help of foreign troops.

In Athens, however, the counter-revolution was unsuccessful. Spartan troops toppled the tyrant and tried to impose an aristocratic government. But, recognizing the popularity of the ousted regime, Cleisthenes, himself an ambitious noble, took up the cudgels against the aristocracy. His reforms institutionalized the anti-aristocratic tendencies of Athenian politics and are often considered to mark the advent of democracy. The reforms of the fifth century further accentuated the anti-aristocratic character of Athenian government.

There certainly are differences between tyranny and democracy, but, as was suggested in the body of the work, they are differences of degree rather than of kind. It may be argued that a tyrant could be removed from power only by force, whereas a democratic leader like Pericles or Cleon could be legally deprived of office. That is true, and Pericles was indeed separated from his generalship for a short time. But that is not the point. The point is that a tyrant like Peisistratus was genuinely popular and, moreover, could not have hoped to maintain his position otherwise. This was well understood by another popular dictator, Agathocles, the third-century Syracusan tyrant, who ordered his reluctant troops to heed the wishes of the common people. Agathocles realized that having an army at his back was no substitute for popular support. If Pericles depended for his position upon popular support, so did Peisistratus.

But, it may then be urged, surely the power enjoyed by the citizenry was far greater under a democracy than under a tyranny? In fact, however, the introduction of sortition combined with rotation in the selection of the holders of most offices in fifth-century Athens only diminished their importance while enhancing that of the most important elective magistracy, the generalship. In any case, it is unrealistic to talk about the division of power in this way. The relationship between a popular leader and his supporters is symbiotic, be he a Peisistratus or a Pericles. His popularity is so intricately bound up with his policies and his general political outlook that it would be impossible to say which has led to which. Indeed, it would be folly to try. The tyrant may formulate policy, but it has got to be acceptable to his supporters, the masses. A popular leader must lead and follow at the same time. This view of the reciprocity and interdependence between the tyrant and the masses is often resisted, and the recent history of Europe has made its acceptance more difficult than ever. It is so much more convenient to regard the dictator as an absolute ruler who alone is to blame for any decision taken during his reign. Modern dictators are often portrayed as demoniacal maniacs and confidence tricksters who somehow mesmerized and hoodwinked millions of people into following them. After all, the more blameworthy the dictator the less blame there is attaching to their supporters.

As aristocratic government favoured the interests of the aristocracy, so popular government, including both tyranny and democracy, favoured those of the masses, i.e. the small farmers and artisans. What we are talking about here is not only two different types of government but two different types of politics, which can be discerned whether their adherents are in power or out and which leave their imprint not only upon domestic affairs but also on foreign policy. Aristocratic government is by definition rule in the interest of a minority. There may or may not be resentment against that rule on the part of the subjected majority, but there is always the possibility that such resentment might arise. We ought not, therefore, to be surprised if we find that aristocracies have a cautious attitude to foreign affairs. For foreign war may easily prove a disruptive force internally. Sparta's reluctance to go to war can be well understood simply by looking at the well-known statistics of the battle of Plataea, at which there were seven helots for every Spartiate. The helots could not all be left at home when the Spartiates went on campaign: that would be an open invitation to revolt. But a long campaign would have proved economically quite

CONCLUSION

ruinous, since 35,000 helots had been withdrawn from agriculture.

As caution in foreign policy was evidently the result of a feeling of insecurity, so a feeling of security seems to have encouraged a more ambitious foreign policy. This is well demonstrated by Spartan foreign policy immediately after the Persian and Peloponnesian Wars. Feeling invincible she was emboldened to embark upon a more aggressive foreign policy than usual, though it would be true to say that on both occasions this new and short-lived spirit of adventure is traceable more to the ambition of individual Spartan leaders – notably the regent Pausanias in the earlier period and Lysander in the later – rather than to that of the state as a whole.

Popular government, on the other hand, was generally prone to an active and aggressive foreign policy. Tyranny marked the high watermark of the power of such states as Samos, Megara and Corinth. It was under her tyrants that Athens first became prominent and her power reached its culmination under Pericles.

Aristocratic power was regionally based, resting as it did upon the social, economic and religious predominance of individual families and clans. Popular government, on the other hand, intent upon smashing the aristocratic power base, tended to encourage national unity and patriotism, and the active foreign policy which it generally pursued was an expression of this spirit. When viewed in this light it can hardly be seen as coincidental that it was under a popular government that Athens grew into an empire.

Psychologically too there was a fundamental distinction between aristocratic and popular government. Pride in belonging to a group is a universal human characteristic and an aristocracy can easily satisfy such feelings merely by being an aristocracy. Greek nobles did not need to be persuaded of their own innate superiority, which indeed was implicitly recognized even by people who repudiated the concept of aristocratic government. But from what corporate spirit could an ordinary citizen draw pride? The persistence of aristocratic social values prevented him from anticipating the modern inverted snobbery of class consciousness. In any case he would not have had any concept of class except in the negative sense that he was not a noble. There was no one he could look down upon in his own state – except slaves, who hardly counted as human at all. So his feeling of superiority had to be developed in relation to alien subject peoples. No wonder, then, that what began as national pride should have grown beyond patriotism into nationalism and imperialism.

Underlying this basic dichotomy, however, was a single current of political thought – an aristocratic current. From Homer to Alexander and beyond birth was the principle criterion of worth among the Greeks. In more senses than one, this attitude to politics ran in their blood.

NOTES
BIBLIOGRAPHY
INDEX

NOTES

ABBREVIATIONS

The works of the ancient authors are abbreviated in the notes according to conventional usage. Secondary sources are sometimes referred to in the notes by a shortened title or, after several citations of the same work, by the name of the author alone. The following abbreviations refer to the most frequently cited journals, collections of inscriptions and the like.

AJP	American Journal of Philology.
Ant. Class.	L'Antiquité classique.
ASI	Ancient Society and Institutions: Studies Presented to Victor Ehrenberg on his 75th birthday, ed. E. Badian (Oxford, 1966). Individual articles do not appear in the bibliography.
BCH	Bulletin de Correspondance Hellénique.
BICS	Bulletin of the Institute of Classical Studies (London).
CAH	Cambridge Ancient History.
CIG	Corpus Inscriptionum Graecarum.
CPh	Classical Philology.
CQ	Classical Quarterly.
CR	Classical Review.
Et. Mag.	Etymologicum Magnum, ed. T. Gaisford (Oxford, 1848).
FGrH	F. Jacoby, Fragmente der griechischen Historiker (1923 ff.).
FHG	C. Müller, Fragmenta Historicorum Graecorum (1841–70).
HSCP	Harvard Studies in Classical Philology.
IG	Inscriptiones Graecae.
JHS	Journal of Hellenic Studies.
Meiggs-Lewis	A Selection of Greek Historical Inscriptions, ed. R. Meiggs & D. Lewis (Oxford, 1969).
PA	J. Kirchner, Prosopographia Attica, 2 vols (1901–3).
POxy	Oxyrhynchus Papyri, eds. B. P. Grenfell & A. S. Hunt (1898 ff.).
P-W	A. Pauly, G. Wissowa & W. Kroll, Real-Encyclopädie der klassischen Altertumswissenschaft (1893 ff.).
SEG	Supplementum Epigraphicum Graecum.
SIG	W. Dittenberger, Sylloge Inscriptionum Graecarum, 3rd edn (1915–24).
TAPA	Transactions of the American Philological Association.
Tod, GHI	A Selection of Greek Historical Inscriptions, ed. M. N. Tod (Oxford, 1933).

CHAPTER I

1 *Od.* IV, 60-64.
2 *Od.* IV, 611-12.
3 *Od.* VI, 187; *Od.* XX, 227.
4 Cf. Calhoun, *CPh* 29 (1934), 203.
5 *Od.* XXIII, 64-66. Cf. XXII, 414.
6 *Od.* XXIII, 121.
7 *Od.* XXIV, 251-55.
8 *Il.* II, 216-19. The context makes it very plain that Thersites was a commoner.
9 Eumaeus: *Od.* XV, 403 ff. There also are some words in Homer which seem to be used only in a moral sense, e.g. δειλός (cowardly); ἐλεγχείη (ignominy, shame); ἀναιδής (shameless). But this does not affect the argument. The main proponent of the idea that Homeric society had no aristocracy is Calhoun, *CPh* 29 (1934), 192-208 and 301-16, and also in Wace & Stubbings' *Companion to Homer*, 434 ff. (with a hostile editorial footnote on page 438!).
10 *Il.* II, 198-202.
11 *Od.* XXI, 314-17.
12 *Od.* XXI, 321-28.
13 *Od.* VIII, 159 ff.
14 *Od.* I, 386-87 and 392-98.
15 *Od.* XXIV, 114 ff.
16 *Od.* XVI, 247 ff.
17 Odysseus: *Od.* XXII, 421. Alcinous: *Od.* VII, 103.
18 *Od.* VIII, 390-95; XIII, 13-15.
19 *Od.* VI, 293 ff.
20 *Il.* XX, 179 ff. Homer treats the Trojans in exactly the same way as he does the Greeks. So far as the poems are concerned, in culture, religion and social organization they were Greeks. And perhaps they really were. The 52-foot deep mound of Hissarlik in what is now northwestern Turkey, which was first excavated by Heinrich Schliemann about a century ago, turned out to have eight different stratified layers, the seventh of which (counting from the bottom) is thought to have been Homer's Troy, Troy VIIa as it is known to the archaeologists. It is a continuation of the civilization of Troy VI, the foundation of which marks the introduction to the area of the horse and of Grey Minyan Ware pottery – at about the same time, *c.* 1800 BC, as these two distinctive features made their debut in Greece itself on the opposite shore of the Aegean. If the Trojans were not Greeks, then they were at least descended from common stock.
21 Mycenae: *Il.* VII, 180; XL, 46; *Od.* III, 304. Troy: *Il.* V, 551; VI, 576. Trojans: *Il.* IV, 509; XII, 440; VII, 361; VIII, 110; VIII, 525; VIII, 516; XIX, 318; XX, 180; IV, 352; XIX, 237; X, 424; XVII, 418.
22 *Il.* I, 158-60.
23 *Od.* XXIV, 118.
24 *Il.* II, 108.
25 *Il.* II, 569 ff.
26 Argos: In catalogue: *Il.* II, 559. Odysseus' fame: *Od.* I, 344; IV, 726, 816.
27 E.g. *Il.* II, 115; IX, 22.
28 It is often thought that the statement that Agamemnon was master of 'many islands and the whole of Argos' is at variance with the description of his kingdom in the catalogue, e.g. Page, *Homeric Iliad*, 127 ff. But if the explanation I offer in the text is accepted there is no clash. The site of the seven cities (*Il.* IX, 149 ff.) is not known for certain. Since they obviously cannot be forced into Agamemnon's own kingdom, however hard one tries, some scholars (e.g. Leaf in his commentary on the *Iliad*) have claimed them for Menelaus' kingdom of Lacedaemon (Sparta), since he was at least Agamemnon's brother. But even that will not do, in view of Agamemnon's own description of them as

being in Pylos (*Il.* IX, 152). Thryoessa: *Il.* XI, 711.
29 *Il.* IX, 156.
30 Crethon and Orsilochus: *Il.* V, 541.
31 *Il.* II, 102.
32 *Il.* II, 185 ff.
33 *Il.* II, 204–6.
34 *Il.* IX, 391–92.
35 *Il.* IX, 96 ff.
36 *Il.* X, 196.
37 *Il.* II, 404 ff.
38 *Il.* IX, 484 ff.
39 Echepolus: *Il.* XXIII, 296. Euchenor: *Il.* XIII, 669.
40 A variant of this view maintains that there are three strata: (i) A very few vestiges of *Realien* of genuine Mycenaean vintage, notably the boar's tusk helmet. (ii) Early Dark Age material, which Homer takes to be Mycenaean and which makes up the bulk of the epics. (iii) Elements contemporary with Homer himself, to be found particularly in similes. See G. S. Kirk, *Proc. Camb. Philol. Soc.* (1961), 34–48. Therefore, instead of dating the traditional elements in Homer to Mycenaean times, this interpretation places them early on in the post-Mycenaean period. If this view is right, it does not affect my argument, which maintains first, the similarity between Homeric society and that of the Mycenaean tablets, and secondly, the continuity between Mycenaean times and Homer's own age.
41 Finley, *Odysseus*, 167, and *idem*, *Historia* 6 (1957), 139.
42 Ventris & Chadwick, *Documents*, 141 ff. especially 146 ff. Crete: ibid., Tablet No. 83. Pylos: ibid., Nos 57–60, 75, 198, 199, 250, 257.
43 *Il.* II, 559 ff.
44 See the eminently reasonable discussion in R. Hope Simpson & J. F. Lazenby, *The Catalogue of Ships in Homer's Iliad* (1970), 153 ff. Sparta was a regional state in classical times and so, in a sense, was Athens, but neither was typical.
45 Ventris & Chadwick, op. cit., 411.
46 Ibid., document No. 152 = Er 01 (312).
47 *Od.* XI, 185. Finley, *Historia* 6 (1957), 148 ff.
48 Finley, ibid.
49 *Il.* XX, 182 ff.
50 *Il.* IX, 578.
51 See for example, *Il.* XX, 248–50.
52 *Od.* VI, 293.
53 See Ventris & Chadwick, op. cit., 236 ff.
54 *Il.* II, 494, 512, 517, 563, 620, 651, 678, 732.
55 Diomedes and Sthenelus: *Il.* II, 563.
56 Pakija: Ventris & Chadwick, op. cit., No. 114 – En 02 (609); Aptara: ibid., No. 47 = Am. 826 (K lix).
57 See Ventris & Chadwick, op. cit., 232 ff.
58 Ibid., Nos 115 ff.
59 Ibid., Nos 131 ff.
60 Ibid., No. 148 – Ep 04 (617).
61 See *Il.* I, 147.
62 Ventris & Chadwick, op. cit., Nos 56–60.
63 L. R. Palmer, *Trans. Philol. Soc.* (1954), 51.
64 Ventris & Chadwick, op. cit., 121.
65 Ibid., No. 214 = Ld 571 (G xlii).
66 Heq^{u}etas attached to a 'platoon' of ten men: ibid., No. 59 = An. 656, lines 15–16.
67 See the discussion on these officials in Ventris & Chadwick, op. cit., 122. *Moropa*: Ventris & Chadwick, Nos 43, 58, 258 = Palmer, *Mycenaean Greek Texts*, No. 177. *Korete* and *parokorete*: Ventris & Chadwick, No. 257 = Palmer, No. 173. *Damokoro*: Ventris & Chadwick, No. 235; but cf. Palmer, 412, *s.v.*
68 Ventris & Chadwick, op. cit., No. 38 – As. 1516.

69 Ibid.
70 Ibid., No. 40 = An. 22 (261). The name of the man thought to be a *pasireu* reappears in Jn 03 (Pylos).
71 Ventris & Chadwick, op. cit., No. 258 = Kn. 01 (Jo 438). See Palmer, *Mycenaeans and Minoans*, 100 f.
72 Ventris & Chadwick, op. cit., 121, 359.
73 Cf. Hope Simpson & Lazenby, op. cit., 2; G. S. Kirk, *Songs of Homer* (1962), 183–88.
74 Ceos: see Taylour, *The Mycenaeans*, 69. For the view that Homer is anachronistic in this regard see Carpenter, *Homeric Epics*, 27 f.
75 Prosymna: H. L. Lorimer, *Homer and the Monuments* (1950), 104. Pylos: *To Ergon tēs Archaiologikēs Hetaireias* (1957), 89 ff.; Perati: Myres & Gray, *Homer*, 270; Rhodes, Naxos and Crete: Vermeule, *Greece*, 301–5; Perati: Desborough, *The last Mycenaeans*, 115, 228; Rhodes and Cos: ibid., 157.
76 See Lorimer, op. cit., 107.
77 For the standard view see, for example, Kirk, op. cit., 183 f. See now Hope Simpson & Lazenby, op. cit., 3 f. Mycenaean throwing-spears: Snodgrass, *Early Greek Weapons*, 160.
78 See, for example, Kirk, op. cit., 124.
79 See further, Hope Simpson & Lazenby, op. cit., 4 f.
80 One such proponent is Finley both in his *Odysseus* and in *Historia* 6 (1957), 133–59.
81 See Ventris & Chadwick, op. cit., 109 f.
82 Finley, *Historia* 6 (1957), 134 f. on *Od*. XIV, 96 ff.
83 *Od*. IV, 71 ff.
84 Finley, art. cit., 133 and 136.
85 See Carpenter, *Greek Civilization*, 39 ff.
86 Desborough, *The Last Mycenaeans*, 224. See also Snodgrass, *Dark Age*, 311.
87 Desborough, loc. cit.
88 Ibid., 228.
89 Thuc. I, 12.

CHAPTER II

1 Starr, *Historia* 10 (1961), 129.
2 See my book on the subject, entitled: *The Senatorial Aristocracy in the Later Roman Empire* (1972).
3 Catalogue of Ships: *Il*. II, 496 ff.; Ithaca: II, 632 ff.; Salamis: II, 557 ff.; Diomedes: II, 559 ff.; Agamemnon: II, 569 ff.; Sparta: II, 581 ff.
4 Arist. *Pol*. 1311b, 27 ff. (V.8.13). See also Paus. III, 2.1; Strabo 582; Sappho fr. 203 (Lobel-Page), *ap*. Athen. X, 425 a; Alcaeus fr. G.2.
5 Alcaeus fr. E.1.23–4; Z.121, cf. Sappho fr. 213.
6 D. L. Page, *Sappho and Alcaeus* (1955), 174 f., cf. Strabo, XIII, 617.
7 Strabo XIV, 633; Hdt. IX, 97.
8 Arist. fr. 556 (Rose 1886); Nic. Damasc. *FHG*, III, 388 = Jac. *FGrH*, 90F, 52–3.
9 Glaucus: *Il*. VI, 119, 215 ff.
10 Caucones are distinguished from Pylians by Homer, *Od*. III, 357 ff.
11 Strabo XIV, 633; Hdt. V, 65.3; Hellanicus fr. 10, *FHG*, I, 47 – *FGhH*, 4 F, 125; Paus. II, 18.9. Modern scholars often reject the Athenian connection, e.g. Busolt, *Griech. Geschichte* I (1885), 214 f. = 2nd edn I, 287, n. 3; Töpffer, *Attische Genealogie*, 225 ff. But it fits in very well with what we now know from archaeological sources about the shift in population from the Peloponnese to Attica.
Sources: Paus. IV, 2.5, II, 18.7, VII, 2.1; *Od*. XI, 286; Strabo 633. See Töpffer, *Attische Genealogie*, 320.
12 Strabo 633.
13 Arist. *Pol*. 130 5b, 18–19; Hdt. VIII, 132. See also the 3rd-century

NOTES 193

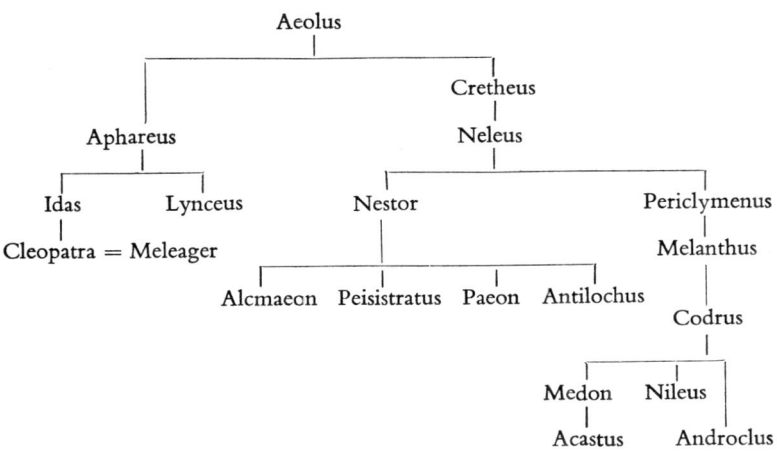

Genealogical Table

Chian inscription *BCH* III, 244.
14 Thuc. II, 80.5.
15 Ibid.
16 See Bickerman, *Chronology*; Clinton, *Fasti Hellenici*, Vol. I, 129, note m; Dunbabin, *JHS* 68 (1948), 59–69, esp. 62; Will, *Korinthiaka*, 259 ff.
17 Paus. II, 4.4..
18 Diod. VII, fr. 9, *apud* Georgius Syncellus, 336–38. Cf. Eus.-Hieron. *Chron.* s.a. 1235; Strabo VIII, 378 (VI.21); Nic. Damasc. fr. 58, *FHG* = *FGrH* 90 F 57.
19 Hdt. V, 92.
20 On Cypselus' date see Busolt, *Griech. Geschichte* I, 446 (first edn) = I, 638 (2nd edn). 119 years: Eus.-Hieron. s.aa. 1240, 1359. 90 years: Diod. VII, fr. 9; Eus. *Chron.* I, 221 (ed. Schöne).
21 See Will, op. cit., 299 f. On Cypselus see p. 121–3.
22 For a discussion of the chronology see Will, op. cit., 259 ff.
23 Neleids in Athens: Paus. II, 18.7;

VII, 2.1.
24 Eus. *Canon*, 298–305; Eus. *Chron.* I, 134.
25 Thuc. II, 15.
26 *Il.* II, 546–58; *Od.* III, 278.
27 Arist. *AP*, 57.4.
28 Arist. *AP*, 3.1.
29 Hignett, *Athenian Constitution*, 41; Jacoby, *Atthis*, 172, 348. See Hignett's critique of the theory expounded by Jacoby, op. cit., 44.
30 Paus. IV, 5.10. See also Paus. IV, 13.7; Justin II, 7.1; Vell. I, 2.1.
31 Paus. I, 3.1. Cf. J. G. Frazer ad Paus. IV, 5.10; Arist. *AP* 3.1 and note ad loc. by Sandys.
32 Paus. I, 3.3. Cf. Frazer ad loc. Cf. Vell. I, 2.1. Eus. *Chron.* I, 189–90; Justin 2.7. Parian Marble: *IG* XII, v. 444, lines 46 ff. = *CIG* II, 2374.
33 Justin 2.7.1; Vell. I, 2.1.
34 Plato, *Menexenus* 238D.
35 See Eus.-Hieron. *Chron.* s.a. 950 (from birth of Abraham) = 1068/7 B C.
36 Arist. *AP*, 3.3.

37 Ibid.
38 Eus.-Hieron. *Chron. s.a.* 950 = 1068/7 BC; Justin 2.7.1; Vell. I, 2.1.
39 Paus. VII, 25.1.
40 Arist. *AP*, fr. 7 (Loeb); cf. Paus. IV, 5.10.
41 It is of no consequence for my present purpose to ascertain whether the polemarchy was introduced before the archonship, as Aristotle believed (*AP* 3.3), or vice versa, as modern scholars tend to argue (e.g. Hignett, op. cit., 42).
42 Eus.-Hieron. *Chron. s.a.* 1264 = 752 BC, 1333 = 683 BC (the last year of the last ten-year archon); Africanus *apud* Syncellum, *apud* Clinton, *Fasti Hellenici, s.a.* 683.
43 Cf. Whibley, *Greek Oligarchies*, 121, where it is assumed that the Medontids were in a similar position in Athens to that occupied by the Bacchiads in Corinth and the other royal clans discussed above.
44 On the antiquity of the Medontids see Hignett, op. cit., 41. Cf. Wilamowitz, *Hermes* 33 (1898), 119 ff. See also Wade-Gery, *Essays*, 100 f.
45 Eus. *Chron.* I, 189–90; Paus. IV, 13.7.
46 For a list of archons see P-W *s.v.*
47 See Hignett, op. cit., 38 ff.
48 Plut. *Thes.* 25.2. See the discussion by Wade-Gery, op. cit., 91 ff. On whether Plutarch is here based on Aristotle, cf. Jacoby, *Atthis*, 247, n. 49.
49 Thuc. II, 15.2.
50 Wade-Gery, op. cit., 94 ff., twists Thucydides' words in order to make him say so explicitly.
51 Bekker's *Anecdota*, 257.
52 Plut. *Thes.* 25.
53 Arist. *AP*, 3.1.
54 Arist. *AP*, 8.2.
55 Isocr. VII, 22. Hignett, op. cit., 78 f.
56 Arist. *AP*, 4.2.
57 See Sandys' comment ad loc. Cf. Kenyon ad loc. The quotation is from Wade-Gery, op. cit., 101.
58 Arist. *Pol.* 1273b, 41 ff. – II, 9.2.
59 Arist. *AP*, 8.2. See Kenyon's explanation of this, ad loc.
60 Arist. *AP*, 7.1.
61 Hdt. VIII, 41.2–3. See Sealey, *Historia* 9 (1960), 158.
62 See M. I. Finley, *The Ancestral Constitution* (1971).
63 Draco's reforms are dated to the 39th Olympiad (624–21) by Tatian, Clement of Alexandria, Eusebius and Suidas, probably all derived from Apollodorus. For details see Cadoux, *JHS* 68 (1948), 92. Diod. IX, 17, dates Draco 47 years before Solon, who is rather vaguely said to have 'lived in the time of the tyrants'. The scholiast to Aeschines I.6 dates Draco 100 years before Solon, but this is thought to be a textual corruption of 'seven years', which may again refer to the 47 years that Diodorus mentions.
64 Arist. *AP*, 7.2.
65 Sealey, art. cit., 155–80, esp. 161; Hignett, op. cit., 99 f.; Wüst, *Historia* 8 (1958), 1–11; W. J. Woodhouse, *Solon the Liberator* (1938); French, *CQ* n.s. 6 (1956), 11–25, *JHS* 77 (1957), 238–46, and *Greece & Rome* 6 (1959), 46–57; E. Ruschenbusch, *Historia* 7 (1958), 398–424; Murakawa, *Historia* 6 (1957), 187.
66 Sealey, art. cit., 160 ff.
67 See Hignett, op. cit., 99 f.
68 E.g. Sealey, art. cit., 161.
69 Plut. *Solon* 19.2 ff.
70 Plut. *Solon* 19.3.
71 Hignett, op. cit., 80.
72 Arist. *AP*, 3.6, 8.4; Hignett, op. cit., 80 ff.
73 Plut. *Thes.*, 25.
74 Those who equate Eupatrids with *gennētai*; Francotte, *La Polis Grecque*, 10; Töpffer, *Attische Genealogie*, 170 n. 2. Eupatrids as a single *genos*: Hignett, op. cit., 315 ff.

75 Wade-Gery, op. cit., 86 f.
76 Arist. *AP*, fr. 5 (Loeb).
77 Hdt. I. 146. For the sources for the Ionian tribes see Busolt-Swoboda, *Griech. Staatskunde*, 118–20, 132 and Busolt, *Griech. Geschichte*, I² 279, n. 3; 280, n. 1. See Hignett, op. cit., 50 ff.
78 Hdt. V,68.1; *Od.* XIX, 175–77, *Il.* II, 668; Tyrtaeus fr. 1 (Diehl), line 12; Busolt-Swoboda, op.cit., 130.
79 Diod. I, 28.5. See also the definitions given by Plutarch, Aristotle and the *Anecdota* cited above.
80 Hignett, op. cit., 315. Cf. Wade-Gery, op. cit., 109, 116.
81 Plut. *Thes.* 25; Bekker's *Anecdota*, 257; Diod. I, 28.5; Arist. *AP*, 13.2.
82 Solon is discussed in Ch. V.
83 See Whibley, *Greek Oligarchies*, 115 ff.
84 See White, *JHS* 74 (1954), 36–43; Labarbe, *Ant. Class.* 31 (1962), 153–88; Barron, *CQ* n.s. 14 (1964), 210–29.
85 Plut. *Quaest. Graec.* 57.
86 Revolution: Thuc. I, 115.2–117.3. Exiled Samians: Thuc. III, 32.2, IV, 75.1, III, 19.2.
87 Thuc. VIII, 21.
88 Thuc. VIII, 73, cf. VIII, 63.
89 Thuc. VIII, 21.
90 Thuc. VIII, 73. See Bradeen, *Historia* 9 (1960), 257–69, esp. 265 f.; G. de Ste Croix, *Historia* 3 (1954–55), 25. Bradeen believes that the aristocracy was probably in power without a break from 440 to 412, but, though Thucydides does not mention a change in government among the terms that the Athenians imposed on Samos in 439 (Thuc. I, 117), the evidence about the Samian exiles seems conclusive.
91 Hdt. VII, 155.
92 Dion. Hal. VI, 62.
93 Arist. fr. 219, *FHG* II, 170. Timaeus fr. 56, *FHG* I, 204.
94 Aristotle and Timaeus, ibid.
95 Hdt. VII, 155.
96 Plut. *Quaest. Graec.* 32, *Mor.* 298C.

97 Arist. *Pol.* 1290b, 10 ff. = IV, 3.8.
98 Arist. *Pol.* 1289b, 31 ff. = IV, 3.1, cf. Rose fr. 603 = Strabo 447.
99 Arist. *Pol.* 1297b, 16 ff. = IV, 10.10.
100 Arist. *Pol.* 1289b, 39 f. = IV, 3.2.
101 Chalcis: Strabo X, 447 = Rose fr. 603: Plut. *Per.* 23; Hdt. V, 77. Cyme: Heraclid. Pont. xi, 6, *FHG* II, 217.
102 Heraclid. Pont. xxii, *FHG* II, 218.
103 Heraclid. Pont. xi, 6, *FHG* II, 217.
104 C. Roebuck, *CPh* 48 (1953), 13.
105 See V. Ehrenberg, 'Myrioi', P-W XVI, 1, 1097 ff.
106 See Whibley, *Greek Oligarchies*, 134 ff.
107 Locri: Polyb. XII, 16. Croton: Iamblich. *Pyth. Vit.* 35.260; Val. Max. VIII, 15.1. Rhegium: Heraclid. Pont. xxv 4, *FHG* II, 219. Acragas: Diog. Laert. VIII, 2.66. See Dunbabin, *Western Greeks*, 68 ff., 316 ff.
108 Polyb. XII, 16.
109 Meiggs-Lewis 20 = Tod 24 = SIG 47. See Graham, *Colony and Mother-City*, 40–60, 226 ff.
110 Polyb. XII, 5.6 f.
111 Dunbabin, op. cit., 184.
112 Arist. *Pol.* 1270a 36 = II, 5.1–2.
113 Plato, *Leg.* V. 738A–B. See also Plato *Ep.* VII, 337C. He is criticized by Arist. *Pol.* 1265a 10 f. = II, 3.2, where the figure in Plato's *Laws* is wrongly given as 5,000. Aristotle also misrepresents Plato, *Repb.* 423A = IV, 2.
114 Epidaurus: Plut. *Quaest. Graec.* I. For dating see Halliday's commentary, 48. Heraclea: Arist. *Pol.* 1305b 11 = V, 5.2. Syracuse: Diod. XIX, 5. Massalia: Strabo IV, 179; cf. *SIG* 200, 42.
115 Locris: *IG* IX, 1. 334–40 (5th century; cf. Whibley, op. cit., 134, n. 3). Rhegium: Heraclid. Pont. *FHG* II, 219. Cyme: Heraclid. Pont. *FHG*

II, 217. Heraclea: Arist. *Pol.* 1305b 12 = V, 5.2. Synhedrion: Strabo IV, 179; Diod. XVI, 65; XIX, 5. Iamblich. *Pyth. Vit.* 35.260.
116 Arist. *Pol.* 1350b 11 = V, 5.2–3. See Whibley, op. cit., 123.
117 Arist. *Pol.* 1274b 5 – II, 9.7.
118 Arist. *Pol.* 1274a 32 ff. – II, 9.6.
119 Arist. *Pol.* 1278a 25 – III, 3.4; 1321a 28 = VI, 4.5.
120 Thuc. I, 12. Thucydides' account has often been impugned. See Gomme's commentary ad loc.
121 *Il.* II, 494 ff.
122 See Page, *Homeric Iliad*, 136. Hope Simpson & Lazenby, *Catalogue of Ships*, 19 ff. Gomme, loc. cit.
123 See *Illustrated London News*, 28 November 1964. For the connection between Thales and Anaximander, the Cadmean royal house and the East, and also between Hesiod and the East, see Thomson, *The First Philosophers*, 137. Paus. IX, 12.2.
124 Thuc. I, 12; Hdt. VII, 176.4; Strabo IX, 401 ff.
125 Arist. frs. 497–98 (Rose). See Wade-Gery, *JHS* 44 (1924), 55–64; Westlake, *Thessaly*, 24 ff., 104 f., 114.
126 Plato, *Crito* 15, 53D.
127 Hdt. VII, 6, with How & Wells's commentary. Westlake, op. cit., 30 and *JHS* 55 (1935).
128 Thessaly: Thuc. IV, 78.3. Thebes: Thuc. III, 62.3, cf. Thuc. IV, 126.2, VI, 38.3.
129 Arist. *Pol.* 1292b 6 ff. = IV, 5.1.
130 See Thuc. IV, 126.2 and Gomme's note ad loc. Also A. W. Gomme, *CR* n.s. 1 (1951), 135 f.
131 *SIG* (3rd edn), No. 274.
132 *Il.* II, 676–79.
133 See, for example, Xen. *Hell.* VI, 1.19.
134 *Il.* II, 748 ff., 683 ff.; *Il.* IX, 484.
135 Hdt. VIII, 43.
136 Xen. *Hell.*, loc. cit. The term may be interpreted as being used also to refer to the Argive Orneatae. Hdt. VIII, 73, and How & Wells ad loc.
137 Scholiast on Arist. *Vesp.* 1271.
138 E.g. Pollux III, 83.
139 See Plut. *Quaest. Graec.* 1. For peasant dress see *Od.* XXIV, 231. Athenaeus XIV, 74, 657D. *Leg. Gort.* 2.8 *et al.* See Halliday, *Plutarch*, 39 ff.; Whibley, *Greek Oligarchies*, 182.
140 Timaeus fr. 59, *FHG* I = Athenaeus XII, 3, 518D = *FGrH* 566 F48.
141 Thespiae: Heraclid. *Pont.* xliii, *FHG* II, 224. Thessaly: Arist. *Pol.* VII, 11.2 = 1331a 32 ff.
142 Arist. *Pol.* 1278a, 15 ff. = III, 3.3.
143 Polyb. XII, 5 ff. See discussion in Dunbabin, *Western Greeks*, 183 ff.
144 Alcman fr. 146 (Edmonds) = 115 (Bergk).
145 Hdt. V, 68. See Halliday, op. cit., 41.
146 Arist. *Pol.* 1306a, 10 ff. = V, 5.7.
147 Thuc. V, 47.9.
148 Cauer-Schwyzer, *Dialectorum Graecorum Exempla*, No. 409.6. See U. Kahrstedt, *Nachr. v. d. Gesell. d. Wiss. zu Göttingen* (1927), 166; Murakawa, *Historia* 6 (1957), 389.
149 Olympia V, *Die Inschriften*, ed. Dittenberger & Purgold, No. 2. See Jeffery, *Local Scripts*, 218–20.
150 Diod. XI, 54.1; Jeffery, loc. cit.
151 See H. Swoboda, 'Elis', P-W V, 2427; G. Busolt, *Forschungen zur Griechischen Geschichte*, 61; Murakawa, *Historia* 6 (1957), 389.
152 Plut. *Praecepta Gerendae Reip.* 10, *Mor.* 805D.
153 Plato's pupil: Plut. *Adv. Colotem* 32, *Mor.* 1126C.
154 See, for example, Gomme's commentary on Thuc. V, 47.9; Murakawa, loc. cit.
155 Olympia V, *Inscriften*, op. cit., Nos 7.4, 3.8. Jeffery, op. cit., 218 ff.
156 Cauer-Schwyzer, op. cit., No. 415. See Kahrstedt, op. cit., 169, where

it is dated to the late 6th century. Murakawa, loc. cit.
157 *SEG* XI, 336 = *IG* IV, 614. See W. Vollgraff, *Mnemosyne* 59 (1932), 369–93. Hammond, *CQ* n.s. 10 (1960), 33–42; M. T. Mitsos, *Argolike Prosopographia*, s.v. 'Potamos'. Cf. *IG* IV, 1, 506.7.
158 6th century: *SEG* XI, 314; 5th century (*c.* 450); Meiggs & Lewis, No. 42 = Tod No. 33.
159 Paus. II, 19.2. Attempt to identify Melantas with Meltas: W. Vollgraff, *Verh. d. Kon. Ned. Akad. v. Wetensch. Afd. Let.*, n.s. 51.2 (1948), 84 ff.
160 Paus. ibid.
161 Hdt. VII, 149.
162 Paus. II, 19.2. See Andrewes, *CQ* n.s. 1 (1951), 39–45. Cf. the genealogy in Diod. VII, fr. 13 f. In Theopompus, *FGrH* 115 F 393 = Diod. VII, 17, and Satyrus, *FHG* III, 165, fr. 21, Cissus (Ceisus) is the founder of Dorian Argos.
163 Diod. VII, 14.
164 Plut. *Mor.* 340C. Cf. Andrewes, art. cit., 44.
165 For the foundation of the Dorian state see Tomlinson, *Argos*, 65 f.
166 Diod. VII, 13.2. See Andrewes, art. cit.
167 Arist. *Pol.* 1310b, 12 = V, 8.2; Hdt. VI, 127.3; Nic. Damasc., *FHG* fr. 41 = 90 F, 35. See also Ephorus *FHG* fr. 15 = *FGrH* 70 F, 115, 176 = Strabo VIII. Pheidon's relationship to Meltas: see Andrewes, art. cit., 40. Paus. VI, 22.2.
168 Meltas: see Andrewes, art. cit., 39 ff.; cf. *BCH* 80 (1956), 38 f. Pheidon: see Tomlinson, op. cit., 180.
169 Thuc. V, 47.9.
170 Steph. Byz. s.v. Dymanes; *CIG* 1130–31; *IG* IV, 488 (probably 4th century), 517 (*c.* 460–450? – Jeffery, op. cit., 170, No. 32), 596–602 (Roman date); *SEG* XI, 293; Paus. II, 23.3;

28.3–7. See W. R. Halliday, *Annals of Arch. and Anth.* X (1923), 27–32.
171 Hdt. VI, 77–81.
172 Hdt. VI, 83.
173 Pollux *Onomast.* 3.83. See p. 60.
174 5,000: Paus. III, 4.1; 6,000: Hdt. VII, 148.2; 7,777: ridiculed by Plut. *Mor.* 245D. Even 5,000 may be too high, though, since we know that at some time between 487 and 481 Argos could spare 1,000 volunteers to aid Aegina against Athens, Hdt. VI, 92.
175 Plut. *Mor.* 245 F.
176 Arist. *Pol.* 1303a 6 f. = V, 2.8.
177 R. F. Willetts, *Hermes* 87 (1959), 501 f.; W. L. Newman, *The Politics of Aristotle* (1887–1902), IV, 304 n.; cf. Forrest, *CQ* n.s. 10 (1960), 223 n.
178 Forrest, art. cit., 223 ff. Cf. Seymour, *JHS* 42 (1922), 24–30.
179 Herodotus' story is corroborated by Ephorus, *FHG* fr. 98 = *FGrH* 70 F 56. Strabo 373.
180 Paus. VIII, 27.1; cf. Hdt. VIII, 73.
181 See Forrest, art. cit., 224.
182 They were probably not fully Doric, for then they would themselves have been divided into the three Doric tribes, which were to be found in all Dorian states. The Orneatae are described by Hdt. VIII, 73, as 'the only autochthonous Ionians', who had been 'doricised by their Argive rulers and by time.'
183 See Forrest, art. cit., 225, 230 ff.
184 Hdt. VII, 149. Forrest's argument (225 f.) that Herodotus treats the Athenian Cleisthenic council in the same way as in IX, 5.1 will not stand up to scrutiny: the council decision is immediately referred to the assembly, whereas in VII, 149 there is no mention of the assembly.
185 *SEG* XIII, 239; Jeffery, *Local Scripts*, 169, No. 22. The Attic form of the word *Heliaea* was used of the assembly only in its judicial capacity. In Argos, too, it may have been specially

convoked to act in a specific capacity: in a mid-5th century inscription (Meiggs & Lewis, No. 42, line 44) we read of the 'aliaea for sacred business'.
186 Thuc. V, 47.9.
187 Diod. XIX, 63.
188 Thuc. V, 29.1, 31.6.
189 *IG* IV, 554; *BCH* 34 (1910), 331. Thera: *IG* XII, 3.330.
190 Plut. *Quaest. Graec.* 1, *Mor.* 291E.
191 Plut. *Quaest. Graec.* 4, *Mor.* 292A.
192 For the suggestion that *artynae* = *damiorgi* see Tomlinson, *Argos*, 198. For the same reason the 80 are not likely to be the *damiorgi* in disguise. See Gomme ad Thuc. V, 47.9; Murakawa, art. cit.
193 Infantry: Thuc. V, 59.5; 72.4. See Gomme ad V, 72.4. Wörrle, *Untersuchungen*.
194 4th/3rd centuries: *SEG* XI, 293. Roman: *IG* IV, 596–602.
195 E.g. Thuc. V, 59, 4 ff. See Tomlinson, op. cit., 198.
196 Diod. XV, 57.3.
197 Diod. XV, 58.
198 Isocr. *Philip*. 52.
199 On Crete see Willetts, *Aristocratic Society* and also Jeffery and Morpurgo-Davies, *Kadmos* 9 (1970), 118–54. On Ionia see Hunt, 'Feudal Survivals in Ionia', *JHS* 67 (1947), 68–76.

CHAPTER III

1 See Rawson, *The Spartan Tradition*, 139 ff. (Machiavelli), 171 ff. (More), 225 ff. (Montesquieu), 231 ff. (Rousseau).
2 J-J. Rousseau, *Œuvres Complètes* (Pléiade), III, 12.
3 Ibid., 30.
4 Plut. *Apophth. Lac.*, Agesilaus 30, *Mor.* 210E/F.
5 Plut. *Apophth. Lac.*, Agesilaus 72, *Mor.* 214A.

6 Tyrtaeus 10, lines 1–14 (Edmonds).
7 Athenaeus, *Deipnosophistae*, XIV, 630E; Diod. VIII, 36. Tyrtaeus' date: See W. den Boer, *Laconian Studies*, 70 n. E. Schwartz, *Hermes* 34 (1899); cf. H. Weil, *Journ. des savants* (1899), 553 ff.
8 Tyrtaeus fr. 5 (Edmonds); Paus. IV, 6.5; Strabo VI, 277; Schol. on Plato *Leg*. I. 629A. See W. den Boer, op. cit., 69 ff.; Wade-Gery, *ASI*, 296. Cf. Chrimes, *Ancient Sparta*, 290 ff., who argues that Spartan rule over Messenia was a gradual process. Eusebius dates the First Messenian War to 746–16, *Chron*. II, 81–3, 85, ed. Schoene.
9 Paus. III, 3.4, 7.6. See Jones, *Sparta*, 3 f.; Wade-Gery, op. cit., 289, 296.
10 The account given in the text is an eclectic conflation of the various versions: Strabo VI, 278–80; Diod. VIII, 21; Athenaeus *Deipnosoph*. 271C; Dion. Hal. XIX, 1; Justin III, 4.3–11. The traditional date for the founding of Tarentum is 706: Eus. *Chron*. II, 81–3, 85, ed. Schoene.
11 See for example Thuc. I, 101.2; Paus. III, 11.8.
12 Theopompus believed that the helots were of Achaean stock: *FGrH* 115 F 122 = *FHG* fr. 134. For the idea that the helots were of pre-Greek stock see K. O. Müller, *Die Dorier*, II², 29. For a discussion of various views on the subject see Oliva, *Sparta and her Social Problems*, 38 ff.; Oliva, *Historica* 3 (1961), 10 f.
13 Hellanicus 188J; Theopompus, loc. cit.; Athenaeus VI, 272A; Ephorus *ap*. Strab. VIII, 365.
14 *Et. Mag*. 332, 53. See also Toynbee, *Greek History*, 195 ff.
15 E. Meyer, *Kleine Schriften* I², 182. Also in his *Geschichte des Altertums* III², 258. Niese, *Göttingische Gelehrte Nachrichten*, 136. Kahrstedt, *Hermes* 54 (1919), 290 ff.

NOTES

16 *Perioikoi* as Dorians: See Kahrstedt, op. cit., 291; Busolt, *Griech. Geschichte*, I, 519 n.; Niese, op. cit., 135; Michell, *Sparta* (1952), 68; J. A. O. Larsen, P-W XIX, 1, 819; Ehrenberg, *Hermes* 59 (1924), 51 & 56; Hampl, *Hermes* 72 (1937), 16 f.; Solmsen, *Rheinisches Museum für Philologie*, 62 (1907), 335 f. For a review of the literature see Oliva, op. cit., 55 ff.
17 See for example Thuc. IV, 8, IV.53.
18 For a list see Niese, op. cit., 1906, 101. See Hdt. VII, 234; Strabo VIII, 362.
19 Paus. III, 22.5; *CIG* V, i 1108.
20 Xen. *Hell.* V. 3. 9.
21 E.g. Chrimes, op. cit., 285; Lotze, *Metaxu*, 34.
22 Isocr. XII, 181. Toynbee, op. cit., 206. Cf. Jones, op. cit., 8.
23 Thuc. IV, 53.
24 Polyb. II, 65.7; Plut. *Cleom.*, 27.
25 Hdt. I, 82; see also I, 66 (Tegea); Thuc. IV, 56–7; V, 41. For the dating see Wade-Gery, *CQ* 43 (1949), 79–81.
26 Paus. IV, 6.6 ff.; IV, 9–24. See Pearson, *Historia* 11 (1962), 397–426.
27 Plut. *Mor.* 194B. Wade-Gery, *ASI*, 297.
28 490: Plato, *Laws* 698D-E.
29 Michell, op. cit., 44.
30 Jones, op. cit., 17, 170.
31 Arist. *Pol.* 1270b 21 ff. = II, 6.15.
32 Jones, op. cit., 170 f.
33 See below.
34 Arist. *Pol.* 1294a 22 = IV, 6.5.
35 Arist. *Pol.* 1293b 35 ff. = IV, 6.2.
36 *Gerousia*: Plut. *Lyc.* 26; Arist. *Pol.* 1271a 10 = II, 6.18. Ephors: Arist. *Pol.* 1270b 28 – II, 6.16. Though Plutarch's description mentions only the *gerousia*, Aristotle derides both elections as 'childish', so it is safe to assume that the same method was employed in both. See also Jones, op. cit., 170 f.
37 Michell, op. cit., 43.
38 Xen. *Resp. Lac.* 10.7.
39 Plut. *Lyc.* 8.
40 Plut. *Lyc.* 16.
41 Jones, op. cit., 43.
42 Plato, *Laws* III, 684D.
43 Plato, *Laws* III, 685A. Polybius, Ephorus and Justin also trace the equality in land-tenure to Lycurgus: Polyb. VI, 45, 48; Ephorus: *FGrH* 70 F118 = Strabo VIII, 365FF; Justin III, 3.3. Isocrates XII, 179, though, agrees with Plato. See also Isocr. XII, 259.
44 Paus. VI, 2.1 f.; Thuc. V, 50; Xen. *Hell.* III, 2.21.
45 Xen. *Mem.* 1.2.61; Plut. *Cimon*, 10.5.
46 Hdt. VI, 103. On Cimon see J. K. Davies, *Athenian Propertied Families* (1971), 300.
47 Xen. *Hell.* VI, 4.11.
48 Arist. *Pol.* 1270a 17 = II, 6.10; also 1307a 35 = V, 6.7. Plutarch, writing of the mid-third century, goes even further in claiming that 'most' of the wealth of Sparta was in the hands of women. Plut. *Agis*, 7.5.
49 Arist. *Pol.* 1270a 24 = II, 6.11.
50 Jones, op. cit., 42.
51 Arist. *Pol.* 1270a 20 = II, 6.10.
52 See n. 43, above.
53 Polyb. VI, 45.
54 Polyb. VI, 46.
55 Plato, *Laws* 684E–685A.
56 Xen. *Resp. Lac.* 10.8.
57 E.g. Jones, op. cit., 43.
58 Busolt-Swoboda, 634 n. 2. Cf. Chrimes, *Ancient Sparta*, 286; Kiechle, *Lakonien und Sparta*, 209 n. 4; Pareti, *Storia di Sparta arcaica* I, 197. See also Xen. *Lac. Pol.* 11.4.
59 Plut. *Lyc.* 16.1.
60 Plato, *Laws* XI, 923C.
61 Though elsewhere he does seem to think of the land as divided into ancestral allotments – 5,040 of them in all. *Laws* 737C.
62 Plut. *Lyc.* 16. See U. Kahrstedt, *Griech. Staatsrecht* (1922), 16 n. 3;

Michell, op. cit., 207; Toynbee, *JHS* 33 (1913), 259 f.
63 Heraclid. 2.76, *FHG* II, 211.
64 Polyb. XII, 6.8.
65 Arist. *Pol.* 1271a 26–37; 1272a 13.
66 Plut. *Agis* 5.1.
67 See above, p. 81. Epitadeus' law fictitious: E. Meyer, *Forschungen zur alten Geschichte* (1892), I, 258. See also E. Meyer, *Rhein. Mus.* 41, 589. Misinterpretation of Aristotle: Asheri, *Historia* 12 (1963), 12. Oliva, op. cit., 191. Cf. Toynbee, *Greek History*, 337 ff. Phylarchus: See Gabba, *Athenaeum* 35 (1957), 3 f. Testamentary inheritance: Asheri, art. cit., 13.
68 Plut. *Agis* 5.
69 Michell, op. cit., 216.
70 For a résumé of the state of play see Oliva, op. cit., 63 ff. Cf. Starr, *Historia* 14 (1965), 257–72, especially 271.
71 Hdt. I, 65–66. This date has sometimes been estimated at *c.* 1000 BC. See Forrest, *History of Sparta*, 57; cf. N. G. L. Hammond, *JHS* 70 (1950), 62 ff. Late dating: Huxley, *Early Sparta*, 7, 42 (700); Forrest, *Phoenix* 17 (1963), 168 ff. & *History of Sparta*, 55 ff. (676); Toynbee, op. cit., 225 (after mid-7th century), 413 ff.
72 Arist. *Pol.* 1036b 36 ff.–1307a = V, 6.2.
73 See above, p. 74. Forrest, op. cit., 56 f.; Jones, *Sparta*, 12.
74 Jones, op. cit., 33; followed by Forrest, *History of Sparta*, 58.
75 See A. M. Snodgrass, *JHS* 85 (1965), 110–22.
76 E.g. Tyrtaeus (Edmonds), fr. 10, line 15; fr. 11, lines 11 ff., 35.
77 A. Andrewes, *The Greek Tyrants*, 72 f.; cf. Snodgrass, art. cit., 116.
78 Snodgrass, art. cit., 122.
79 Hdt. I, 65.
80 Ephorus *apud* Strabo X, 480–4; Polyb. VI, 45 ff.; Plato, *Reph.* 544C, 547A ff.; Plato, *Laws* 631B ff., 634 ff.,

780E ff.; Arist. *Pol.* 1271b ff. = II, 7.1.
81 E.g. Andrewes, *Probouleusis* 17 n.: Forrest, op. cit., 53, 65. Cf. Toynbee, op. cit., 329.
82 Arist. *Pol.* 1271b 20 ff. = II, 7.1. Cf. Ephorus fr. 61, *FHG* I, 249 = *FGrH* 70 F 145; Diod. V, 78.3 f.
83 See Toynbee, op. cit., 332.
84 Ephorus *apud* Strabonem X, 482; Arist. *Pol.* 1271b 20 ff. = II, 7.1 ff.
85 Ephorus and Aristotle, locc. citt.
86 See above, p. 23ff.
87 Livy III, 31.8. Cf. R. M. Ogilvie's Commentary ad loc.
88 Hdt. I, 66; Thuc. I, 18.1.
89 Plut. *Lyc.* 11.
90 Plut. *Lyc.* 10.
91 Plut. *Lyc.* 6.4.
92 Ibid. See Wade-Gery, *Essays*, 47 ff.; A. H. M. Jones, *ASI*, 165ff.
93 Plut. *Lyc.* 6.1.
94 See J. H. Oliver, *Demokratia, the Gods and the Free World* (1960), 20; Butler, *Historia* 11 (1962), 385–96.
95 Wade-Gery, op. cit., 37, 54 ff.; Jones, op. cit., 172; Forrest, *Phoenix* 17 (1963), 157.
96 Plut. *Lyc.* 6.5. Cf. Wade-Gery, op. cit., 62. On the kings see Hdt. VI, 56–60.
97 Diod. VII, 14 (12.6) = Tyrtaeus fr. 4 (Edmonds).
98 Arist. *Pol.* 1272a 11 = II, 7.4.
99 Arist. *Pol.* 1273a 6 ff. = II, 8.3. See Wade-Gery, op. cit., 51–4; A. Andrewes, *ASI*, 3.
100 Thuc. I, 87.
101 Xen. *Hell.* II, 2. 19; II, 4.38; III, 2.23; IV, 6.3; V, 2.11, 20; V, 2.33; VI, 3.3; VI, 4.3.
102 E.g. Andrewes, op. cit., 6 f.
103 Plut. *Lyc.* 6.4. Cf. Jones, op. cit., 165 ff.; Butler, *Historia* 11 (1962), 386 ff.
104 Jones, op. cit., 170.
105 Xen. *Hell.* III, 2.23; IV, 6.3.
106 Diod. XI, 50 (477 BC); Plut.

Agis, 8 ff. (242 BC). See Jones, op. cit., 168 f.; Andrewes, op. cit., 4 f.
107 Plut. *Agis*, 11.1.
108 Jones, op. cit., 169.
109 Thuc. I, 79.
110 Xen. *Hell.* II, 4.38; V, 2.11, 20; V, 2.34; VI, 4.3.
111 Cic. *de Reph.* II, 58; *de Leg.* III, 16.
112 See Michell, *Sparta*, 119 ff.
113 Thera: *IG* XII, iii, 322, 326, 330, 336. Perioecic cities: *IG* V, i, 331–2, 961 ff. Messenia: Polyb. IV, 4.
114 Hdt. I, 65; Xen. *Lac. Pol.* 8.3; Plato, *Ep.* VIII, 354B. But cf. Plato, *Laws* 691D–692A. Ephorus, *FGrH* 70 F 149 = *FHG* fr. 64, I, 249; Strabo X, 481 f.; Isocr. XII, 153; Justin III, 3.2.
115 Arist. *Pol.* 1313a 26 = V, 8.22. This view was taken up by several later authors. See Kiechle, *Lakonien und Sparta*, 222 nn. 4–6.
116 Eus. *Chron.* II, 78, 81 (ed. Schoene); Diogenes Laertius I, 68; Plut. *Lyc.* 7.
117 Xen. *Lac. Pol.* 15.7.
118 Xen. *Lac. Pol.* 15.6.
119 Plut. *Cleom.* 10.
120 Fines: Plut. *Agesilaus* 2, 5; Scholiast *ad* Aristophanes, *Nub.* 859. Impeachment: Paus. III, 5.2; Plut. *Agis* 19. Arrest: Thuc. I, 131; cf. Plut. *Agis* 18–19. Deposition: Plut. *Agis* 11. See also Hdt. VI, 56.
121 King's power: Hdt. VI, 56. Ephors: Plut. *Lyc.* 28.
122 Hdt. VI, 57. Cf. Thuc. I, 20, who denies that the kings had two votes apiece in the *gerousia*.
123 Demetrius of Scepsis, *ap.* Athenaeus IV, 141e, f.
124 Xen. *Lac. Pol.* 4.3.
125 Hdt. I, 65. Cf. Polyaenus II, 3.11; Pollux VIII, 111 (on Athens). Michell, *Sparta*, 236 f., believes that the *triecas* was a body of thirty men under two officers.
126 Tyrtaeus I, lines 10–13, ed. Diehl (2nd edn).
127 E.g. Hdt. IX, 53; Arist. fr. 541 (Rose, 1886).
128 N. G. L. Hammond, *JHS* 70 (1950), 50 ff.; den Boer, *Laconian Studies* (Amsterdam, 1954), 173.
129 Arist. fr. 541 (Rose, 1886).
130 Paus. III, 16.9.
131 Hdt. IX, 53; Thuc. I, 20.
132 Hdt. III, 55.
133 See Michell, op. cit., 100.
134 Beattie, *CQ* 45, n.s.1 (1951), 46–58.
135 Paus. III, 16.9. Amyclae: IF v. 26; Neapolis: IG v. 677, 680.
136 Beattie, art. cit. For further discussion see *Laconian Studies*, 170 ff.; Michell, op. cit., 97 ff.; Toynbee, op. cit., 260 ff.; Wade-Gery, *CQ* 38, 120.
137 Wade-Gery, art. cit., 122.
138 Hdt. I, 67.
139 Plut. *Solon* 10.
140 Nicias: Thuc. V, 19, 404: Arist. *AP* 38.4 (ten); Xen. *Hell.* II, 4.38 (fifteen).
141 Presiding over assembly: Thuc. I, 87; Xen. *Hell.* II, 2.19; III, 2.23. Supervising other officials: Xen. *Lac. Pol.* 8.4; Arist. *Pol.* 1270b 7 ff. = II, 6.14. Judges: Arist. *Pol.* 1275b 10 ff. = III, 1.7 f. Finance: Plut. *Lys.* 16; *Agis* 6; Diod. XIII, 106. Crypteia: Plut. *Lyc.* 28. Foreign Affairs: Xen. *Hell.* II, 2.13, V, 2.11; Polyb. LV, 34.5 f.
142 See Xen. *Hell.* II, 3.34. Re-election: Plut. *Agis* 16.
143 Arist. *Pol.* 1270b 7 ff. = II, 6.14.
144 Arist. *Pol.* 1270b 21 ff. = II, 6.15 (quoted above, n. 31); 1294b 30 = IV, 7.5.
145 Hdt. I, 65.
146 Age of six: Plut. *Lyc.* 16 (not eight, as in Jones, op. cit., 34). See Michell, op. cit., 167. Discipline: Xen. *Lac. Pol.* II, 2 ff. Plut. *Lyc.* 16 ff.
147 Plut. *Lyc.* 10 ff.
148 Plut. *Lyc.* 16.

149 Hdt. IX, 28. Also Hdt. IX, 10, 29.
150 Gomme's figures for 5th-century male citizens and metics of military age (18 to 59) and adult male slaves have been followed here, rather than his conjectural totals including women and children, which give a different ratio. A. W. Gomme, *The Population of Athens in the Fifth and Fourth Centuries BC* (1933), esp. 26. Cf. A. H. M. Jones, *Athenian Democracy* (1957), 76 f.
151 Estimates of the Spartan population: 10,000: Arist. *Pol.* 1270a 37 f. = II, 6.12. 9,000: Plut. *Lyc.* 8, 16. 8,000: Hdt. VII, 234. Plataea: IX, 28; Mantinea: Thuc. V, 16.68; Leuctra: Xen. *Hell.* VI, 4.15 f. For further discussion see Toynbee, *Greek History*, 396 ff.; Forrest, *Sparta*, 131 ff.
152 Thuc. VII, 21.28. Estimate of slave population: Gomme, op. cit., 20 ff.
153 The Spartans' love of freedom was proverbial. E.g. Hdt. VII, 135.
154 Plut. *Lyc.* 18.
155 Michell, *Sparta*, 96 f.
156 Plato, *Laws* IV, 712 D-E.
157 Iso. *Areopagiticus* 61 (152).
158 Cic. *de Repb.* II, 23.
159 Arist. *Pol.* 1294b 32 ff. = IV, 7.5.
160 Arist. *Pol.* 1294b 15 ff. = IV, 7.4 f.
161 Pseudo-Plut. *Mor.* 194B; Aelian. *Varia Historia* XII, 42. See Wade-Gery, *ASI*, 295. Also, Pearson, *Historia* 11 (1962), 397-426.
162 Plut. *Quaest. Graec.* 5. Other similar clauses: Thuc. V, 23, III, 54, II, 27; Xen. *Hell.* V, 2.3.
163 See Chapter I.
164 For an example of Spartan hauteur in this connection see Agesilaus' speech quoted above, p. 73.
165 See, for example, B. Russell, *Power* (1938), 129; G. Watson, *The English Ideology* (1973), 30.
166 A. de Tocqueville, *L'Ancien Régime et la Révolution* (1856; editions Gallimard 1952), 277 f.
167 See the discussion in Oliva, *Sparta*, 139 ff.; Kiechle, *Messenische Studiem*, 92 ff.; Huxley, *Early Sparta*, 89 ff.; den Boer, *Historia* 5 (1956), 162-77, and *Laconian Studies*, 18; Pearson, *Historia* 11 (1962), 401 ff.; Wade-Gery, *ASI*, 289 ff.
168 Plato, *Laws*, III, 698 D-E.
169 Paus. IV, 6.3.
170 Paus. IV, 23.6. Anaxilas: Hdt. VI, 23, VIII, 165.
171 Huxley, op. cit., 88. See also Dickins, *JHS* 32 (1912), 24 ff.; Ehrenberg, P-W III, 2A, 1348 f.; Wallace, *JHS* 74 (1954), 32 ff. Cf. Grundy, *JHS* 32 (1912), 267.
172 Hdt. VI, 61 ff., 74.
173 Thuc. I, 132.4.
174 Date of Pausanias' death: see discussion in Oliva, op. cit., 151. Earthquake: Diod. XI, 63. Date of earthquake: see Gomme's *Commentary on Thucydides*, I, 401-8.
175 See, for example, K. J. Neumann, *HZ* 96 (1906), 75.
176 Diod. XI, 63-4.
177 Diod. XI, 63.4, 64.1, 64.4; Plut. *Cimon* 16.7. Followed by N. G. L. Hammond, *Historia* 4 (1955), 379.
178 Thuc. I, 101.2.
179 Xen. *Hell.* III, 3.4 ff.
180 Xen. *Hell.* III, 3.5 ff.
181 Xen. *Hell.* III, 3.11.
182 Blackball theory: Toynbee, *JHS* 33 (1913), 261. Mess-dues theory: Busolt-Swoboda, *Griech. Staatskunde*, 659, n. 4.
183 Xen. *Hell.* III, 3.9.
184 *Neodamōdeis* as freed helots: for evidence see Ehrenberg, P-W XVI, 2 (1935), 2396.
185 *Neodamōdeis* as 'new citizens': Chrimes, *Ancient Sparta*, 39, 48; U. Kahrstedt, *Griech. Staatsrecht* (1922), 46. Cf. Oliva, *Sparta*, 169. See Hesychius s.v. *damōdes*.

NOTES

186 Separate companies for *neodamōdeis*: e.g. Xen. *Hell.* VI, 1.14.
187 Cf. Willetts, *CPh.* 49 (1954), 27.
188 Thuc. IV, 26.5-6.
189 Thuc. IV, 80.5.
190 Thuc. V, 34.1.
191 Thuc. V, 67.1.
192 Thuc. IV, 80.3-4.
193 Diod. XIV, 13.2; Plut. *Lysander* 24, 26; Arist. *Pol.* 1301b 20 = V, 1.5.
194 Plut. *Lysander* 20, 35.
195 Ephorus *FGrH* 70 F 118; Paus. *FGrH* 582 F 3. The interpretation depends on the reading, which is very much in doubt. See Ehrenberg, *Neugrunder des Staates*, 14 & 124, n. 9. Kiechle, *Lakonien und Sparta*, 220. Pausanias & the ephorate: Arist. *Pol.* 1301b 20 = V, 1.5; 1333b 32 = VII, 13.13.
196 Xen. *Hell.* III, 5.25.
197 Plut. *Lys.* 19.
198 Plut. *Comparison of Lysander & Sulla*, 3.
199 Plut. *Lys.* 16 ff.; op. cit., 3.
200 Plut. *Lys.* 16. The literal meaning of the riddle is, 'there are many owls lurking beneath Ceramicus', this being a region of the city of Athens. In Greek this is *Keramikos*, whereas the word for a tile is *Keramos*. This gives the riddle a double point.
201 Plut. *Lys.* 17.
202 Diod. VII, 12.5.
203 See, for example, Forrest, *History of Sparta*, 124 f., 137.
204 Ibid., 124, 126.
205 See above, p. 18 ff.
206 Xen. *Hell.* VI, 4.11.
207 Arist. *Pol.* 1270a 30 = II, 611. On mess-dues see n. 65.
208 Xen. *Hell.* VI, 4.15; cf. Xen. *Ages.* 2.24.
209 Hdt. IX, 10-11.
210 Toynbee, *Greek History*, 403.
211 Plut. *Agis* 5.
212 The three schools: 100 citizens: M. Cary, *CQ* 20 (1926), 186. 700 citizens: Beloch, *Griechische Geschichte*, IV, 1, 325; H. Bentson, *Griech. Geschichte* (1965), 408; Fuks, *Athenaeum* 40 (1962), 245 ff. Plutarch's figures unreliable: Ehrenberg, P-W III, 2A, 1420.
213 See Fuks, art. cit., 249; Oliva, *Sparta*, 212.
214 Plut. *Agis* 8. Eurotas valley and 'civic land': F. Bolte, P-W III, 2A (1929), 1321 f.; Oliva, 35 ff., 51 ff., 107 ff., 222.
215 Cf. Fuks, *CPh.* 57 (1962), 162.
216 Plut. *Agis* 11-13.
217 Plut. *Agis* 11.
218 Plut. *Agis* 14.
219 Plut. *Agis* 16.
220 Plut. *Agis* 19.
221 Plut. *Agis* 21.
222 Plut. *Cleom.* 2.1.
223 Plut. *Cleom.* 7.8.
224 Plut. *Cleom.* 10.
225 Plut. *Cleom.* 11.
226 Plut. *Cleom.* 11.
227 Paus. II, 9.1.
228 *Gerousia*: IG V, i. 92 ff. *Patronomi*: IG V, i. 48 ff.
229 E.g. H. Schaeffer, P-W XVIII, 4 (1949), 2296, 2304. Cf. Oliva, *Sparta*, 245.
230 Plut. *Cleom.* 23.1.
231 Daubies, *Historia* 20 (1971), 665-96.
232 The linguistic argument hinges on the *men ... de* construction; but it is far from conclusive. Daubies, art. cit., 668 ff. Freed helots would get political rights: ibid., 695.
233 Cf. Daubies, art. cit., 694 f.
234 E.g. Beloch, op. cit., IV, 1, 714.
235 For the date see Oliva, *Sparta*, 262. Numbers: Plut. *Cleom.* 28.8. For the total of the Spartan army see Walbank's *Historical Commentary on Polybius* I (1957), 273, 279.
236 Plut. *Cleom.* 37 ff.; Polyb. V, 39.
237 Polyb. II, 70.1. Also Paus. II, 9.2. Cf. Plut. *Cleom.* 30.1. Polybius natur-

ally considers Cleomenes as the destroyer of the 'ancestral constitution'. Polyb. II, 47.3, IV, 81.14.
238 See Finley, *The Ancestral Constitution*.
239 See especially Shimron, *CQ* 14 (1964), 235. Also, Shimron, *Historia* 13 (1964), 149 f. Cf. F. W. Walbank, *ASI*, 303–12; Oliva, op. cit., 264 ff.
240 Plut. *Cleom.* 10.
241 Polyb. V, 9.9–10.
242 Polyb. IV, 23.
243 Polyb. IV, 34–5.
244 Polyb. IV, 81.
245 Lycurgus' war: Polyb. IV, 36, 60, 80 f. Lycurgus & revolution: See Walbank, op. cit., ad IV, 35.3–7, 14.
246 Shimron, *CQ* 14 (1964), 236 f. Cf. Oliva, op. cit., 265, 270.
247 Nabis' royal title: *BCH* 20 (1896), 502–22; *SIG*[3] 584. Poralla, *Prosopographie*, 164 f.
248 Polyb. XIII, 6; Livy XXXIII, 44.8, XXXIV, 32.3. Hostile modern accounts: M. Holleaux, *CAH*, VIII, 147; Gabba, *Athenaeum* 35 (1957), 24 f.; H. E. Stier, *Roms Aufstieg zur Weltmacht und die griechische Welt* (1957), 22 f.
249 Polyb. XIII, 6.3–4.
250 Polyb. XVI, 13.1.
251 Liv. XXXIV. 31.11 ff.; XXIV, 32.9.
252 E.g. Jones, *Sparta*, 158.
253 E.g. Liv. XXIV, 27.2 ff.
254 Liv. XXXVIII, 34.
255 Plut. *Phil.* 16; Paus. VIII, 51.3.
256 Plut. *Phil.* 16.
257 Polyb. XIII, 6.
258 Liv. XXXVIII, 34.6.
259 Cf. W. S. Robins, *UBHJ* 6 (1958), 93–8; Chrimes, *Ancient Sparta*, 38 f.; Shimron, *CPh* 61 (1966), 1–7; R. F. Willetts, *CPh* 49 (1954).
260 Strabo VIII, 365.
261 Plut. *Cleom.* 23.1.
262 Strabo VIII, 363, 366; Diod. LIV, 7.2. See *JRS* 51 (1961), 112–18.

263 See Chrimes, op. cit., 84 ff.
264 Liv. XXXIV, 36; XXXV, 13.2; XXXVIII, 31.2.
265 E.g. the (as yet unpublished) Trevelyan lectures given by G. de Ste Croix in Cambridge in 1973 on 'Class Conflict in the Greek World'.
266 Arist. *Pol.* 1272b 19 ff. = II, 7.8.
267 Arist. *Pol.* 1269a 39 ff. = II, 5.3.
268 See Chapter V.
269 Arist. *Pol.* 1308a 13 ff. = V, 7.3.

CHAPTER IV

1 Plato, *Repb.* 565C–566B, 563E.
2 Arist. *Pol.* 1310b 8 ff. = V, 8.2–3.
3 Nic. Damasc. *FGrH* 90 F 57.
4 Arist. *Pol.* 1315b 28 = V, 9.22; Nic. Damasc. 58.7. Cf. Andrewes, *Greek Tyrants*, 49.
5 Nic. Damasc. 58.6 f.
6 Diod. VIII, 24; *P.Oxy.* XI, 1365 = *FGrH* 105 F 2.
7 Arist. *Rhet.* 1357b = I, 2.7.
8 Arist. *Pol.* 1305a 18 ff. = V, 4.5. Cf. Ure, *Origin of Tyranny*, 267, for an ingenious and far-fetched interpretation of this event.
9 Arist. *Pol.*, loc. cit.
10 Plut. *Solon* 29.1.
11 Arist. *AP*, 13.4; Arist. *Pol.* 1310b 30 = V, 8.4.
12 Hdt. I, 59–60; Arist. *AP*, 14.
13 Hdt. I, 62.
14 Diod. XIII, 91; Arist. *Pol.* 1305a 27 = V, 4.5, 1310b 30 = V, 8.4.
15 Diod. XIV, 7.
16 Arist. *AP*, 16.6.
17 Arist. *Pol.* 1313a 38 ff. = V, 9.2.
18 Plut. *Sept. Sap. Conv.*, *Mor.* 146B ff.
19 Hdt. V, 92; cf. Arist. *Pol.* 1284a 26 ff. = III, 8.3, 1311a 20 f. = V, 8.7.
20 Arist. *Pol.* 1291b 24 = IV, 4.1.
21 Thuc. VIII, 24.4.
22 Tod, *Greek Historical Inscriptions* I, 1 = Meiggs-Lewis, 8. See Quinn, *Historia* 18 (1969), 22–26.

23 Theognis 183-92 (Edmonds).
24 Ure, op. cit., 9, 299 f.

CHAPTER V

1 Oliver, *Demokratia*, vii. Some examples of works which in varying degrees idolize democracy: Jones, *Athenian Democracy*; Gomme, *More Essays*; Agard, *What Democracy Meant to the Greeks*; Forrest, *Emergence of Greek Democracy*; Ste Croix, *Peloponnesian War*; Finley, *Democracy Ancient and Modern*.
2 Category 1: Grote, *History of Greece*; Gomme, Finley, Forrest, opp. citt. Category 2: Sealey, *Essays in Greek Politics*; Frost, *Historia* 13 (1964), 385-99.
3 Jones, op. cit., 49, 46.
4 Frost, art. cit., 388.
5 Plut. *Per.* 11.3.
6 Arist. *AP*, 28. See Connor, *The New Politicians*, 6 n.
7 Plut. *Solon*, 13.2-3.
8 Arist. *AP*, 5.3.
9 Plut. *Solon*, 14, 5-6 = Solon frs. 32, 33; Arist. *AP*, 12.4 = Solon frs. 36, 37.
10 Archon: Arist. *AP*, 5.2; Plut. *Solon*, 14.2.
11 Solon fr. 37 (Edmonds) = Arist. *AP*, 12.5. Cf. Arist, *AP*, 12.1 = Solon fr. 5-6 (Edmonds).
12 Arist. *AP*, 12.1 = Solon fr. 5 (Edmonds). Cf. Forrest, op. cit., 160; French, *JHS* 77 (1957), 242; Sealey, op. cit., 15.
13 Arist. *AP*, 7.3; Plut. *Arist.* 1.2. Cf. Hignett, *Athenian Constitution*, 101.
14 Arist. *AP*, 13.4.
15 So Busolt, *Griech. Geschichte* (1893-1904), II², 305, and *CAH* IV, 60 f.
16 Arist. *AP*, 13.5.
17 Hdt. V, 70-72; Thuc. I, 126. 3-12; Plut. *Solon*, 12.
18 Arist. *AP*, 19.

19 Arist. *AP*, 19.4 f.; Hdt. V, 64; Thuc. VI, 53.3.
20 Hdt. V, 66.
21 Cleisth. Arist. *AP*, 20.5-21.1. Isagoras: Arist. *AP*, 20.1.
22 Arist. *AP*, 20.2.
23 Hdt. V, 70.
24 Marriage-tie: Marcellinus *V. Thucyd.* 18. See Davies, *Athenian Propertied Families*, stemma I.
25 B. D. Meritt, *Hesperia* 8 (1939), 59, No. 21, line 5. See Eliot & McGregor, *Phoenix* 14 (1960), 27 ff. Hdt. V, 62, VI, 123. Cf. Davies, op. cit., 375.
26 Hdt. VI, 121.
27 Hdt. V, 72; Arist. *AP*, 20.3; Scholiast on Aristophanes, *Lysistrata*, 273. See Wade-Gery, *CQ*, 27 (1933), 18.
28 Hdt. V, 66.
29 Hdt. V, 66; Arist. *AP*, 21. Cf. Hdt. V, 69. See Bicknell, *Studies*, 3.
30 Bicknell, op. cit., 4 ff.
31 Arist. *AP*, 21.3, 21.2; *Pol.* 1319b 26 = VI, 2.11.
32 See Davies, op. cit., 369 f.
33 See How & Wells, Appendix XVI, Vol. II, 343 ff.
34 Arist. *AP*, 28. See Connor, op. cit., 6 n.
35 See Fornara, *Athenian Board of Generals*, 42 ff.
36 Plut. *Cimon*, 15; 10.8.
37 Arist. *AP*, 27.3; Theopompus *FGrH* 115 F 89; Plut. *Cimon*, 10, 1-3.
38 Sealey, op. cit., 59 ff.; Connor, op. cit., 18 ff.; also Frost, *Historia* 13 (1964).
39 Arist. *AP*, 27.4; Plut. *Per.* 9.2.
40 Sealey, op. cit., 70.
41 Plut. *Per.* 11.4-12.7.
42 Plut. *Per.* 11.5. Cf. Frost, art. cit., 389 ff.
43 Sealey, op. cit., 66, 96, 98.
44 Ar. *Vesp.* 1033, *Pax* 756.
45 Ar. *Vesp.* 1238, with scholium.
46 Plut. *Arist.* 2.5. Cf. Connor, op.

cit., 27 n. On Aristeides' political leanings see Hignett, op. cit., 184 f.
47 Plut. *Arist.* 2.4; *Mor.* 807B.
48 Plut. *Mor.* 807B.
49 Ibid.
50 Plato, *Repb.* I, 332D; also *Crito*, 49B–C.
51 Aesch. *Choeph.* 123; Pindar, *Pyth.* II, 83; Xen. *Mem.* II, 3.14, II, 6.35; Isocr. I, 26.
52 Plut. *Mor.* 806F.
53 Plut. *Mor.* 807A.
54 Plato, *Repb.* 331E.
55 Ar. *Vesp.* 242.
56 Ar. *Eq.* 732.
57 Arist. *AP*, 28.3; Plut. *Nic.* 8.3. Theopompus, *FGrH* 115 F 92.
58 Ar. *Eq.* 44 and scholium.
59 Connor, op. cit., 194 ff.
60 Plut. *Mor.* 300C.
61 Plut. *Mor.* 800C; Plut. *Per.* 7.4.
62 Plut. *Per.* 7.4.
63 Sealey, op. cit., 61.
64 Plut. *Per.* 9–15.
65 Cratinus: See Schwarze, *Beurteilung des Perikles*, 55 f. Hermippus: Ibid., 101 ff. A work which I have found most useful for comedy is B. H. Garnons Williams's unpublished Oxford B. Litt. dissertation, *The historical evidence contained in Aristophanes and in the fragments of the Old Attic Comedy* (1933), which was kindly loaned to me by the author.
66 *PSI* 11 (1935) No. 1212, line 22 ff. See Schwarze, op. cit., 43 f.
67 Schwarze, op. cit., 44, 50.
68 Telecleides, *apud* Plut. *Per.* 16.2; Ar. *Eq.* 164 ff. See Schwarze, op. cit., 96 f., 170 f.
69 *Scholium* ad Ar. *Ach.* 67.
70 Garnons Williams, op. cit.
71 Ar. *Ach.* 703; *Vesp.* 947.
72 Eupolis, frags. 249, 274. Plut. *Per.* 16.1.
73 Thuc. II, 65.9.
74 Fine: Thuc. II, 65.3; Plut. *Per.* 35.4; Diod. XII, 45. Fifteen years: Plut. *Per.* 16.3.
75 See, e.g., Gomme, *More Essays*, 178; Jones, op. cit., 127.
76 Jones, op. cit., 118. Thuc. I, 31–44, 139–45; III, 36–49; IV, 17–22; V, 44–6; VI, 8–26. See Staveley, *ASI*, 275–88, Hammond, *Studies*, 346 ff.; Fornara, op. cit., K. J. Dover, *JHS* 80 (1960), 61–77.
77 501/0: Arist. *AP*, 22.2–3. Marathon: Arist. *AP*, 22.2; Hdt. VI, 111 487/6: Arist. *AP*, 22.5; 458/7: Arist. *AP*, 26.2.
78 J. K. Davies, 112 f., 403 ff.
79 Deinarchus I, 71. Cf. Hignett, *Athenian Constitution*, 191, 224.
80 See Fornara, op. cit., 19, 44 ff.
81 On rotation see Diod. XIII, 97.6; Hdt. VI, 110. Cf. Xen. *Hell.* I, 6, 29 ff. See Dover, art. cit.
82 Thuc. II, 22.1; also II, 59.3.
83 Thuc. IV, 118.14. See Gomme ad loc.
84 Tod 61 = Meiggs-Lewis 65, line 56.
85 *IG* II^2, 27 = *SIG* 132. See Hignett, op. cit., 245 f.
86 Gomme, op. cit., 178.
87 See, e.g., H. J. Eysenck, *British Journal of Sociology*, 2–3 (1951), 189–209.
88 See especially Thuc. III, 44.
89 Thuc. II, 63.1–2. Cf. II, 41.4; 64.3; III, 40.4.
90 Plut. *Per.* 12.2. On *apragmon* see Ehrenberg, *JHS* 67 (1947), 46–67.
91 On the date see, e.g., Bowersock, *HSCP* 71 (1966), 33–46; Gomme, op. cit., 38–69.
92 Ps-Xen. *AP* I, 14–18.
93 *Scholium* ad Ar. *Ach.* 378.
94 Ar. fr. 65.
95 Ar. fr. 82.
96 Ar. *Vesp.* 666–75, translated by M. Hadas in his edition of *The Complete Plays of Aristophanes* (1962). See also Ps-Xen. *AP* I, 16 ff.

97 Cf. Gomme, op. cit., 70–91.
98 Frost, *Historia* 13 (1964), 388.
99 Ibid., 392 ff.
100 Ceryces: See MacKendrick, *The Athenian Aristocracy*, 49 f., 88 f. n. 46. Herodes Atticus: See Bowersock, *Greek Sophists*, 23 and Ch. VII. Woloch, *Historia* 18 (1969), 503–10.

CHAPTER VI

1 Plato, *Repb.* V, 473D.
2 Plato, *Protagoras* 319B–D.
3 Plato, *Repb.* VIII, 558C.
4 Ps-Xen. *AP* I, 2.
5 Ps-Xen. *AP* I, 3.
6 Ps-Xen. *AP* I, 6–8.
7 Ps-Xen. *AP* I, 10–12.
8 Plut. *Per.* 37.3; Arist. *AP*, 26.4. See C. Hignett, *Athenian Constitution* (1952), 343 ff.
9 Ps-Xen. *AP* I, 9.
10 Thuc. II, 37.1. It has been suggested that what Pericles is saying here is that poverty and obscurity of birth do not prevent one from holding public office 'at all events' (*ge*) 'if one is able to benefit the city'. (Adkins, *Moral Values*, 105, 141 f.). This, of course, gives the passage quite different overtones and rather limits the degree of equality claimed by Pericles. The modern writer concerned does not even have the courtesy to inform his readers, however, that this translation depends entirely upon a modern alteration of the ordinary Greek adversative *de*, as read by all the MSS, into *ge* – a change which, as Gomme points out (ad loc.), is by no means necessary for either sense or style; indeed, the MS. reading is eminently Thucydidean in style.
11 Donlan, *Historia* 22 (1973), 147.
12 Phocylides fr. 16 = 10D; Theognis 148; Arist. *Eth. Nic.* 1129b 27. Scholium ad loc. (Heyl, 210; Edmonds, *Elegy & Iambus* I, 180).
13 Theognis 145–8.
14 Adkins, *Merit & Responsibility*, 78.
15 Ibid., 79.
16 Cf. Havelock, *Phoenix* 23 (1969), 49–70.
17 Adkins, *Moral Values*, 42.
18 Theognis, 869–72.
19 Plut. *Arist.* 2; *Mor.* 807B.
20 Plut. *Mor.* 807B.
21 Havelock, art. cit.
22 Plato, *Repb.* I, 331D.
23 Plato, *Repb.* I, 331E.
24 Plato, *Repb.* I, 332D.
25 Xen. *Mem.* II, 3–14; II, 6.35.
26 *Od.* III, 52.
27 Just. *Inst.* I, 1.
28 Adkins, opp. citt.; Havelock, art. cit. Cf. Lloyd-Jones, *The Justice of Zeus.*
29 E.g. *Od.* VI, 120; IX, 215; XIX, 111.
30 Theognis, 147, 869–72.
31 Pindar, *Nem.* VI, 8–11; cf. XI, 38–42.
32 Eur. *Electra*, 367–85.
33 J. D. Denniston (ed.), Eur. *Electra* (1939), *ad* 367–72.
34 Eur. *Electra*, 43–6.
35 See above, p. 15.
36 Eur. *Electra*, 1249, 1284–7.
37 Ar. *Ranae*, 1477–8.
38 Plato, *Repb.* I, 335B–E. Note: The *Republic* is written in the first person throughout with Socrates as the narrator.
39 E.g. Adkins, opp. citt.; Havelock, art. cit. See above.
40 Plato, *Repb.* IV, 433A–B.
41 Plato, *Repb.* IV, 433E–434C.
42 Plato, *Repb.* III, 415A–C.
43 Arist. fr. 94 (Rose, 1886).

BIBLIOGRAPHY

GENERAL

Beloch, J., *Griechische Geschichte*, 4 vols (Berlin, 1912–31).
Bickerman, E. J., *Chronology of the Ancient World* (London, 1968).
Busolt, G., *Griechische Geschichte*, 4 vols (Gotha, 1893–1904).
—— and Swoboda, H., *Griechische Staatskunde*, 2 vols (Munich, 1920 & 1926).
Cambridge Ancient History, vols II–VII (Cambridge, 1925 ff.).
Clinton, H. F., *Fasti Hellenici*, 3 vols (Oxford, 1834–51).
Daremberg, C. and Saglio, E. (eds), *Dictionnaire des antiquités* (Paris, 1877–1919).
Francotte, H., *La Polis grecque* (Paderborn, 1907).
Gilbert, G., *Handbuch der Griechischen Staatsaltertümer*, 2 vols (Leipzig, 1893–95).
Glotz, G., *La Cité grecque* (Paris, 1928).
Gomme, A. W., *A Historical Commentary on Thucydides*, 4 vols (Oxford, 1945–70).
Greenidge, A. H. J., *A Handbook of Greek Constitutional History* (London, 1896).
Grote, G., *A History of Greece*, 8 vols (London, 1862).
Hasebroek, J., *Trade and Politics in Ancient Greece* (London, 1933).
Meyer, E., *Geschichte des Altertums* (Stuttgart & Berlin, 1893–1902).
Töpffer, J., *Attische Genealogie* (Berlin, 1889).
Wade-Gery, H. T., *Essays in Greek History* (Oxford, 1958).
Whibley, L., *Greek Oligarchies: Their Character and Organisation* (Cambridge, 1896).

CHAPTER I

Calhoun, G. M., 'Classes and Masses in Homer', *CPh* 29 (1934), 192–208 and 301–16.
Carpenter, Rhys, *Folk Tale, Fiction and Saga in the Homeric Epics* (Cambridge, 1946).
——, *Discontinuity in Greek Civilization* (Cambridge, 1966).
Desborough, V. R. d'A., *The Last Mycenaeans and their Successors* (Oxford, 1964).
——, *The Greek Dark Ages* (London, 1972).
Finley, M. I., *The World of Odysseus* (London, 1956).
——, 'Homer and Mycenae: property and tenure', *Historia* 6 (1957), 133–59.
——, *Early Greece: the Bronze and Archaic Ages* (London, 1970).
Kirk, G. S., *Songs of Homer* (Cambridge, 1962).
Lorimer, H. L., *Homer and the Monuments* (London, 1950).
Myres, J. L. and Gray, D. H. F., *Homer and his Critics* (London, 1958).
Page, D. L., *History and the Homeric Iliad* (Berkeley, 1959).

Palmer, L. R., *Mycenaean Greek Texts* (Oxford, 1963).
——, *Mycenaeans and Minoans* (London, 1965).
Simpson, R. Hope and Lazenby, J. F., *The Catalogue of Ships in Homer's Iliad* (Oxford, 1970).
Snodgrass, A. M., *Early Greek Weapons and Armour* (London, 1964).
——, *The Dark Age of Greece* (Edinburgh, 1971).
Taylour, Lord William, *The Mycenaeans* (London, 1964).
Ventris, M. and Chadwick, J., *Documents in Mycenaean Greek* (Cambridge, 1956).
Vermeule, E., *Greece in the Bronze Age* (Chicago, 1964).
Wace, A. J. B. and Stubbings, *A Companion to Homer* (London, 1962).

CHAPTER II

Andrewes, A., 'Ephoros Book I and the Kings of Argos', *CQ* n.s. 1 (1951), 39–45.
Burn, A. R., *The Lyric Age of Greece* (London, 1960).
Cadoux, T. J., 'The Athenian archons from Kreon to Hypsichides', *JHS* 68 (1948), 70–123.
Dunbabin, T. J., *The Western Greeks* (Oxford, 1948).
Forrest, W. G., 'Themistokles and Argos', *CQ* n.s. 10 (1960), 221–41.
French, A., 'The economic background to Solon's reforms', *CQ* n.s. 6 (1956), 11–25.
——, 'Solon and the Megarian Question', *JHS* 77 (1957), 238–46.
Graham, A. J., *Colony and Mother-City in Ancient Greece* (Manchester, 1964).
Greenhaigh, P., *Early Greek Warfare* (Cambridge, 1973).
Halliday, W. R., *The Greek Questions of Plutarch* (Oxford, 1928).
Hammond, N. G. L., 'An early inscription at Argos', *CQ* n.s. 10 (1960), 33–42.
Hignett, C., *A History of the Athenian Constitution to the end of the Fifth Century B.C.* (Oxford, 1952).
Hunt, D. W. S., 'Feudal survivals in Ionia', *JHS* 67 (1947), 68–76.
Jacoby, F., *Atthis* (Oxford, 1949).
Jeffery, L. H., *The Local Scripts of Archaic Greece* (Oxford, 1961).
——, and Morpurgo-Davies, A., 'BM 1969. 4-2.1, a new Archaic inscription from Crete' and *Kadmos* 9 (1970), 118–54.
Murakawa, K., 'Demiurgos', *Historia* 6 (1957), 385–415.
Ruschenbusch, E., 'Patrios politeia', *Historia* 7 (1958), 398–424.
Sealey, R., 'Regionalism in Archaic Athens', *Historia* 9 (1960), 155–80.
Seymour, P. A., 'The Servile Interregnum at Argos', *JHS* 42 (1922), 24–30.
Starr, C. G., *The Origins of Greek Civilization*, 1100–650 BC (New York, 1961).
——, 'The decline of the early Greek kings', *Historia* 10 (1961), 129–38.
Thomson, G., *The First Philosophers* (London, 1955).
Tomlinson, R. A., *Argos and the Argolid* (London, 1972).
Vollgraff, W., 'De titulo Argivo antiquissimo anno MCMXXVIII recuperato', *Mnemosyne* 59 (1932), 369–93.
Westlake, H. D., *Thessaly in the Fourth Century B.C.* (London, 1935).
White, M., 'The Duration of the Samian Tyranny', *JHS* 74 (1954), 36–43.
Will, E., *Korinthiaka* (Paris, 1955).
Willetts, R. F., *Aristocratic Society in Ancient Crete* (London, 1955).

Wörrle, M., *Untersuchungen zur Verfassungsgeschichte von Argos im 5 Jahrhundert v. chr.* (Munich, 1964).
Wüst, F. R., 'Gedanken über die Attischen Stande: ein Versuch', *Historia* 8 (1959), 1–11.

CHAPTER III

Andrewes, A., *Probouleusis* (Oxford, 1954).
Asheri, D., 'Laws of inheritance, distribution of land and political constitutions', *Historia* 12 (1963), 1–21.
Butler, D., 'Competence of the demos in the Spartan Rhetra', *Historia* 11 (1962), 385–96.
Chrimes, K. M. T., *Ancient Sparta* (Manchester, 1952).
Daubies, M., 'Cléomène III, les hilotes et Sellasie', *Historia* 20 (1971), 665–96.
den Boer, W., *Laconian Studies* (Amsterdam, 1954).
Dickins, G., 'The growth of Spartan policy', *JHS* 32 (1912), 1–42.
Ehrenberg, V., 'Spartiaten und Lakedaimonier', *Hermes* 59 (1924), 23–73.
——, *Neugründer des Staates* (Munich, 1925).
Forrest, W. G., 'The date of the Lycourgan reforms in Sparta', *Phoenix* 17 (1963), 157–79.
——, 'Legislation in Sparta', *Phoenix* 21 (1967), 11–19.
——, *A History of Sparta 950–192 B.C.* (London, 1968).
Fuks, A., 'Agis, Cleomenes and equality', *CPh* 57 (1962), 162–66.
——, 'The Spartan citizen-body in the mid-century B.C.', *Athenaeum* 40 (1962), 244–63.
——, 'Social Revolution in Greece', *Parola del Passato* III (1966), 437–48.
Gabba, E., 'Studi su Filarco', *Athenaeum* 35 (1957), 3–55, 193–239.
Grundy, G. B., 'The policy of Sparta', *JHS* 32 (1912), 261–69.
Hampl, F., 'Die lakedaemonischen Periöken', *Hermes* 72 (1937), 1–49.
Huxley, G. L., *Early Sparta* (London, 1962).
Jones, A. H. M., *Sparta* (Oxford, 1967).
Kahrstedt, U., 'Die spartanische Agrarwirtschaft', *Hermes* 54 (1919), 279–94.
Kiechle, F., *Messenische Studien* (Kallmünz, 1959).
——, *Lakonien und Sparta* (Munich, 1963).
Lotze, D., *Metaxu Eleutherōn kai Doulōn* (Berlin, 1959).
Michell, H., *Sparta* (Cambridge, 1952).
Niese, B., 'Neue Beiträge zur Geschichte und Landeskunde Lakedämons', *Göttingische Gelehrte Nachrichten* (1906), 101–42.
Oliva, P., 'On the problem of the helots', *Historica* 3 (1961), 5–34.
——, *Sparta and her Social Problems* (Prague-Amsterdam, 1971).
Pareti, L., *Storia di Sparta Arcaica* (Florence, 1917).
Pearson, L., 'The pseudo-history of Messenia and its authors', *Historia* 11 (1962), 397–426.
Poralla, P., *Prosopographie der Lakedaimonier* (Breslau, 1913).
Rawson, E., *The Spartan Tradition in European Thought* (London, 1969).
Shimron, B., 'Polybius and the reforms of Cleomenes III', *Historia* 13 (1964), 147–55.
——, 'The Spartan polity after the defeat of Cleomenes III', *CQ* 14 (1964), 232–39.

Shimron, B., 'Nabis of Sparta and the helots', *CPh* 61 (1966), 1–7.
Solmsen, F., 'Vordorisches in Lakonien', *Rheinisches Museum für Philologie* 62 (1907), 329–38.
Starr, C. G., 'The credibility of early Spartan history', *Historia* 14 (1965), 257–72.
Toynbee, A. J., 'The growth of Sparta', *JHS* 33 (1913), 246–75.
——, *Some Problems of Greek History* (London, 1969).
Wallace, W. P., 'Kleomenes, Marathon, the Helots and Arcadia', *JHS* 74 (1954), 32–35.
Willetts, R. F., 'The Neodamodeis', *CPh* 49 (1954), 27–32.

CHAPTER IV

Andrewes, A., *The Greek Tyrants* (London, 1956).
Barron, J. P., 'The sixth-century tyranny at Samos', *CQ* 14 (1964), 210–29.
Berve, H., *Die Tyrannis bei den Griechen*, 2 vols (Munich, 1967).
Bradeen, D. W., 'The Lelantine War and Pheidon of Argos', *TAPA* 78 (1947), 223–41.
Cadoux, T. J., 'The duration of the Samian tyranny', *JHS* 76 (1956), 105–6.
Drews, R., 'The first tyrants in Greece', *Historia* 21 (1972), 129–44.
Gwynn, A., 'The character of Greek colonisation', *JHS* 38 (1918), 88–123.
Hammond, N. G. L., 'The family of Orthagoras', *CQ* 6 (1956), 45–53.
Labarbe, J., 'Un décalage de 40 ans dans la chronologie de Polycrate', *Antiquité Classique* 31 (1962), 153–88.
Mossé, C., *La Tyrannie dans la Grèce Antique* (Paris, 1969).
——, *La Colonisation dans l'Antiquité* (Paris, 1970).
Page, D., *Sappho and Alcaeus* (Oxford, 1955).
Quinn, T. J., 'Political groups at Chios: 412 BC', *Historia* 18 (1969), 22–30.
Snodgrass, A. M., 'The hoplite reform and history', *JHS* 85 (1965), 110–22.
Ure, P. N., *The Origin of Tyranny* (Cambridge, 1922).
Westlake, H. D., *Timoleon and his Relations with Tyrants* (Manchester, 1952).
——, *Essays on the Greek Historians and Greek History* (London, 1969).
White, M. E., 'The duration of the Samian tyranny', *JHS* 74 (1954), 36–43.
——, 'Greek Tyranny', *Phoenix* 9 (1955), 1–18.
Wormell, D. E., 'Studies in Greek Tyranny, I: The Cypselids', *Hermathena* 66 (1945), 1–24.

CHAPTER V

Agard, W. R., *What Democracy Meant to the Greeks* (Madison, 1960).
Bicknell, P. J., *Studies in Athenian Politics and Genealogy* (Historia Einzelschriften, No. 19; Wiesbaden, 1972).
Bowersock, G. W., 'Pseudo-Xenophon', *HSCP* 71 (1966), 33–46.
——, *Greek Sophists in the Roman Empire* (Oxford, 1969).
Bowra, C. M., 'Euripides' Epinician for Alcibiades', *Historia* 9 (1960), 68–79.
Bradeen, D. W., 'The popularity of the Athenian Empire', *Historia* 9 (1960), 257–69.
——, 'The fifth-century archon list', *Hesperia* 32 (1963), 187–208.
Broneer, O., 'Excavations on the north slope of the Acropolis', *Hesperia* 7 (1938), 161–263.

Calhoun, G. M., *Athenian Clubs* (Bulletin of Univ. of Texas, 262, 1913).
Calhoun, G. M., *The Business Life of Ancient Athens* (New York, 1926).
Caspari, M. O. B., 'On the revolution of the Four Hundred at Athens', *JHS* 33 (1913), 1–18.
Chrimes, K. M. T., 'On Solon's property classes', *CR* 46 (1932), 2 ff.
Connor, W. R., *The New Politicians of Fifth-Century Athens* (Princeton, 1971).
Davies, J. K., *Athenian Propertied Families* (Oxford, 1971).
Davison, J. A., 'Notes on the Panathenaea', *JHS* 78 (1958), 23–42.
Dover, K. N., '*Dekatos autos*', *JHS* 80 (1960), 61–77.
Eliot, C. W. J. and McGregor, M. F., 'Kleisthenes: eponymous archon 525/4 BC', *Phoenix* 14 (1960), 27–35.
——, *Coastal Demes of Attica* (Toronto, 1962).
Fine, J. V. A., *Horoi* (*Hesperia*, Supplement 9; Princeton, 1951).
Finley, M. I.,*Studies in Land and Credit in Ancient Athens* (New Brunswick, 1951).
——, 'The Athenian Demagogues', *Past and Present* 21 (1962), 3–24.
——, *The Ancestral Constitution* (Cambridge, 1971).
——, *Democracy Ancient and Modern* (London, 1973).
——, *The Ancient Economy* (London, 1973).
Fornara, C. W., *The Athenian Board of Generals from 501 to 404* (Historia Einzelschriften, No. 16; Wiesbaden, 1971).
Forrest, W. G., *The Emergence of Greek Democracy* (London, 1966).
French, A., 'The economic background to Solon's reforms', *CQ* 6 (1956), 11–25.
——, 'Solon and the Megarian Question', *JHS* 77 (1957), 238–46.
——, 'The party of Peisistratos', *Greece & Rome*, 2nd ser. 6 (1959), 46–57.
——, *The Growth of the Athenian Economy* (London, 1964).
Frost, F. J., 'Pericles, Thucydides son of Melesias and Athenian politics before the war', *Historia* 13 (1964), 385–99.
Fuks, A., *The Ancestral Constitution* (London, 1953).
Geagan, D. N., 'The Athenian Constitution after Sulla' (*Hesperia*, Supplement 12; Princeton, 1967).
Ghinatti, F., *I Gruppi Politici Ateniesi fino alle guerre Persiane* (Rome, 1970).
Gomme, A. W., *The Population of Athens in the Fifth and Fourth Centuries* (Oxford, 1933).
——, *More Essays in Greek History and Literature* (Oxford, 1962).
Hammond, N. G. L., *Studies in Greek History* (Oxford, 1973).
Hands, A. R., 'Ostraka and the law of ostracism', *JHS* 79 (1959), 69–79.
Hignett, C., *A History of the Athenian Constitution to the end of the Fifth Century B.C.* (Oxford, 1952).
Jones, A. H. M., *Athenian Democracy* (Oxford, 1957).
Kagan, D., *The Outbreak of the Peloponnesian War* (Ithaca and London, 1969).
Kirchner, J., *Prosopographia Attica* (Berlin, 1901–3).
Knight, D. W., *Some Studies in Athenian Politics in the Fifth Century BC* (Historia Einzelschriften, No. 13; Wiesbaden, 1970).
Lewis, D. M., 'Cleisthenes and Attica', *Historia* 12 (1963), 22–40.
Losada, L. A., *The Fifth Column in the Peloponnesian War* (Leiden, 1972).
MacKendrick, P., *The Athenian Aristocracy 399 to 31 BC* (Cambridge, Mass., 1969).

Mattingly, H. B., 'The Athenian Coinage Decree', *Historia* 10 (1961), 148-88.
——, 'Athens and Aegina', *Historia* 16 (1967), 1-5.
Meiggs, R., 'The dating of fifth-century Attic inscriptions', *JHS* 86 (1966), 86-98.
——, *The Athenian Empire* (Oxford, 1972).
Mossé, C., *Athens in Decline* (London, 1973).
Oliver, J. H., *Demokratia, the Gods and the Free World* (Baltimore, 1960).
——, 'Reforms of Cleisthenes', *Historia* 9 (1960), 503-7.
Ostwald, M., *Nomos and the Beginnings of the Athenian Democracy* (Oxford, 1969).
Quinn, T. J., 'Thucydides and the unpopularity of the Athenian Empire', *Historia* 13 (1964), 257-66.
Rhodes, P. J., *The Athenian Boule* (Oxford, 1972).
Ruschenbusch, E., *Solonos Nomoi* (*Historia Einzelschriften*, No. 9; Wiesbaden, 1966).
Ryder, T. T. B., 'Pericles and the radical democracy', *Handbook of Classical Teachers* (of Ireland), (1972-73).
Ste Croix, G. E. M. de, 'The character of the Athenian Empire', *Historia* 3 (1954/5), 1-41.
——, *The Origins of the Peloponnesian War* (London, 1972).
Sanctis, G. de, *Atthis: Storia della Repubblica Ateniese* (Turin, 1912).
Sartori, F., *Le Eterie nella Vita Politica Ateniese* (Rome, 1957).
Schwarze, J., *Die Beurteilung des Perikles durch die attische Komödie und ihre historische und historiographische Bedeutung* (Munich, 1970).
Seager, R., 'Alcibiades and the charge of aiming at tyranny', *Historia* 16 (1967), 6-18.
Sealey, R., *Essays in Greek Politics* (New York, 1967).
Staveley, E. S., *Greek and Roman Voting and Elections* (London, 1972).
Sundwall, J., *Epigraphische Beiträge zur sozial-politischen Geschichte Athens im Zeitalter des Demosthenes* (Leipzig, 1906).
Thomsen, R., *Eisphora* (Copenhagen, 1964).
Thomson, G., *Aeschylus and Athens* (London, 1941 and 1973).
Vanderpool, E., *Ostracism at Athens* (1970).
Westlake, H. D., *Individuals in Thucydides* (Cambridge, 1968).
——, 'The subjectivity of Thucydides: his treatment of the Four Hundred at Athens', *Bulletin of John Rylands Library*, 56 (1973), 193-218.
Wilamowitz-Möllendorff, U. von, *Aristoteles und Athen*, 2 vols (Berlin, 1893).
Williams, B. H. Garnons, *The Historical Evidence Contained in Aristophanes and in the Fragments of the Old Attic Comedy* (Unpublished B. Litt. dissertation; Oxford, 1933).
Woloch, M., 'Four leading families in Roman Athens', *Historia* 18 (1969), 503-10.
Woodhouse, W. J., *Solon the Liberator* (Oxford, 1938).

CHAPTER VI

Adkins, A. W. H., *Merit and Responsibility: A Study in Greek Values* (Oxford, 1960).
——, *Moral Values and Political Behaviour in Ancient Greece* (London, 1972).
Bambrough, J. R. (ed.), *Plato, Popper & Politics* (Cambridge, 1966).
Bonner, R. J., *Aspects of Athenian Democracy* (New York, 1933).

Cole, A. T. J., 'The Anonymus Iamblichi and his place in Greek political thought', *HSCP* 65 (1961), 127–63.
Cross, R. C. and Woozley, A. D., *Plato's Republic: A Philosophical Commentary* (London, 1964).
Dodds, E. R., *The Greeks and the Irrational* (Berkeley, 1951).
——, *The Ancient Concept of Progress* (Oxford, 1973).
Donlan, W., 'The tradition of anti-aristocratic thought in early Greek poetry', *Historia* 22 (1973), 145–54.
Ehrenberg, V., 'Origins of democracy', *Historia* 1 (1950), 515–48.
——, *Society and Civilization Greece and Rome* (Cambridge, Mass., 1964).
Gouldner, A. W., *Enter Plato* (New York, 1965; London, 1967).
Guthrie, W. K. C., *A History of Greek Philosophy*, 3 vols (Cambridge, 1962).
——, *The Sophists* (extract from previous work) (Cambridge, 1971).
Havelock, E. E., *The Liberal Temper in Greek Politics* (New Haven, 1957).
——, '*Dikaiosyne*: an essay in Greek intellectual history', *Phoenix* 23 (1969), 49–70.
Headlam, J. W., *Election by Lot at Athens* (Cambridge, 1933).
Jaeger, W., *Paideia* (English translation, 3 vols, Oxford, 1944–6).
Lloyd-Jones, H., *The Justice of Zeus* (Berkeley, 1971).
Mahaffy, J. P., *Social Life in Greece from Homer to Menander* (London, 1883).
Morrison, J. S., 'Antiphon', *Proceedings of the Cambridge Philological Society*, 187 n.s. 7 (1961), 49–58.
Podlecki, A. J., *The Political Background of Aeschylean Tragedy* (Ann Arbor, 1966).
——, 'The political significance of the Athenian "tyrannicide"-cult', *Historia* 15 (1966), 129–41.
Popper, K., *The Open Society and its Enemies* (London, 1945).
Quass, F., *Nomos und Psephisma* (Zetemata, No. 55; Munich, 1971).
Shorey, P., *What Plato Said* (Chicago, 1933).
Strasburger, H., 'Der soziologische Aspekt der homerischen Epen', *Gymnasium* 60 (1953), 97–114.
Strauss, L., *Socrates and Aristophanes* (New York and London, 1966).
Vlastos, G. (ed.), *Plato: A Collection of Critical Essays*, 2 vols (New York, 1971).
——, *Platonic Studies* (Princeton, 1973).
Walcot, P., *Greek Peasants, Ancient and Modern* (Manchester, 1970).
Woodhead, A. G., *Thucydides on the Nature of Power* (Cambridge, Mass., 1970).
Zuntz, G., *The Political Plays of Euripides* (Manchester, 1955).

INDEX

Acanthus 92
Achaea 38
Achaean League 119
Achilles 19, 21, 22, 29
Acragas (Agrigentum) 55
Aegina 127f.
Aegisthus 171
Aeneas 22, 29
Aethe 23
Agamemnon 15, 17, 19, 21, 22, 28, 39
agathoergoi 96f.
agathos 14ff., 165, 175
Agesilaus 72, 73
Agis IV 92, 112ff.
agōgē 87, 89, 98, 114
Ajax 21
Alcaeus 40
Alcibiades 132, 145, 149, 152, 154, 156
Alcinous 18, 21, 22
Alcmaeonids 46, 122, 136
Alcman 73
Aleuas 58
Amphimedon 17
anax 22, 28, 33f.
Anaxagoras 155
Anaxilas (Anaxilaus) 104
Anchises 22
Androclus 41
Antigonus Doson 116
Antilochus 21
Antinous 17
Apollonia (Black Sea) 52

Apollonia (Chalcidice) 92
Apollonia (Ionian Gulf) 52, 53
Arcadia 104
archagetas 36
Archeanactidae 40
Archidamas 92
archon 44
Areopagus Council 47, 49, 140
aretē 165, 174, 175, 178
'Argos' 20
Argos 21, 39, 51, 57, 62, 64ff., 70
Aristeides 132, 142, 145, 149
aristocracy: Athenian 130ff.; concepts of 158ff.; by conquest 57ff.; definition 9ff.; of first settlers 51ff.; of fixed size 55f.; military 54; royal-clan 40ff.; Spartan 77ff.
Aristomenes 104
Aristophanes 153f., 172f.
Aristotle 10, 173, 180f.
Aspasia 148
Athens: Cleisthenes 137ff.; democracy 140ff.; the Five Thousand 56; monarchy 42ff.; population 99; Solon 133ff.; in Samos 52; and Sparta 92, 87ff.; tyranny 123ff.
Attica 37, 38
Augustus 118

Bacchiads 41f., 122
basileus 14, 17, 21f., 33, 36
Basilidae 41

Boeotia 57
Boulē (Athens) 150
Boutadae 140
Bouzygae 140
Brasidas 107
Brasideii 107
Brauron 124, 138
Byzantium 52, 60

Callias 145, 156
Callicrates 132
Ceos 35
Cephalus 168, 173
Ceryces 156
Chalcis 54
Chaonians 41
Chilon 116f.
Chios 40, 41, 127f.
Cimon 132, 140ff., 145, 149, 155
Cinadon 105f.
Clazomenae 40
Cleanactidae 40
Cleisthenes (Athenian statesman) 50, 132, 137ff., 145
Cleomenes I 104, 137, 138f.
Cleomenes III 112ff.
Cleon 132, 142, 143f., 145f., 149, 151ff., 155f.
Cleophon 132, 156
Clytemnestra 171
Cnidus 56
Cnossus 27
Codrus 41, 44f.
Colophon 54, 55
Conon 156
Corcyra 151
Corinth 23, 39; Bacchiads 40, 41f.; Cypselus 121ff.; *kunaphaloi* 60; Periander 125f.
Cos 35, 38
Council of Five Hundred 139, 140
Croton 55
Cyclades 37

Cyme 54, 55, 56
Cyprus 37
Cypselus 42, 121ff.
Cyrene 52
Cyzicus 51

Dark Age 26, 37
Delian League 152
Delos 35
Demaratus 104
Demetrius of Phalerum 156
democracy 130ff.
Demosthenes (Athenian general) 144, 149
dikaiosunē 165ff., 173ff., 178
Diocles 20, 22, 57
Diodotus 151
Diomedes 20, 22, 28, 39, 41
Dionysius (Syracusan tyrant) 123, 124f.
Dodecanese 38
Dorians 37, 57
Draco 47ff.
dunasteia 59, 143

Echepolus 23
Electra 171f.
Elis 57, 62f.
Epaminondas 101
Ephesus 40, 41
Ephialtes 49, 132, 140, 142f., 145
Epidaurus 56, 57, 60, 62
Epirus 40, 41, 58
Epitadeus 110
eqeta 32
equality 158ff., 167ff.
Eratosthenes 26
Eretria 54
Erythrae 40, 41
esthlos 14f.
Euchenor 23
Eupatrids 46, 50, 51, 135
Euripides 170ff., 180f.

INDEX

Euryalus 17
Eurycles, C. Julius 118
Eurymachus 16, 17

feudalism 27, 31

gamoroi 52
geomoroi 52
gerousia 33, 79, 97
Glaucus 41
Gortyn 60
gumnētes 60, 67ff.
guslari 26
Gylippus 109
Gymnopaedia 80

Helenus 22
helots (Sparta) 75f., 77
hepetēs 32
heq^{u}etas 32
Heraclea 56, 60
Herodes Atticus 157
hetaireia 142
hetairos 32
hippagretai 95
Hipparchus 136
Hippias 136f., 139
Hippodamus of Miletus 56
Homer 13ff., 169
homoioi ('Equals') 79, 98, 105ff.
hupomeiones 105f.
Hyberbolus 152, 156

Idomeneus 21, 22
Iliad 15ff., *passim*
Ion 50
Ionia 37
Isagoras 132, 137ff.
Istrus 56
Ithaca 17, 18, 22, 39

Justinian 169

kakos 14ff., 171
krupteia 97

Laconia 37
Laertes 14, 17
Laodamas 40
lawagetas 30, 33
Leipsydrium 136f.
Leonidas 92, 113
Leontini 123
Leuctra 80, 110f.
Linear B tablets 27ff.
lochoi 95f.
Locri (Italy) 55, 61
Locris 21, 55, 56
Lycurgus 81ff., 88ff., 97ff., 120, 135
Lysander 107f.

Magnesia 54
Mantinea 62, 107
Marathon 104, 124
Marcus Aurelius 157
Massilia 56
Medontidae 43f.
Megacles 136, 138
Megara 123
Meleager 29
Menelaus 13, 21, 22, 36
merchants, status of 17
Meriones 21
meritocracy 159
Messenia 20, 37, 77, 101, 119
Messenian Wars 77, 101; First 74, 94;
    Second 86, 104, 135; Third 105
metics 101, 163
Miletus 38, 40, 51, 126f.
Miltiades 132, 145, 149
Mycenae 20, 37, 77, 101, 119

Nabis 112ff.
Nausicaa 13
Naxos 35, 38
Neleids 40, 41

neodamōdeis 105ff., 115
Nestor 20, 21, 22, 36
Nicias 132, 142, 144, 145, 149, 152, 153, 156

ōba 95f.
Odysseus 13ff., *passim*
Odyssey 13ff., *passim*
Old Oligarch 152, 162f.
Orestes 40, 171f.
Orthagoras 122f.

paidonomos 98
Panaetius (tyrant of Leontini) 123
Parthenon 142
pasireu 33
Patroclides 122
patronomos 114, 119
Pausanias (Spartan regent) 104f.
Pausanias (Spartan king) 108
Peisander 53, 142
Peisistratus (Athenian tyrant) 123ff., 132, 145
Peisistratus (son of Nestor) 13, 169
Peleus 22, 23
Peloponnesian War 52, 109, 151f.
Penelope 14, 16
penestai 53, 60
Penthilus 40
Perati 35, 38
Periander (Corinthian tyrant) 125f.
Pericles 122, 132, 141ff., 145, 146ff., 152, 154ff., 163f.
Perinthus 51
perioikoi (Sparta) 59f., 66, 68f., 76f., 79, 93, 99, 102, 105, 112ff., 119
Phaeacians 18
Phalaris 55
Pharsalus 58, 62
Pheidias 155
Pheidon of Argos 66
Pherae 20, 22
phiditia 84, 87, 112f.

Philoetius 13
Philolaus 57
Philopoemen 117
Phoenix 23
Phthia 22
Pindar 170
Plataea 98f., 110f.
Plato 10, 160ff., 168, 173ff.
Pleistarchus 104
polemarch 44
Polemarchus 143f., 168f., 173
Praxiergidae 140
Priam 19, 22
Priene 52
Prosymna 35
Protagoras 167
prutanis 36
Pylades 172
Pylos 21, 22, 27, 35, 37

rex sacrorum 29
Rhegium 55, 56
Rhodes 37, 38
Rome 88
Russell, Bertrand 9

Salamis 21, 39
Samos 51f., 147
Scepsis 40
Scheria 14, 18
Sicilian expedition 151
Sicyon 23, 51, 57, 60, 61, 122f.
Simonides 143, 168f.
Socrates 168, 173
Solon 47ff., 132, 133ff.
Sparta 21, 37, 57; aristocracy 77ff.; and Athens 92, 98ff., 151; constitution 89ff.; council and assembly 91ff., 95, 112; ephors 91, 93ff.; great *Rhetra* 89f., 93; helots 75f., 77, 102ff.; *homoioi* 79; *klēroi* (*klāroi*) 79ff., 112f.; Lycurgan system 81ff., 109f., 112ff.; population 99

INDEX

strategia 148f.
sussitia 87, 89, 98, 106, 110, 113, 114
Sybaris 60f.
Syracuse 51f., 53, 56, 60, 124f.

tagos 58
Taras (Tarentum) 74
Tegea 101
Telemachus 13, 17, 37, 169
telestēs 30f.
temenos 28ff., 34
Theagenes 123
Thebes 57, 92, 101
Themistocles 132, 143, 145, 149, 167, 168f.
Theognis 128, 164ff., 168ff.
Thera 51, 53, 57
Theramenes 132
Thersites 14f.
Theseus 43, 46, 50
Thespiae 61
Thesprotians 41, 58

Thessaly 40, 53, 57, 58f., 61
Thrasybulus (Milesian tyrant) 126f.
Thucydides, son of Melesias 132, 147, 148, 155
Timotheus 156
Tiryns 18, 28
Tomi 51
triecas 95
trittues 50, 139
Trojan War 26
Troy 18f.
tyranny 121ff.
Tyrtaeus 73

Union of Soviet Socialist Republics 159f.

wanaka 28
Wilamowitz-Möllendorff, U. von 26

Xanthippus 132, 149